THE BRITISH LABOUR GOVERNMENT AND THE 1976 IMF CRISIS

The British Labour Government and the 1976 IMF Crisis

Mark D. Harmon
Assistant Professor of Politics
University of California at Santa Cruz
California

First published in Great Britain 1997 by
MACMILLAN PRESS LTD
Houndmills, Basingstoke, Hampshire RG21 6XS and London
Companies and representatives throughout the world

A catalogue record for this book is available from the British Library.

ISBN 0-333-67818-4

First published in the United States of America 1997 by
ST. MARTIN'S PRESS, INC.,
Scholarly and Reference Division,
175 Fifth Avenue, New York, N.Y. 10010

ISBN 0-312-17624-4

Library of Congress Cataloging-in-Publication Data
Harmon, Mark D.
The British labour government and the 1976 IMF crisis / Mark D.
Harmon.
p. cm.
Includes bibliographical references and index.
ISBN 0-312-17624-4
1. Monetary policy—Great Britain. 2. Great Britain—Economic
policy—1945– 3. Great Britain—Politics and
government—1964–1979. 4. International Monetary Fund. I. Title.
HG939.5.H257 1997
332.4'941—dc21   97–8582
                                                           CIP

This book is printed on paper suitable for recycling and made from fully managed and
sustained forest sources.

10   9   8   7   6   5   4   3   2   1
06   05   04   03   02   01   00   99   98   97

Printed and bound in Great Britain by
Antony Rowe Ltd, Chippenham, Wiltshire

Contents

List of Figures

List of Tables

Preface and Acknowledgments

There were essentially two factors that led to my initial interest in the 1976 UK–IMF crisis. As a graduate student in international relations seminars, I became convinced that many of the external influences on state action that are presented within the literature as 'international cooperation' are more accurately described and understood as relations of coercion. Accordingly, I began this project looking for a case in which I could explore the nature of 'structural power' in contemporary international affairs, including the ways in which choices are framed and possibilities foreclosed. In addition, I was interested in examining the conflict between economic liberalism and social democracy as a way to understand why left-of-center governments in advanced industrial states so frequently are unable to sustain themselves in power; this case study allowed me to examine closely a left-of-center government's accommodation to external pressures for policy change at the expense of the interests of its domestic supporters.

While working on this project, I incurred numerous debts and obligations that I would like to acknowledge. For funding my research in Europe, I am grateful to have received a Pre-Dissertation Fellowship from the Council for European Studies, a Grant-in-Aid of Research from the Mellon-West European Studies Program at Yale, and a Dissertation Research Support Grant funded jointly by the Yale Center for International and Area Studies and the Council of West European Studies Mellon Fund. I was fortunate to have received a Mellon Fellowship administered through the Institute for Social and Policy Studies at Yale, and I am also grateful for a travel grant from the Gerald Ford Foundation. I also acknowledge varying levels of research support from Yale University and from the University of California at Santa Cruz.

I have benefited enormously from the assistance of numerous librarians and archivists. At Yale, Sue Lorimer, JoAnn Dionne, Judy Carnes, and Maureen Malone-Jones answered my frequent questions quickly and cheerfully. Karen Holzhausen and Diane Windham Shaw, archivists at the Ford Presidential Library and at the David Bishop Skillman Library at Lafayette College respectively, were extremely helpful, as was Stephen Bird at the Labour Party's archives in London. I also wish to acknowledge my gratitude to Mary Wood and the staff at the Library of the Royal Institute of International Affairs. I am extremely grateful for the quite considerable assistance of Tony Benn and Ruth Winstone, who trusted me with access to the private political diaries of Tony Benn prior to their publication, as well as the several individuals who agreed to be interviewed by me on an off-the-record basis for this project. I also thank Kathleen Burk for suggesting the utility of a visit to the Ford Presidential Library, Karen Holzhausen for informing me about the availability of William Simon's papers, and Edmund Dell for reading and commenting on the manuscript.

My work on this project has benefited from several individuals who have provided advice, criticism, and reassurance. Foremost among them have been my PhD advisers David Cameron, Sylvia Maxfield, and Bruce Russett, who have always been supportive and encouraging. Isebill Gruhn, Chip Hauss, Diane Kunz, Joseph LaPalombara, Andrei Markovits, Robert Meister, Thomas Risse-Kappen, and H. Bradford Westerfield also at various stages have contributed important and welcomed insights for which I am grateful. Among my cohort at Yale, Tom Hartley, Dorothee Heisenberg, Chris Howell, Dave Kinsella, Philip Marlow, Shoon Murray, Wolfgang Reinicke, Ian Robinson, Susan Scarrow, and Jeff Winters all have been helpful. I also wish to acknowledge my parents, Richard and Jean Harmon, who have been my most reliable supporters; without their love and encouragement, there is no doubt that this project would never have been brought to completion. Although I would like to blame all of the people mentioned above for the work's shortcomings (except perhaps my parents), regrettably I alone am responsible.

Mark Harmon
Santa Cruz, California

1 Sovereignty, Regimes, and 'Cooperation'

In late November and early December 1976, at the height of one of the most intense financial and political crises in the United Kingdom since World War Two, Prime Minister Jim Callaghan was under sharply conflicting pressures. On one side, he faced external demands from the International Monetary Fund (IMF) that his Government commit to further deflationary economic policy measures as a condition of the $3.9 billion IMF loan it was seeking; on the other side, he found adamant resistance to deflation among the majority of ministers in his Government. In a transatlantic telephone conversation with US President Gerald Ford on 1 December, Callaghan related his predicament and attempted a bit of gallows humor. Ford a few weeks earlier had been defeated in the 1976 US Presidential election and was in his final weeks in office. Callaghan joked with Ford that 'it's just a question of which of us remains in office longer.' The President, knowing that the British Cabinet would take a decision on the IMF policy demands the next day, replied drily, 'you might be out of office first' (Benn 1989: 672). When the British Cabinet decided on the following day to cut the size of the Public Sector Borrowing Requirement (PSBR) by £1.5 billion for the next fiscal year, Callaghan sent Ford a cable that outlined the differences that still remained between the Government's decisions and the IMF's demands. The Cabinet meeting had been 'long and difficult,' the Prime Minister confessed, 'and I do not yet know whether I shall be able to carry all the Cabinet with me ... I must tell you that I am not sanguine, and I can only hope the IMF really understand the consequences' (Callaghan 1976b).

In the end, Callaghan and his Government survived the crisis. The United Kingdom received approval for the IMF loan it was seeking, and there were no ministerial resignations over the deflationary conditions that accompanied the loan. But it was not persuasive economic argument that won the debate within the British Cabinet. At the first full Cabinet session at which the loan conditions were discussed, a majority of the ministers who spoke (10 out of 13) argued for a rejection of the IMF's terms, and the cuts were deeper than the Prime Minister wanted or thought necessary (Callaghan 1987: 433; Crosland 1982:

1

377–8; Bernstein 1983: 561–6; Benn 1989: 653–5; Healey 1989: 430). Although a majority of the Cabinet ultimately gave sanction to the deflationary policy package, key ministers remained to the end unpersuaded by the economic arguments for the policy shift (Callaghan 1987: 438–9).

One of the key questions underlying Cabinet opposition was the issue of who and what would be the determinants of British economic policy in a global economy characterized by increasing interdependence. US Treasury Secretary William Simon (1975b: 1457, 1463–5) had given public voice to such questions when he observed a year earlier that governments needed

> to learn better how to live in an interdependent world – how to balance economic interdependence and national independence. All nations are linked together economically. When our policies are mutually supportive we are all better off. When they are mutually incompatible we all suffer.
>
> Yet we are not yet ready for one world politically and we may never be. We wish to retain our sovereignty. For example, although monetary policy in the United States affects the economies of the European countries, and vice versa, neither Europeans nor Americans can allow domestic monetary policies to be determined by the other.

Yet as part of the settlement with the IMF in December 1976, the British Government yielded its right to determine British fiscal and monetary policies as it saw fit, and Secretary Simon was a key be-hind-the-scenes player in 'set[ting] the parameters' by which the financial and political crises in Britain were resolved (Whitehead 1985: 197). Both preceding and following the crisis, the direction of British fiscal and monetary policy was determined to a large extent by exter-nal actors – by the requirements of 'market confidence' and by the stipulations attached to the IMF loan. Notwithstanding the determined resistance of the British political authorities to deflationary policy changes, limits were set on the size of Britain's public sector deficit and on the extent of British domestic credit expansion (an indirect monetary growth measure) for the years 1977–79.

Former IMF official Fred Hirsch writing about the crisis a few months after its resolution noted that although 'reformist governments in ex-posed financial conditions do not have much room for manoeuvre, . . . that is an argument for reducing the exposure, and not only diluting the reformism' (*The Guardian*, 18 February 1977, 'Did the Treasury?' p. 10). But rather than diminish the British economy's international exposure, the Government in its IMF letter of intent pledged just the opposite: 'The Government remains firmly opposed to generalized restrictions on trade and does not intend to introduce restrictions for balance of payments purposes. . . . The Government does not intend to introduce any multiple currency practices or impose new or intensify existing restrictions on payments and transfers for current international transactions' (Healey 1976e: para. 24). Despite the preference of a significant Cabinet minority to restrict the economic interdependence and exposure that had stymied the achievement of the Government's economic policy goals, the Government after 1976 formally and explicitly committed itself to the IMF to maintain openness and interdependence as a condition of financing.

The IMF settlement of December 1976 did succeed in restoring confidence in the Callaghan Government's management of the British economy. The pound sterling had been under 18 months of intermittent, but frequently intense, selling pressure, falling from above $2 throughout 1975 to reach a low point of $1.56 in October 1976. After settlement with the IMF in December 1976, exchange market pressure on sterling changed direction sharply, and by 1978 the pound was again trading in the $2 range. However, restoration of confidence in sterling occurred simultaneously with the erosion of the Government's domestic political support. As Callaghan ruefully recounts in his memoirs (1987: 447), 'not for the first time as overseas confidence grew in our ability to pull Britain around, so we began to lose the support of the electorate.' Criticism was especially sharp among the Labour Party's traditional backers. Preceding and to a greater extent following the IMF crisis, 'alternative economic strategy' proposals were put forward by the Government's left-wing trade union and Labour Party supporters that constituted implicit indictments of the Government's economic policy. As early as July 1976, the Trades Union Congress (TUC) made public its unhappiness with the Government by testily reminding Chancellor of the Exchequer Denis Healey that 'it should not need emphasis that the confidence of the trade union Movement in the course of economic policy is of equal weight to the need for confidence on the part of the financial community at home and abroad' (TUC 1976a: 311). By early 1977, the TUC Economic Committee was bluntly charging that 'the reason why the economy was not meeting the TUC's targets was because [TUC] policy recommendations were not carried out' (Middlemas 1991: 168), and the TUC was implicitly impugning the Government's good faith in fulfilling the terms of its Social Contract partnership with the trade unions that had been instrumental in bringing the Government to power in 1974. Both within and outside the Labour Party by the late 1970s, pressures were growing to make future Labour Governments more accountable to its supporters, especially *vis-à-vis* economic policy (see Kogan and Kogan 1982: 26–39; Heffer 1986: 25–7, 31; Seyd 1987: 28–31).

When the Government attempted to impose another, stricter round of incomes policies on wage settlements in late 1978 and early 1979, the trade union rank-and-file in the public sector staged the widespread and highly publicized strikes of the so-called Winter of Discontent. The industrial unrest constituted a clear and embarrassing repudiation of the Labour Government's macroeconomic strategy by its own traditional supporters. When the Callaghan Government lost a March 1979 vote of confidence in Parliament and elections were held, a decisive 5.5 per cent of the overall electorate shifted from Labour to the Conservatives (Butler and Kavanagh 1980: 343, 392). According to Ivor Crewe (1982: 10), the 1979 general election was 'the most emphatic rejection of the Labour Party for almost half a century. Not since the débâcle of 1931 had Labour suffered such an adverse swing or seen its share of the vote (at 36.9 per cent) or of the electorate as a whole (at 28.0 per cent) fall so low. . . . The Labour Party also took a severe knock as the parliamentary representative of the working class. . . . The heaviest desertions from Labour occurred among manual rather than non-manual workers, especially among the younger generation and skilled workers.' The 1979 electoral defeat and internal party strife triggered subsequent developments that were to threaten Labour's position in British politics as the main opposition party to the Conservatives when several of the party's senior members left Labour in the early 1980s to found the Social Democratic Party. Labour was defeated in the subsequent three general elections and remained out of power for over a decade and a half.

How did this happen? How could a party that pledged in its 1974 election manifestos 'to bring about a fundamental and irreversible shift in the balance of wealth and power in favour of working people and their families' (Labour Party 1974a: 15; 1974b: 30) preside over sustained conditions of rising unemployment and declining and stagnant living standards, ultimately to be repudiated by those whose economic interests it had been elected to defend? The explanation offered here is that Labour's inability to sustain itself must be seen in the context of the combination of bilateral, multilateral, and structural external economic pressures that the Government could neither effectively resist nor successfully reconcile with the sustenance of its domestic political support.

Time and again in 1975 and 1976, the British Government was pressured into responding to crises of confidence in sterling by negotiating restrictive incomes policies and by undertaking agonizing public expenditure reductions. The Government's accommodating response to pressures for deflation ran counter to the United Kingdom's bipartisan postwar macroeconomic policy orientation of promoting economic growth during periods of relative slack through Keynesian demand stimulation. Although Keynesian demand management was never as successful in the UK as it was in other advanced industrialized countries, Britain nonetheless achieved average real GDP growth rates of 3.1 per cent during 1960–68 and 3.3 per cent during 1968–73; but during 1973–79, average real GDP growth in the UK fell to 1.5 per cent, lower than every other OECD economy except Luxembourg, New Zealand, and Switzerland (OECD 1989a: 44). In the chapters that follow, I examine the external pressures exerted on British economic policy during the first three years of the 1974–79 Labour Government and the political and economic crises that external pressures brought about.

INTERNATIONAL SOVEREIGNTY, POLICY SUSTAINABILITY, AND EXTERNAL PRESSURES

The core element of any meaningful definition of international sovereignty involves the assertion of final political authority within a given territorial unit (Krasner 1988: 86). As one British Cabinet minister commented during a 1975 Cabinet discussion of the UK's membership in the European Community, 'Sovereignty is not omnipotence. It is the right to make your own laws' (Castle 1980: 342; Benn 1989: 312). One of the questions that guides this case study is whether this core element of state sovereignty – the right to make your own laws and policies – is still meaningful, given the increasingly interdependent international political economy. To what degree and under what conditions are fundamental economic policy choices influenced, constrained, and determined in response to external pressures?

There are, of course, innumerable circumstances in contemporary global affairs in which the assertion of a state's ultimate sovereign authority is circumscribed, not least through the existence and effective operation of international law. However, international law is made on the principle of unanimity in which no state's behavior is bound by law without its initial consent, and thus when states cede their ability to 'make their own laws' by agreeing to be constrained by international law, a degree of formal legal sovereignty nonetheless remains (Henkin 1968: 33). The sovereign assertion of final political authority can also be circumscribed by the existence and operation of international regimes.[1] For national sovereign choice to be real, alternative policy options must be available. In operational terms, sovereignty comes down to a question of the ability to pick between alternative courses of action that are within acceptable cost parameters. But if costs can be manipulated, the range of effective choice can be significantly constrained, and the operational meaning of sovereignty is substantially diminished.

State autonomy, defined as 'states conceived as organizations claiming control over territories and people [which] may formulate and pursue goals that are not simply reflective of the demands or interests of social groups, classes, or society' (Skocpol 1985: 9), is a closely related concept, and in some important ways international sovereignty can be conceptualized as the extension of the concept of state autonomy to a global level of analysis. Theda Skocpol (1985: 14) stresses that state autonomy is not fixed, but rather that it ebbs and flows not only because of the occurrence of crises (e.g., war, economic depression) that can and do disrupt the previous capacity-limiting or capacity-enabling arrangements, but also 'because the very *structural potentials* for autonomous state actions change over time, as the organization of coercion and administration undergo transformations, both internally and in their relations to societal groups and to representative parts of government' (original emphasis). In addition, the degree of state autonomy varies over policy domains, and states do not have similar autonomy and capacity across issue-areas. Accordingly, Skocpol (1985: 19–20) argues that questions of state autonomy need to be investigated narrowly with a domain-specific focus, and she cites Peter Katzenstein's work (1978) on the foreign economic policies of advanced industrialized states as a good example.

Both of these points – that state autonomy varies over time and over policy-domain – can and should be usefully extended to the investigation of the contemporary nature of state sovereignty. If international sovereignty is conceptualized as the autonomy of political authority in a given political unit – the right to make your own laws and policies – one might begin the analysis by asking autonomy from whom or from what? Conceptualizing international sovereignty as autonomy from other nation-states, international organizations, and/or transnational actors over-simplifies, as there are 'structural' influences and pressures that can and do circumscribe sovereign choice. It is here that the neo-Marxist and neo-pluralist 'relative autonomy' critiques of pluralist conceptions of the liberal democratic state can be usefully brought into a discussion of international sovereignty.

Pluralists (e.g., Dahl 1961, Polsby 1963) have been sharply criticized for setting forth a conception of the democratic state as a neutral arena in which organized groups compete with each other for access to state power and authority. C.B. Macpherson (1977: 77, quoted in Carnoy 1984: 36) for instance has suggested thinking about democracy as 'simply a market mechanism: the voters are the consumers; the politicians are the entrepreneurs.' Anthony Downs (1957: 3–141) has mapped out most completely the conception of popularly elected governments in liberal democracies as analogous to self-interested agents in a free marketplace, in which rival political parties compete for voters by supplying alternative policy products. Voters demand through the ballot box the policies of the party offering the most attractive programs. Market feedback mechanisms exist in which parties that fail to offer appealing policies see competitors succeed: they either restructure themselves and their policy offerings to be more attractive to voters during elections or fail and thereby 'go out of business.'

One of the problems with market analogies as a framework to understand liberal democratic political systems is that the analogy transposes the supposedly value-free character of economic liberalism onto investigations of the determinants of state action. Taken to its extreme, the liberal democratic state is conceptualized as a neutral arena or as an unbiased authority structure in which governments, parties, and policy alternatives succeed or fail in the democratic marketplace of political competition. This conception has come under sharp attack, both normatively and empirically. From a normative perspective, Theodore Lowi (1967: 6; 1969: 22–41) has argued that what emerged in the United States in the postwar period was what he termed 'interest group liberalism,' in which public authority was delegated to unaccountable private interests, who in turn employed it to further their own ends, and it is increasingly problematic to distinguish independent public authority exercised by state officials from the influence and power of entrenched interests (see also McConnell 1966: 339–40, 363–8). From an empirical basis, Marxist and non-Marxist scholars have argued that the implicit pluralist premise of the liberal democratic state as a value-free arena is misleading. Far from being an unbiased instrument, state action in capitalist polities benefits the long-term interests of capitalists over other societal groups, and indeed the state itself assumes a policy orientation favorable to the capitalist classes on most political and economic issues (Miliband 1969: 1–22; Lindblom 1977, 1982; Jessop 1978).

Crucial to Marxist and neo-Marxist arguments about the biased nature of the democratic capitalist state is the idea of 'relative autonomy.' It is conceded that Marx and Engels' charge from the *Communist Manifesto* that 'the executive of the modern State is but a committee for managing the common affairs of the whole bourgeoisie' (Marx and Engels 1848: 475) is misplaced, as it can be shown that capitalist states possess a significant degree of latitude in many policy-domains. Indeed, the argument that the state acts on behalf of the capitalist-class-as-a-whole is conceptually problematic, as the capitalist classes are divided among and against themselves in significant ways, and it is not clear how and whether a capitalist class interest as-a-whole emerges (for an extended discussion of these issues, see Jessop 1982, 1990: 79–104). Although the concept of 'relative autonomy' allows Marxists to get away from the *Manifesto*'s narrowly deterministic conception of the state, it raises important theoretical and empirical difficulties of its own. As Fred Block (1987: 83) explains:

> the central problem with this formulation is the difficulty of specifying the limits of 'relative autonomy.' The phrase suggests that if the state managers were to exceed certain limits, the capitalist class – or factions thereof – would act to bring the state back into line. But the disciplinary action would appear to depend on the degree of consciousness, consensus, and political capacity of the capitalist class, or its most important factions. . . . Alternatively, if the argument is that there are structural limits on the degree of state autonomy, then it should be possible to identify concrete structural mechanisms that prevent the state from exceeding its normal authority. Thus far, there has been little said about what those structural features might be.

The investigation and delineation of the 'concrete structural mechanisms' constraining state action has been central to the study of social democracy and democratic socialism within liberal capitalist democracies in Western Europe (see Miliband 1961; Coates 1975; Przeworski 1980, 1985; Esping-Anderson 1985; Przeworski and Sprague 1986; Przeworski and Wallerstein 1988; Jessop 1990: 170–89). A common theme that emerges from this work is the importance of the capitalist state's reliance upon a reasonable and stable level of economic activity to finance itself and its functions – what James O'Connor (1973: 6–9) has called the 'social capital expenditures' necessary to facilitate private capital accumulation and the 'social expenses' necessary to maintain social harmony and manage the social discontent that arises from economic dislocation in capitalism. The level and nature of wealth-producing economic activity in capitalist states is determined largely by private investment decisions, which in turn are heavily contingent upon expectations of future economic activity, private sector profit levels, and 'confidence.' Crudely put, the investment decisions taken by holders of capital in the private sector can constitute a kind of veto that capitalists collectively hold when they decide when, where, and how to direct their capital. The popularly elected governments that preside over the state and at least nominally articulate state power are held responsible and accountable by their electorates for economic prosperity. As a steady flow of investment capital is essential for the growth of productivity levels, and as productivity growth in turn allows for the possibility of higher standards of living, it becomes imperative for governments to assure continued investment that sustains economic growth and prosperity.

Charles Lindblom (1982) has argued that because state economic policy-makers have to regard investment as paramount, markets 'imprison' policy-makers. A government that does not regard investment and the maintenance of investor confidence as the overarching imperative will see its popular support erode. 'For a broad category of political/economic affairs, [the market] imprisons policy making, and imprisons our attempts to improve our institutions. It greatly cripples our attempts to improve the social world because it afflicts us with sluggish economic performance and unemployment simply because we begin to debate or undertake reform' (Lindblom 1982: 6; see also Lindblom 1977: 170–233). A focus on confidence offers a useful framework for the analysis of the 'concrete structural mechanisms' that limit state action, a framework with which one can investigate the limits of relative autonomy and the bounds beyond which policy-makers are unable to cross. Undoubtedly, a structural constraint stemming from the necessity to maintain confidence is most pressing on governments that are most ambitious in the scope of the reformist policy changes they would like to achieve.[2]

A useful non-Marxist discussion of structural constraint can be found in the concept of macroeconomic sustainability. Economists in the Organization for Economic Cooperation and Development (OECD) have noted that while sustainability 'is difficult to define precisely,' nevertheless 'the premise is that if a given course of policy encounters difficulties, it is because accumulating evidence suggests that the chosen course is, for one reason or another, unsustainable. The question of when, and how, governments come to recognize a particular situation as unsustainable, and the way such recognition influences subsequent

policy choices' is of interest (OECD 1988: 7; see also Krugman 1988).
A more technical, more quantitative, and ostensibly more apolitical
discussion of 'debt sustainability' has been offered by the Commission
of the European Communities (1990: 106–10) in its 1990 report on
the feasibility of economic and monetary union in Europe. The Commission acknowledges, however, that 'the empirical assessment of
sustainability is not straightforward because it is inherently a forward-
looking condition: at any point in time, whether or not a budgetary
policy meets the sustainability criterion depends on the future course
of taxes, spending, and macroeconomic variables like the growth rate
and the real interest rate.'

It might be argued that questions of structural constraint and
sustainability are really matters of fiscal and financial balance in which
problems emerge when national economies run continuing non-cycli-
cal current account and/or balance of trade deficits that follow from
overly stimulatory macroeconomic policies and when state expenditures consistently exceed the resources available in the national exchequer. But reducing the concept of sustainability to continuing
imbalance ignores extended periods of supposedly 'unsustainable'
macroeconomic policies. In the United States, for example, annual fiscal deficits in excess of $100 billion have been incurred since 1982,
with deficits in excess of $200 billion occurring sporadically in the
Reagan, Bush, and Clinton administrations. Indeed, the level of total
US debt more than doubled during the Reagan Presidency (1981–89),
surpassing $2 trillion and amounting to over 43 per cent of American
gross domestic product in 1988; under Presidents Bush and Clinton,
the overall size of the debt has continued to grow. But the United
States has been able to finance its deficits without difficulty; there has
been neither a confidence crisis nor a political crisis that has forced
the 'unsustainability' of US fiscal policy onto the American political
agenda. Sustainability, it appears, is more than a question of fiscal and
external balance; the American experience of sustaining the unsustainable
during the 1980s suggests that fiscal and external deficits are unproblematic as long as unconditional financing can be secured, and that the
financial community's confidence in the policies of a particular government is crucial to the sustainability of those policies.

The OECD (1988: 9) finds clear examples of unsustainable macroeconomic policies in what it euphemistically calls 'weak currency episodes' in Britain, France, and Italy in the mid-1970s and the early
1980s:

For reasons varying from one episode to another, but ultimately related to socio-political factors, the authorities . . . used macroeconomic policy to support real demand and incomes even after the terms-of-trade losses due to the oil shocks had occurred. They could not seriously tackle the root causes of their problems until the situation approached crisis conditions and the need for remedial action, on the internal as well as on the external side, became evident and broadly accepted by the unions and the population at large. The climax and the irresistible push to act came with a run on the currency, which raised fears of an uncontrollable spiral between depreciation and inflation. While in these episodes there was probably no dilemma in a fundamental economic sense between internal and external requirements, the deterioration of the balance of payments was typically perceived by the authorities as creating a policy dilemma up to the point where a currency crisis called forth a policy U-turn.

Governments that had sought to mitigate recessions through stimulatory fiscal policy actions found that they could not sustain this policy choice. Currency pressure and a loss of confidence brought forth a policy U-turn in which domestic demand and real income levels were suppressed in order to restore a greater degree of fiscal and external balance.

In the UK in 1976, the policy U-turn occurred in an atmosphere of acute political crisis, with the Government engaged in arduous and acrimonious economic policy discussions and negotiations with other governments, with multilateral international organizations, and with its domestic supporters. The pressures that directed a government with 'unsustainable' economic policies into a U-turn can be investigated as empirical evidence of the 'concrete structural mechanisms' that constrain state autonomy and sovereignty in significant and politically consequential ways. A central concern of the chapters that follow is to demonstrate the operation of these mechanisms at a state-to-state level, at a multilateral level, and at a structural level.

INTERNATIONAL REGIMES, INTERNATIONAL COOPERATION, AND THE ASSUMPTION OF VOLUNTARISM

In various policy realms, states and non-state actors interact with each other through regularized patterns of behavior that over time have evolved into institutionalized practices and customs that scholars have labeled international regimes. Stephen Krasner (1983: 2) has defined regimes as sets of

> implicit or explicit principles, norms, rules, and decision-making procedures around which actor expectations converge in a given area of international relations. Principles are beliefs of fact, causation, and rectitude. Norms are standards of behavior defined in terms of rights and obligations. Rules are specific prescriptions or proscriptions for action. Decision-making procedures are prevailing practices for making and implementing collective choice.

Analytically, regimes are linked to questions of national sovereignty in several ways. Regime-consistent patterns of behavior can be resistant to sovereign assertions of national authority when the sets of implicit or explicit principles, norms, rules, and decision-making procedures are institutionalized, yet in certain policy domains, regimes are essential to the effective realization of sovereign national choice (Krasner 1988: 76; see also Young 1989).

Robert Keohane (1984: 59) has argued that the 'essence of regimes' lies in 'injunctions about behavior' that are politically consequential and that are specific enough so that violations and changes can be identified. Somewhat differently, John Ruggie (1983: 198) sees international economic regimes as a fusion between national power and 'legitimate social purpose' that project multilateral authority into the international arena. Regimes for Ruggie (1983: 196) are 'part of the language of state action' and 'a concrete manifestation of the internationalization of political authority.' Conceived as behavioral injunctions and as projections of international authority, regimes have clear constraining effects upon state sovereignty by limiting 'the discretion . . . to decide and act on issues that fall within the regime's domain' (Ruggie 1983: 196). These constraints are one of the primary observable effects of international regimes which act as 'intervening variables' (albeit, with feedback mechanisms) between 'basic causal variables' (e.g., international power distributions) and 'related behavior and outcomes' (Krasner 1983: 5–10, 357–67; Keohane 1984: 64). As Krasner (1978: 87) has argued regarding American involvement in the international commercial and monetary regimes of the 1970s, 'the international economic system is no longer congruent with the underlying political power that sustains it. There is too much openness, too much interdependence.' Regimes mediate between basic causal variables (declining American power) and observable outcomes (continued economic openness) to explain the incongruence.

A focus on regimes as 'injunctions about behavior' and as manifestations of 'legitimate social purpose' involves elements of analysis that presuppose the existence of an international community organized around a set of shared values and/or beliefs (see Ruggie 1983). Regime analysis does not begin with institutions, but rather with principles shared among the participants that underpin institutions (Cowhey 1990: 177). Shared principles imply a social community, and it is this implied community extending across policy domains that makes regime analysis theoretically challenging to the traditional power-centric and state-centric realist concerns of international relations (Keeley 1990: 83–4; Haggard and Simmons 1987: 492; Young 1986: 107; on realism, see Morganthau 1948; Waltz 1959, 1979).

The challenges that the regime concept poses to the traditional focus upon power-centrism, state-centrism, and the implications of anarchy within the realist international relations literature occur not only at the conceptual level but at the normative level as well. Robert Keohane (1984: 5–7) is the most direct on this point: by focusing upon regimes, he is normatively concerned with the analysis of alternative mechanisms to maintain international peace and order in the face of declining US power and the attendant likelihood of the emergence of greater international conflict. Regimes are potential alternative mechanisms for maintaining post-hegemonic peace and order. Whereas realist balance-of-power theories of peace maintenance are built upon the characteristics of different polarity structures and the successful balancing of states in an anarchic global system (Carr 1939; Waltz 1964, 1969; Deutsch and Singer 1964; DePorte 1979), regime analysis is premised upon a normative base of international community, cooperation, and the joint realization of common interests (Keohane 1984: 5–7).

Regimes are not necessarily inconsistent with realist assumptions about national 'self-help,' however (Waltz 1979: 91, 105–7; Keohane 1984: 61–3). Keohane (1984: 65–109) offers a functionalist explanation to regime emergence and persistence in which regimes facilitate the long-run maximization of national self-interest. The essence of functionalism is that anticipated effects explain causes; with respect to regimes, the anticipated positive benefits that ensue from international cooperation explain why behavioral patterns of international cooperation occur and why they persist (see also Axelrod 1984). Indeed, the existence of a regime can alter the contours upon which national self-interest calculations occur in favor of regime cooperation. Reductions in information costs, the benefits derived from stability, the building up of behavioral expectations, the ideological biases built into and sustained by the regime – all of these factors can lead national authorities to prefer to conduct policy in ways consistent with cooperative regime arrangements and be resistant to other less cooperative potential policy options (Krasner 1983: 361–4; Haas 1983: 49–50; Keohane 1984: 8).

Interest definition is by nature resistant to precise measurement, and growing interdependence in the postwar international political economy has made the determination of states' interests *vis-à-vis* global economic policy issues increasingly complex. Moreover, with transnationalization, the distinctions between the state as a domestic actor and the state as an international actor have become conceptually problematic as the 'gate-keeper' image of the state as a regulator of domestic–external interactions is becoming increasingly obsolete (Keohane and Nye 1977: 33–5; Pempel and Tsunekawa 1979: 259–60; see Putnam 1988 and Evans, Jacobson, and Putnam 1993 for work that addresses these points). With respect to international economic regimes, the delineation and determination of the interests of the governing authorities is complicated still further by the diffusion of liberal economic ideas that have tended to increase the perceived benefits of mutual economic openness over closure and to diminish the perceived advantages of non-cooperation relative to unreciprocated cooperation (Ruggie 1983, cited by Oye 1986: 6; see also Gilpin 1987: 26–31, 389–94; Prestowitz 1988: 390–400).

Functionalist explanations of international regimes posit that state actors realize that they can 'do well' (self-interest maximization) by 'doing good'[3] (international cooperation). Stephen Haggard and Beth Simmons (1987: 492) see this element of regime theory as a kind of realist/neo-liberal synthesis within the literature, as a reconciliation of realism's emphasis on the *realpolitik* pursuit of interest with neo-liberalism's more normative concerns about the development and enhancement of international cooperation. Robert Keohane himself, while acknowledging the passing of an exclusively national conception of self-interest (Keohane and Nye 1977: 33–5), nonetheless argues that regimes 'should be comprehended chiefly as arrangements motivated by self-interest' (Keohane 1984: 63) and suggests a clear functional relationship between the self-interest calculations of national authorities and the construction and maintenance of frameworks for international cooperation.

Functionalist explanations of the emergence of international regimes have focused on international analogues to rational choice 'Prisoners' Dilemma' games in which there is an implicit assumption of voluntarism among the players[4] (see Keohane 1984: 65–84). While voluntarism is frequently not made explicit within the analysis, John Keeley (1990: 85–6) has noted that the essential functionalist notion of regime formation is one of 'freely shared judgments freely converging to a consensus. . . . lead[ing] to an interpretation of regimes as broadly voluntary, benevolent, cooperative and legitimate associations.' As Oran Young (1986: 109) explains, 'actors frequently experience powerful incentives to accept the behavioral constraints associated with institutional arrangements in order to maximize their own long-term gains, regardless of their attitudes toward the common good. . . . It is easy to comprehend why actors would willingly abandon a truly anarchical social environment for a world featuring recognized social institutions.'

Functionalist voluntarism, however, leads to an underemphasis both on the role of coercion in regime formation and on the importance of discipline and the manipulation of incentives and punishments in sustaining regime arrangements. The normative bias in favor of cooperation within the regime concept tends to confuse international 'cooperation' with what might be more appropriately characterized as manipulative coercion and the discipline of enforcing cooperation (Young 1986: 110). The respective conceptions of regimes by Ruggie and Keohane as the 'internationalization of political authority' and as 'injunctions about behavior' suggest implicit costs and punishments that ensue when policy choices are not consistent with the sets of implicit or explicit principles, norms, rules, and decision-making procedures that define the regime.

Moreover, regime analysis is often framed in the language of microeconomics, further complementing the implicit assumption of voluntarism (Young 1986: 109–10). Robert Keohane (1984: 240), for example, argues that 'to be successful, [post-hegemonic] institutions require not just a pattern of underlying common interests but a sufficiently favorable environment that the *marginal* contributions of international institutions – to minimizing transaction costs, reducing uncertainty, and providing rules of thumb for government action – can make a crucial difference' (my emphasis). The market analogy with its voluntarist premises is perhaps most explicit when Keohane (1983: 142) outlines a 'demand' theory for international regimes by incorporating hegemonic stability theory 'within a supply-demand approach that borrows extensively from microeconomic theory.' Through such borrowings, actors are conceptualized as freely making decisions regarding the extent of participation in international regime frameworks by calculating benefits and costs at the margins, with international regime frameworks conceived as freely formed cooperative structures that can be 'produced' and 'consumed' in greater or lesser degrees. Actors participate in the regimes, and the regimes persist over time, because the marginal benefit of regime participation exceeds the marginal cost.

REGIMES, COERCION, AND STRUCTURAL CONSTRAINT: OUTLINE OF THE ARGUMENT

Given the voluntarist premises within the regime concept as well as the normative value-biases in favor of international cooperation, the roles of coercion, manipulation, and discipline are relatively under-emphasized in the literature.[5] Susan Strange (1988: 31) argued for a conception in international relations theory of what she calls structural power, in which the possessor is able to alter the range of choices available to others. I am sympathetic to her argument, and in the chapters that follow I show through a case study of the 1976 UK–IMF crisis that international coercion, manipulation, and discipline can and do occur at multiple levels within 'cooperative' regime frameworks. For example, at the structural level, runs on the currency and a loss of confidence in the future value of assets denominated in that currency can occur in the face of real or perceived movements away from the liberal norms that embody the postwar regimes that govern international economic relations. At the bilateral and multilateral levels, 'help' to states experiencing balance of payments difficulties and/or a crisis of confidence is made available only with strings. It is clear from the case study that alongside the more cooperative elements, regime frameworks also present opportunities for coercion, manipulation, and discipline, and that the international regime concept and the international cooperation literature more generally mislead rather than clarify when the coercive nature of external pressures on national policy authorities is mis-specified as 'international cooperation'[6] (see Young 1986: 107, 110; Strange 1983: 349). With respect to national macroeconomic policy making, the constraints that manifest themselves to influence the range of choices and to foreclose certain policy options take many forms – the state-to-state influence and coercion that take place through international 'coordination' and 'consultations' regarding national macroeconomic policies, the conditionality that accompanies official multilateral loan assistance, and the policy pressures that stem from declining levels of confidence in the macroeconomic policies of a popularly elected government. Through a case study of the 1976 IMF crisis in the United

Kingdom, I seek to make explicit the voluntarist premises of international regime theory and to modify the regime concept by focusing on the constraints operating which limit the policy choices of national authorities and on the limits of state autonomy and sovereignty within the international political economy.

The case study chapters are organized chronologically at two levels of analysis: the systemic level of regime formation and evolution within the international political economy (Chapters 2, 4, and 7), and the domestic politics level of macroeconomic policy-making in the United Kingdom (Chapters 3, 5–6, and 8–10). Chapter 2 reviews the establishment of the International Monetary Fund in the postwar international monetary system with a focus on the conditional character of official IMF balance of payments financing that had emerged by the late 1960s. The chapter outlines the extent of British borrowings from the Fund in the 1950s and 1960s and the piecemeal extension of IMF conditionality to British drawings. I argue that the institutionalization of conditionality within the IMF and its gradual extension to cover British borrowings were 'imposed' rather than 'voluntarist' elements within postwar official financing arrangements. Chapter 3 reviews the record of the 1964–70 British Labour Government in selected macroeconomic policy domains and assesses the formative impact these experiences had on the leftward drift of Labour Party policy while Labour was in opposition in the early 1970s. I focus in particular on the development and evolution of Labour's Social Contract partnership with the TUC and Labour's policy shifts *vis-à-vis* the exchange rate. I argue that the central lesson that leading figures within the Party drew was that the 1964–70 Government had been a disappointment because potentially high rates of economic growth had been consistently foregone in an effort to maintain sterling's external value and because a rift had been allowed to develop between the Government and its trade union supporters. After Labour lost the 1970 general election, deflationary macroeconomic policy for the sake of balance of payments purposes and sterling stability as well as Labour's approach to the TUC underwent a substantial rethinking.

Chapter 4 returns to the systemic level to assess how IMF conditionality and official balance of payments financing facilities were transformed as a result of the 1971–73 collapse of the fixed-rate Bretton Woods monetary system and the 1973–74 Organization of Petroleum Exporting Countries (OPEC) energy price shock. I argue that in 1974 a new emphasis emerged regarding payments financing that held that a less conditional access to medium-term financing and a slower adjustment strategy were the preferred manner in which to deal with the massive external payments imbalances that confronted most developed and developing countries as a result of higher energy costs. Chapter 5 examines how the newly elected British Labour Government made the new financing-over-adjustment norm central to its economic strategy and reviews the policy orientation and political circumstances of the first several months of Labour's period in power, paying particular attention to fiscal policy, external borrowing, and the Government's problematic Social Contract partnership with the trade unions. This period was characterized by unproblematic, readily available external financing, little or no loan conditionality, and relatively little external pressure on the specific elements of domestic economic policy in the UK. I argue that with the new emphasis on financing-over-adjustment, the Government was able to maintain domestic demand and thereby reconcile the interests of its domestic political supporters with the terms of trade losses and global economic recession of 1974–75. The macroeconomic situation began to change in June and July 1975 with a substantial and sustained run on the pound. Chapter 6 reviews how British economic policy in 1975 became increasingly redirected towards the requirements for maintaining external confidence, both in the Government's downwardly revised public expenditure plans and in the 'voluntary' incomes policy arrangement the Government was able to extract under exchange market pressure from its trade union supporters. Up through March 1976, there was an increasing degree of 'structural' pressure exerted on policy decisions in the UK through the perceived requirements of external confidence. Although financing was becoming more worrisome and more problematic, there was as yet no explicit bilateral coercion or multilateral conditionality *vis-à-vis* the British authorities' economic management.

Chapter 7 again returns to the systemic level of analysis to show how the requirements for official balance of payments financing became qualitatively tougher in late 1975 and through 1976. The tightening of conditionality occurred largely in response to changed attitudes in the US Treasury and in the IMF about the levels of official and unofficial deficit financing that were occurring and concern about the slow pace of adjustment among deficit countries. The less conditional official financing arrangements and emphases of 1974 and 1975 were largely abandoned. Chapters 8 through 10 focus upon the 1976 UK–IMF crisis itself. I outline the different but interrelated levels of external pressure that were directed at the British Government during 1976 and show how the pressures for policy change operating at different levels tended to reinforce each other to bring about a deflationary reorientation of British economic policy. The crisis began in March 1976 with a new run on sterling, in which the pound fell from over $2 at the start of 1976 to reach a record low of $1.56 in October. The escalating stages of the confidence crisis prior to the Government's application for an IMF loan in September are outlined in Chapter 8: under intermittent but at times intense currency market pressure, the Government successively negotiated a second year of wage restraint with the TUC, obtained a short-term stand-by credit of $5.3 billion (to which the United States attached conditions), went through yet another round of public expenditure cuts, and moved hesitantly towards the public announcement of monetary growth targets. Nevertheless, pressure on the Government for additional policy retrenchment grew sharper in late September when sterling slipped beneath $1.70 just as the Labour Party's 1976 Annual Conference was beginning. Chapter 9 discusses the Government's crisis announcement to apply for an upper credit tranche IMF loan, the early negotiations between British and IMF officials for the loan, and the Prime Minister's efforts to arrange an additional support mechanism that would stabilize the potentially volatile official sterling balances that were held in London. The Government considered a range of policy alternatives, and Cabinet opposition to additional deflation was strong. Chapter 10 reviews the negotiation of the final settlement that resolved the crisis, involving eleventh-hour visits to Britain by the US Treasury Secretary and the IMF Managing Director, and intense and exhausting Cabinet sessions in which the Government ultimately yielded to the pressures for further deflation. The terms accompanying the IMF loan and the sterling balances support mechanism restored confidence in the pound, but explicitly constrained the Government's economic policy autonomy for almost the entirety of its remaining period in power.

In the conclusion, I draw from the materials presented in the case study to argue that international regimes under certain conditions are more appropriately conceptualized as coercive power instruments within a hierarchically organized world economy rather than as a framework for self-interested actors to cooperate and thereby to provide themselves with post-hegemonic collective goods stemming from international cooperation. International regime theory misleads more than clarifies, I argue, when it mis-specifies as international cooperation what are in essence highly coercive relationships.

2 IMF Conditionality and the United Kingdom, 1944–70: 'My Appeal was Essentially Based on Bogus Dignity'[1]

Robert Gilpin (1987: 122) has characterized the conflict between domestic economic autonomy and international economic stability as the 'fundamental dilemma' of international monetary relations, arguing that 'the manner in which this dilemma has or has not been resolved in large measure defines the subsequent phases in the history of the international monetary system.' This chapter examines the postwar evolution of the mechanisms by which conflicts between domestic economic autonomy and international monetary imperatives were reconciled, and how these mechanisms affected Britain up through the early 1970s.

Scholars have pointed to two sets of economic priorities held by participants at the July 1944 international monetary conference that produced the plans for the Bretton Woods international monetary system: first, the major capitalist victors of World War Two were committed to achieving strong rates of postwar economic growth and conditions of domestic full employment; second, the economic nationalism that had characterized international economic relations during the 1930s was to be avoided (Ruggie 1983; Gilpin 1987: 131). The emphasis was on achieving multilateral free trade and currency convertibility, but premised upon state action to secure desired national macroeconomic goals, including sustained growth and full employment. 'Unlike the economic nationalism of the thirties, [the postwar international economy] would be multilateral in character; unlike the liberalism of the gold standard and free trade, its multilateralism would be predicated upon domestic intervention' (Ruggie 1983: 209). Susan Strange (1983: 347) by contrast has argued that such a focus upon overarching principles and values is bound to be misleading, and she points to the Bretton Woods monetary system as an example of the static bias of such an approach:

> Facile generalizations about 'the Bretton Woods regime' abound – but they bear little resemblance to the reality. It is easily forgotten that the original [IMF] *Articles of Agreement* were never fully im-

plemented, that there was a long 'transition period' in which most of the proposed arrangements were put on ice, and that hardly a year went by in the entire postwar period when some substantial change was not made (tacitly or explicitly) in the way the rules were applied and in the way the system functioned.

Strange is correct in that the ways in which domestic economic autonomy and international monetary stability were reconciled evolved over the Bretton Woods period. As Kenneth Dam (1982: 128–30) comments, the Bretton Woods 'rules of the game' were never as rigid and inflexible as they seem retrospectively. Nevertheless, Benjamin Cohen (1983: 317) has argued that certain principles and norms of a 'balance of payments financing regime' can be discerned. For Cohen, the defining principle of the balance of payments financing regime in the context of both the Bretton Woods system and the post-Bretton Woods non-system is that the availability of payments financing for deficit countries should not be unlimited (Cohen 1983: 333; Bernstein 1983: 45).

In this chapter, the establishment and evolution of the principle of conditionality within the IMF are examined, with a focus upon the United Kingdom. In contrast to those scholars who characterize the postwar monetary system as part of the postwar 'consensual American hegemony' (Maier 1978: 46) and as the product of 'hegemony by consent [that was] open but reciprocal and agreed upon rather than imposed' (Ikenberry 1992: 290), I argue here that IMF conditionality reflected the interests and preferences of the hegemonic country of the system and was to a considerable degree imposed upon the other participating states despite their objections.[2] The initial agreement upon conditionality was based upon both ambiguity and coercion. As the Fund evolved and as principles were translated into policy to be applied in specific circumstances, there was a significant degree of opposition, especially in the early years.

ESTABLISHING IMF CONDITIONALITY, 1944–58

C. David Finch (1989: 8), an IMF staff member who was involved in arranging various loan agreements between the Fund and the UK, has operationally defined IMF conditionality as 'the practice of withholding access to IMF loans until the adjustment policies of the requesting countries are judged to be adequate.' Given the evolution of IMF conditionality and its central importance to the IMF's operations, it is noteworthy that the term 'conditionality' does not appear within the original *Articles of Agreement* that serve as the legal foundation for the IMF; in fact, conditionality did not become an explicit part of the IMF's constitutional framework until 1969 when the First Amendment to the *Articles* became effective (Dell 1981: 14; Cohen 1983: 321; De Vries 1985, 1: 485).

The monetary framework established at Bretton Woods placed currency market intervention obligations upon central banks so that exchange rates would be kept within narrow fixed margins. It was recognized at Bretton Woods that intervention obligations presupposed central bank holdings of foreign currency reserves, and the representatives were agreed that there should be a procedure by which international liquidity would be supplied in the form of official, prearranged borrowing facilities. The IMF was created in part to assure the availability of this financing (Cohen 1983: 319), as well as to provide official financing for balance of payments imbalances. According to Finch (1989: 8), 'the IMF was intended to be a financial cooperative, with a pool of resources available for use on a revolving basis as differences in the phasing of the business cycle in each country created rotating temporary financing needs. Although there were divergences of views, it was initially expected that the resources, although dispensed over time, would be provided virtually on request.'

Although the question of conditionality was scarcely mentioned during the deliberations at the Bretton Woods conference, the 'automaticity' of IMF loan assistance to countries experiencing balance of payments problems was a major point of contention in discussions that led up to and followed the conference. The British delegation to the June 1944 pre-conference discussions held in Atlantic City, New Jersey was under explicit instruction that deficit countries in the proposed IMF should not be required to pursue 'a deflationary policy, enforced by dear money and similar measures, having the effect of causing unemployment' (Dell 1981: 2). On the contrary, 'the British delegates thought it extremely important that members should be free to pursue desired domestic policies, even though these might have an effect on exchange rates' (Horsefield 1969, 1: 82). The American delegation by contrast wanted some assurance that the IMF's resources would not be wasted and that borrowing foreign currency from the IMF was not an unqualified right. Accordingly, the language in the IMF *Articles* governing the use of Fund resources was the subject of important discussion at the Atlantic City pre-conference meeting. The US delegation sought amendments to the draft *Articles* that changed the text dealing with member borrowing from '[a] member shall be entitled to buy another member's currency from the Fund' to '[a] member may buy the currency of another member country from the Fund,' and from 'the member represents that the currency demanded is presently needed for making payments' to 'the member country initiating the purchase needs the currency requested for making payments' (Dell 1981: 3). The aim of the changes was to make more clear that balance of payments financing was not an unqualified right.

The American amendments were not adopted. 'The United Kingdom had the support of virtually all countries other than the United States in wishing to place strict limitations on the Fund's responsibilities *vis-à-vis* the economic policies of its members': the final text of Article 5, Section 5 of the *Articles* reads that countries seeking balance of payments assistance 'shall be entitled to purchase' foreign currency, and that a country needing assistance 'represents that the currency demanded is presently needed' (Dell 1981: 2–4; Horsefield 1969, 3: 191). Given the failure of the US attempt to amend the language, most governments probably thought that when they approved the Bretton Woods Agreements they were approving the British principle of 'automaticity' in IMF loan facilities (Dell 1981: 4). Indeed, the minutes of the Atlantic City pre-conference meetings indicate that a presumption of substantial national autonomy from Fund direction had been established. The head of the British delegation Lord Keynes 'was asked if "the British recognized that in joining the Fund they were accepting some obligation to modify their domestic policy in the light of its international effects on stability;" he replied that they did – but at their own discretion' (Horsefield 1969, 1: 85). Having been addressed in Atlantic City, the question of automaticity in large measure did not come up when Article 5 of the *Articles* was subsequently discussed at the full Bretton Woods Conference, and there were no reservations filed by any member governments on the subject of conditionality when subsequently ratifying the *Articles* (Horsefield 1969, 1: 101–2; Dell 1981: 6).

Nevertheless, the United States insisted through the late 1940s that members' use of IMF resources was not automatic. The 1949–62 US Executive Director to the Fund, Frank Southard (1979: 17) describes American officials as 'uncompromisingly of the view that a way had to be found for the Fund to require countries to accept performance criteria as a condition to a drawing.' In May 1949, Southard outlined the American position in a memorandum to the other Executive Directors: 'The use of resources of the Fund by any member should be subject to close scrutiny to assure that any purchases conform strictly to the general principles and purposes of the Fund, as well as to the specific provisions of the Articles of Agreement. Any doubt should be resolved in favor of the Fund rather than in favor of the member' (Horsefield 1969, 2: 398). Southard also laid out specific criteria upon which the Fund should make determinations prior to approving a drawing (see Horsefield 1969, 2: 398–9), and the US began to challenge requests for IMF drawings from several countries in the late 1940s on the grounds laid out in Southard's memo (Horsefield 1969, 2: 398–9; Dell 1981: 9). In part because of disagreement between the US and other Fund members, and in part because of the US policy decision (pushed through the Executive Board after 'prolonged debate') that European countries receiving assistance under the Marshall Plan were not to request dollars from the Fund except in exceptional circumstances, a 'virtual freeze' was placed on IMF drawings after April 1948 (Southard 1979: 16; De Vries 1985, 1: 482; Dam 1982: 170–1). Officials inside the Fund and in member countries became 'disturbed at the small extent to which drawings were being made available to assist member countries in the kind of difficulties which the *Articles* had envisaged' (Horsefield 1969, 1: 276). Southard (1979: 17) recounts that the situation by 1951 'was creating great resentment among members. After all, most of them had paid to the Fund in gold . . . and, if they had no assurance of access to Fund resources, they were worse off than nonmembers.'

In November 1950, IMF Managing Director Camille Gutt attempted to break the impasse with a proposal that linked borrowings from the Fund to an undertaking by a member seeking such borrowings to take specific steps to overcome balance of payments difficulties. Although Gutt's proposal was challenged by European and other members of the Fund's governing Executive Board, it was in the end accepted as the only way for the Fund to resume its intended functions in light of the American position[3] (Dell 1981: 8–9; Horsefield 1969, 1: 281). Britain and France, however, withheld their approval from this decision by abstaining. The British argued that the proposal prejudiced the larger issue of the right of members to draw on the Fund; the French position was that the proposal tacitly assumed that members were ineligible to draw from the Fund unless they demonstrated otherwise (Horsefield 1969, 1: 281). 'It was a desire to enlist the cooperation of the US as the principal source of credit that prompted other Fund members to give way to American views . . . rather than any conviction on their part that adoption of the US concept of conditionality was indispensable for a successful functioning IMF' (Dell 1981: 10; see also Southard 1979: 18).

It was only with the acceptance of the principle of conditionality that IMF loan resources became widely available for use by member governments. In 1950, there were no approvals of drawings from the Fund, and there were only two approvals in 1951. The number increased sharply thereafter, however; between 1952 and 1965, 57 members drew from the Fund or arranged IMF stand-by agreements, some of them repeatedly (Horsefield 1969, 2: 460–3). As the use of Fund loan facilities became more frequent, loan conditionality evolved from an abstract principle to an operating policy governing IMF–member state relations. In a 1952 decision, the IMF Executive Board affirmed a statement by the Managing Director that outlined the expectations that would guide loan decision-making and reflected the evolving nature of Fund conditionality.

> The task of the Fund is to help members that need temporary help, and requests should be expected from members that are in trouble in greater or lesser degree. The Fund's attitude toward the position of each member should turn on whether the problem to be met is of a temporary nature and whether the policies the member will pursue will be adequate to overcome the problem within such a period. The policies, above all, should determine the Fund's attitude.
>
> (Horsefield 1969, 3: 228–30; Dam 1982: 120–1)

The Executive Board also outlined expectations concerning undertakings from borrowing states – 'When requesting the use of the resources of the Fund . . . a member will be expected to include in its authenticated request a statement that it will comply with the above principles' (Horsefield 1969, 3: 229) – which included the time frame for the drawing as well as the engagement that 'the policies the member will pursue will be adequate to overcome the problem.' The Fund, in deciding whether to 'postpone or reject the request, or accept it subject to conditions,' would determine the adequacy of the policies to be pursued (Horsefield 1969, 1: 189, 3: 227).

The Executive Board in 1952 also envisaged the stand-by arrangement, which over the following years became the standard framework for the provision of IMF financing. A member anticipating a need for Fund resources would negotiate a stand-by facility rather than an immediate drawing (Horsefield 1969, 3: 228–30; Dell 1981: 10). By distinguishing among what were termed 'credit tranches' comprising 25 per cent increments of a member's borrowing quota, the Executive Board established the policy that there were different levels of member borrowing and that the degree of conditionality was related to the extent of the drawing. The distinction among levels of borrowing made clear the low-conditionality of borrowings in the 'gold tranche' or the first credit tranche in that a member drawing an amount equal to its initial gold in-payment to the Fund 'can count on receiving the over-whelming benefit of any doubt' in the Fund's assessment of its domestic policies. With this provision, a degree of 'automaticity' in the Fund's borrowing policies was retained (Southard 1979: 18–9; Horsefield 1969, 3: 230; Dell 1981: 10; De Vries 1985, 1: 483).

The policy mechanics of IMF conditionality continued to evolve through the 1950s. Beginning with a stand-by request from Chile in 1956, the 'phasing' of drawings was introduced, in which drawings were not disbursed immediately but rather were spread out over a specified period of time, with each successive disbursement contingent upon the satisfactory performance of the borrowing member (Horsefield 1969, 2: 482). There were few objections raised by the Executive Directors to this innovation, and by 1958 phasing clauses were included in the majority of stand-by arrangements, especially those with Latin America (Dell 1981: 11; Horsefield 1969, 1: 431, 2: 481–4). In 1957, binding quantitative performance clauses appeared in an IMF stand-by agreement with Paraguay in which a ceiling was fixed for the total amount of national credit and a maximum budget commitment for government expenditures and public works was specified (Dell 1981: 11–12; Horsefield 1969, 2: 484). Several Executive Directors expressed concern about the inclusion of quantitative performance clauses. In particular, British Executive Director Guy Frederick Thorold noted that the Paraguayan loan was the first time a stand-by arrangement had been linked to bud-getary figures and that he 'would wish the record to show that the decision taken was on the merits of the particular case and was not to be regarded as a precedent for general application': several other non-American Executive Directors felt similarly. However, the US Executive Director strongly favored the specific quantitative conditions, arguing that the Fund through experience had learned the advisability of ad-justing terms to particular situations and circumstances; in the end, the Executive Directors approved the Paraguayan loan with the performance conditions (Horsefield 1969, 1: 431, 2: 485; Dell 1981: 12).

In 1958, a stand-by arrangement with Haiti was considered by the Executive Directors that contained a wider range of specific policy commitments, including a clause stipulating that 'if Haiti, without con-sultation and agreement with the Fund, departs from the budgetary or credit or other policies and intentions set forth . . ., Haiti will not draw further amounts under this stand-by arrangement before consulting the

Fund and agreeing with it the terms on which further drawings may be made' (Horsefield 1969, 2: 485). The US Executive Director supported the conditions, although several Executive Directors expressed misgivings. The Canadian Executive Director for instance objected to the detailed fiscal and monetary conditions, arguing that they 'went too far, involving . . . judgments of specific detail which the Board had not discussed' (Horsefield 1969, 2: 485). Despite these concerns, the Haitian stand-by was approved with its conditions intact, and the use of performance criteria quickly spread to other IMF stand-by arrangements. Also in 1958, the practice was begun whereby an applicant country would send a 'letter of intent' to the Fund formally outlining its proposals for corrective actions, including performance clauses (Horsefield 1969, 1: 433). Over time, IMF letters of intent became sufficiently standardized and routine that IMF Legal Department Director Joseph Gold (1970: 60–4, 271) could produce an 'illustrative stand-by arrangement' that included a letter of intent for an imagined borrower he called Patria.

By the end of the 1950s, the main elements of IMF conditionality were in place. It is clear that the introduction of quantitative conditions into stand-by arrangements was a departure from certain members' conception of the IMF's role; as the IMF official historian concedes, 'binding specific performance conditions for drawings under stand-by arrangements in their early days had to be defended against the charge that they were not in accordance with the concept of an assured line of credit' (Horsefield 1969, 2: 485). The shift from the 'member[s] shall be entitled' language in the 1944 *Articles* to quantitatively defined macroeconomic performance conditions and phasing by the late 1950s was significant and consequential. With the introduction of each new element of conditionality (usually with strong American support), concerns and objections from non-American Executive Directors were raised. But when concessions to the American position were not forthcoming (e.g., 1949–51), the Fund as provider of official financing resources ceased to function. Even after the principles of conditionality were firmly entrenched within the Fund's lending policies, the US continued to exercise an effective veto over the ability of applicant members to draw on the Fund. As US Executive Director Southard (1979: 19–20) recounts, 'the US voice in the Fund was decisive. . . . The practical question in those years, in any prospective large use of Fund resources, was whether the United States would agree – and the answer was obtained by direct inquiry.'

EXTENDING IMF CONDITIONALITY TO BRITAIN, 1956–69

The United Kingdom was the heaviest user of IMF resources during the first 25 years of the Fund's operation, drawing a total of over $7.25 billion between 1947 and 1971 (Horsefield 1969, 2: 464–7; De Vries 1976, 1: 395–6). The UK's heavy use of Fund resources began before the conditionality provisions described above were in place. The British drew $240 million from the Fund in 1947 and $60 million in 1948. Repayment of the 1940s drawings did not begin until 1954, and was not complete until 1959, at which time the UK was also repaying a 1956 drawing (Horsefield 1969, 2: 464–7). Moreover, prior to the late 1960s, the Fund's conditionality practices involving phasing and quantitative stipulations were applied primarily to arrangements with developing countries: the establishment of conditionality preceded its extension to developed country borrowings from the Fund.[4]

In December, 1956 in the aftermath of the Suez crisis, the United Kingdom drew $561.5 million from the IMF and arranged a stand-by for $738.5 million. In arranging the stand-by, the British defined the economic problem to be addressed as the restoration of international confidence in sterling rather than more fundamental domestic economic policy questions. As the IMF's official historian explains, 'while the British authorities believed that measures already taken should ensure a satisfactory current account balance for 1956–57, they were afraid that this result would be endangered if the loss of confidence were not overcome,' and the Fund staff accepted the UK position that the problem was confidence (Horsefield 1969, 2: 412; Southard 1979: 20, 27). Recurring difficulties, however, led the British to seek a renewal of the stand-by in 1957 and again in 1958, and these requests were also approved (Horsefield 1969, 1: 428–9). Although the British stand-bys were arranged during the period when phasing and performance criteria were fast becoming standard features of Fund stand-by arrangements with developing countries, the UK's 1956–58 stand-bys contained neither phasing requirements nor special quantitative stipulations (Horsefield 1969, 1: 430–2).

In the context of a growing balance of payments deficit, the UK again drew from the Fund in 1961 in the amount of $1.5 billion and arranged a Fund stand-by of $500 million (Horsefield 1969, 2: 460–3, 490–1). Although there was neither a published letter of intent nor a public statement between the parties about any attached policy conditions (Crawford 1983: 422), the IMF historian has described the process by which the 1961 arrangements were agreed. The British authorities in requesting the drawing explained to Fund officials that 'further considerable deficits' in the current and long-term capital accounts were likely and that the authorities would have to draw on exchange reserves for financing:

> The UK authorities clearly regarded this balance of payments position as uncomfortable and considered it vital for the United Kingdom to direct its whole economic policy to the goal of re-establishing a balance in external payments. Since attainment of this goal would take some time . . ., the UK authorities looked to the Fund to provide in the meantime that measure of support that might be required to maintain confidence in the pound sterling.
>
> (De Vries 1987: 53)

As in the late 1950s, British authorities were using IMF drawings as a means to shore up external confidence in the currency. Regarding domestic economic policy, the British position was that they were already taking adequate corrective measures, and the Fund staff concurred[5] (De Vries 1987: 53–4).

However, the 1961 stand-by arrangement included what was called a 'major shift' clause that stipulated that 'should any major shift in the direction or emphasis of policy become necessary during the currency of the stand-by arrangement, the [British] Government would, at the request of the Managing Director, be ready to consult with the Fund and, if necessary, reach new understandings before any request for a further drawing is made' (Horsefield 1969, 2: 488, 1: 490). It is important, however, to distinguish the 'major shift' clause from the stricter forms of conditionality that were being applied to developing borrowers during this period. While the 'major shift' clause did refer to changes in 'the direction or emphasis of policy,' the particular policy elements defined quantitatively were not specified. Moreover, the 'major shift' clause was essentially a commitment to 'consult'; by contrast, stand-by agreements with developing countries involved the prospect of a cut-off of Fund drawings in the event of non-compliance.

In 1962, the British requested another IMF stand-by for $1 billion with a justification that continued to be centered around international confidence. As the Fund historian explains, 'the UK authorities [in 1962] requested the new stand-by arrangement to help protect sterling from unforeseen shifts in confidence. . . . In effect the UK authorities were using the Fund's resources as a secondary line of reserves' (De Vries 1987: 55). The 1962 stand-by arrangement was renewed in 1963 and again in 1964, both times for $1 billion (Horsefield 1969, 1: 568). In the letter of intent which was part of the 1964 arrangement, the Conservative Government described its aims succinctly as 'growth without inflation' and included a 'major shift' clause (Horsefield 1969, 1: 572).

Only a few weeks after the 1964 stand-by had been arranged, 'it became apparent to the Fund staff that a substantial drawing . . . was to be expected' (Horsefield 1969, 2: 455). The British economy by mid-1964 was running a substantial balance of payments deficit. At the IMF Annual Meeting held in September 1964, the IMF Managing Director notified the larger member states that the General Arrangements to Borrow (GAB) might need to be activated in order to accommodate a drawing by the UK[6] (Horsefield 1969, 1: 568). An election was due in the UK by autumn 1964. Among European and American financial officials, 'Britain's political constraints were recognized. . . . Everyone understood that little could be expected in the way of policy actions before the election' (Solomon 1977: 87).

The Labour Party won the 15 October 1964 general election narrowly, thereby ending 13 years of Conservative Government in Britain. The inherited economic situation was difficult, however, with the 1964 balance of payments deficit expected to be a record £800 million, a magnitude that undermined confidence in sterling by raising the prospect that the new Government would be forced into devaluation. In late October, a formal proposal to activate the GAB in the event of any UK drawing was sent by the IMF Managing Director to the GAB participants. In late November, the British formally sought to draw the entire $1 billion available under the stand-by arrangement; eight days later, the funds were made available (Horsefield 1969, 1: 568–9).

None of the available accounts of this period (Horsefield 1969; Wilson 1971; Solomon 1977: 86–99; Callaghan 1987) indicate that the election of a new Labour Government and the drawing of the full amount of the stand-by soon thereafter prompted the IMF Managing Director to seek consultation with the British under the 'major shift' clause. However, a three-month central bank credit that had been put together for the UK in November 1964 (see Horsefield 1969, 1: 569; Solomon 1977: 89; Callaghan 1987: 175–6) was extended in February 1965 with a catch: 'it was only on the clear understanding that Britain would go to the Fund as soon as possible that central banks agreed to roll over the short-term debt for a further, and final, three months' (Strange 1976: 127; Crawford 1983: 423). The Fund staff in early 1965 made preparations for a further UK drawing on the order of $1–1.5 billion; in April 1965, the British applied to the IMF for a $1.4 billion drawing (Horsefield 1969, 1: 569; Solomon 1977: 89).

The official IMF historian has described the contents of the British letter of intent that accompanied the 1965 drawing as 'more specific' than the 1964 letter of intent:

> The Government's aims were spelled out as achieving a strong balance of payments, sustaining expansion, avoiding inflation, and repaying debt, and the Chancellor undertook (a) to keep in close contact with the Fund in relation to the United Kingdom's balance of payments position and, if asked by the Managing Director, to discuss this position with the Fund; and (b) to notify the Fund if any shift in the direction or emphasis of financial policy became desirable . . . and, at the request of the Managing Director, to consult the Fund about such shift in policy.
>
> (Horsefield 1969, 1: 572)

Although the British did take certain 'corrective measures' at the same time as they received the 1965 IMF drawing (see Ponting 1989: 72–80; Solomon 1977: 89– 90), these measures were not stipulated as part of the letter of intent. The IMF Executive Board in May 1965, after 'a prolonged discussion of the situation of the United Kingdom,' approved the requested drawing (Horsefield 1969, 1: 569). Conditionality, to the extent that it applied to the British use of Fund financing in the mid-1960s, continued to be more a matter of 'consultations' than 'conditions.'[7]

The British authorities, however, had other substantial external influences on domestic economic policy during this period. The British and American governments in 1965 and 1966 were engaged in extensive bilateral discussions about sterling's weakness, external financing, and domestic economic conditions in Britain (Ponting 1989: 80–1). According to American international financial official Robert Solomon (1977: 90), a 'crisis atmosphere' developed in the foreign exchange market for sterling during the summer of 1965, in which the US Federal Reserve System undertook 'quiet and informal consultations with other central banks' about the provision of assistance to the UK. 'Behind the scenes, an active discussion was taking place within the British Government and between British and American officials on the need for a more stringent incomes or wage-price policy. . . . Gradually a program was formulated involving an incomes policy with "teeth" on the British side and, on the American, leadership in assembling an additional rescue package for sterling' (see also Wilson 1971: 131–3). In June and July 1966, a heavier run on sterling precipitated a £500 million deflationary package of fiscal measures for 1967; to obtain foreign exchange to support sterling, British authorities again drew upon the short-term central bank swap network; there was, however, no direct involvement of the IMF in the Government's 1966 economic policy measures (Crawford 1983: 423–4; Ponting 1989: 284).

The deflationary package along with falling interest rates in the US and West Germany resulted in an improved balance of payments position and kept sterling stable until well into 1967. In fact, the British in early 1967 enjoyed inflows of short-term capital: in March 1967, the UK was able to repay in full the swap drawings and other borrowings from foreign central banks, and in May the Bank of England repaid six months ahead of schedule $400 million of indebtedness that stemmed from IMF borrowings in 1964 (De Vries 1976, 1: 431; Solomon 1977: 92). Due to a number of factors, however, sterling's strength did not last beyond the second quarter of 1967. Imports remained high while exports were sluggish, confidence in the future value of sterling weakened, and the in-flow of short-term capital reversed itself.[8] The drain on British currency reserves became alarming, and in September 1967, the authorities took action to hide the extent of the depletion through official borrowing from central banks and a one-day loan from the US Treasury (Solomon 1977: 93–4).

British officials held preliminary discussions about their financial difficulties with IMF Managing Director Pierre-Paul Schweitzer at the Annual IMF/World Bank meeting in September 1967; these discussions were followed by further talks in Washington about the possibility of financial assistance for the UK from the Fund. Schweitzer told the British that 'there would be great interest in the corrective measures that would be pursued' and that, as the GAB would have to be activated to arrange any UK drawing, the 'full support of other participants' in the GAB would be required (De Vries 1976, 1: 339). It was apparent to the Fund staff that the accumulated pressures on sterling were likely to result in devaluation, and the staff had begun calculations of the magnitude of a sterling devaluation and its likely effects on trade balances (De Vries 1976, 1: 432).

In the face of sustained pressure on sterling, the Chancellor of the Exchequer and the Prime Minister decided in early November 1967 to devalue the pound (Callaghan 1987: 218–19; Wilson 1971: 447–58). American officials were firmly opposed, primarily because of the anticipated effects sterling devaluation would have on speculation against the US dollar (Callaghan 1987: 220; Ponting 1989: 291). But American opposition did not translate into a willingness to provide Britain with unconditional financing. In fact, there had been efforts by central bankers meeting in Basle to avert sterling devaluation by arranging another central bank rescue package; on 13 November, the Governor of the Bank of England reported to the Prime Minister that 'the central banks were agreed that any support for the pound would have to be a major long-term operation involving an IMF stand-by credit of $3 billion which would only be available on stringent conditions. There would have to be strict credit control, a statutory prices and incomes policy, deflation, and an agreement not to float the pound, accompanied by strict IMF monitoring of the economy' (Ponting 1989: 291–2). Rather than accept such a loan, the Prime Minister and the Chancellor reconfirmed their earlier decision to devalue (Ponting 1989: 292; Callaghan 1987: 220–1).

Chancellor of the Exchequer James Callaghan is vague in his memoirs (1987: 220) about the specifics of loan conditionality in November 1967, recounting only that the Government was presented with the option of an American-organized $3 billion loan, accompanied by 'conditions which were not such as I could recommend to the Cabinet.' When it appeared that the Government would not accept the $3 billion with conditions, the possibility of 'a smaller loan of say $2 billion from the IMF, with milder conditions than those initially proposed by the United States' was raised; this too was rejected. According to Prime Minister Harold Wilson (1971: 453), the Americans insisted that any loan to forestall sterling devaluation must be an IMF stand-by of at least $3 billion rather than short-term central-bank credits, but in Wilson's account it was the IMF Managing Director who insisted upon the 'unacceptable and intolerable' conditions.

> Pierre-Paul Schweitzer . . . gave a ruling that . . . the rules of the Fund would require not only the agreement of the main banking countries, as members of the General Agreement [*sic*] to Borrow (GAB), but the imposition of rigid restrictions. M. Schweitzer instanced strict credit controls, a tightening of prices and incomes policy – presumably statutory – a limitation on growth, and an agreement that, while we might during the currency of the loan decide to devalue, we must pledge ourselves never to float. . . . Such conditions had be to rejected as unacceptable and intolerable. . . . M. Schweitzer, under American as well as British pressure, sought to qualify the conditions. But whatever *ex gratia* qualifications there might be, GAB agreement from the Group of Ten principal banking countries would still be required. In our view, this must lead to the most searching intrusions not only into our privacy, but even into our economic independence.

According to the IMF historian (De Vries 1976, 1: 339), it was clear by mid-November that devaluation was 'imminent,' and an IMF loan that would accompany rather than forestall devaluation quickly became the new focus of discussion.[9] On 17 November, a memorandum from the Chancellor of the Exchequer was presented to the Fund requesting the IMF's agreement to a sterling devaluation of 14.3 per cent, stating the UK's intention to seek a stand-by of $1.4 billion, and describing the related economic measures that were being taken (De Vries 1976, 1: 339). The note explained that the British Government had taken 'all possible steps other than devaluation to restore balance of payments equilibrium. . . . These steps had reduced the deficit on current and long-term capital account. But a hoped-for surplus had not materialized' (De Vries 1976, 1: 433). The British pledged that 'additional measures, including severe credit restraints, curtailment of government expenditure, continuation of the price and incomes policies, tightening of hire-purchase restrictions, and increases in taxation in the next budget, would accompany the devaluation' (De Vries 1976, 1: 434).

An IMF staff mission left Washington immediately for London to discuss the terms of the stand-by arrangement[10] (De Vries 1976, 1: 340). Of the seven previous stand-bys arranged for the UK prior to 1967, there is no indication within the IMF histories (Horsefield 1969; De Vries 1976; De Vries 1987) that staff missions had visited the UK prior to the approval of the stand-bys in order to discuss terms. But equally important, there is no indication that the 1967 staff mission had any significant impact on the policy changes that accompanied the stand-by. Mention of the IMF staff visit is omitted from both Callaghan's and Wilson's memoirs, and in fact, the Prime Minister suggests that it was the implications of just such an IMF mission that would 'go through all the books and be free to recommend changes in our policies' that reinforced his decision to devalue (Wilson 1971: 455; Callaghan 1987). In any event, the British sent a letter of intent to the IMF on 23 November (Callaghan 1967). When Roy Jenkins became Chancellor a week later following Callaghan's resignation, Jenkins decided that the letter – which 'had been considered line by line by the Cabinet' – should be made public (Wilson 1971: 469).

The British letter of intent was wide-ranging. Its opening, described as the 'governing paragraph' by the Chancellor (UK Jenkins 1967a: 645), stated that the Government's 'main objectives of policy remain the achievement and maintenance of a strong balance of payments, together with a high rate of economic growth which will make for full employment' (Callaghan 1967: para. 3). The Government also committed itself to measures 'to free resources from domestic use on the scale necessary' to secure a £500 million improvement in the balance of payments per year (Callaghan 1967: paras. 4, 5). The economic policy measures to accomplish the shift in resources were attached to the letter as an annex. Combined with the reduction in purchasing power that the devaluation entailed, the new measures would 'lead to a reduction of home demand by about £750 million to £800 million below what would otherwise have been the case' (Callaghan 1967: para. 7). The Government acknowledged the possibility that further policy measures might be needed to achieve balance of payments surplus: the letter of intent stipulated that reviews and consultations would occur with the Fund on a quarterly basis (Callaghan 1967: paras. 9, 10; De Vries 1976, 1: 341). The Government pledged that the public sector borrowing requirement for the financial year 1968 was to be 'kept under firm control' and would be held 'to not more than £1 billion,' and that the appropriateness of this target and the measures to achieve it were to be reviewed with the Fund (Callaghan 1967: para. 10). The Government also pledged to continue with its prices and incomes policy (Callaghan 1967: para. 12). With respect to monetary policy, the letter stated that it was expected that monetary expansion would be less in 1968 than was estimated for 1967, and that monetary developments in relation to expectations 'will be taken into account in determining appropriate policy actions' (Callaghan 1967: para. 11). The Government also pledged not to resort to any new or intensified restrictions on current payments, and to relax and abolish restrictions that exist 'as soon as the balance of payments allows' (Callaghan 1967: para. 13). Finally, the letter concluded with a statement that 'if . . . present policies should turn out to be inadequate, the Government is firmly determined to take such further measures as may be necessary to achieve these goals. If, in the opinion of the Government of the United Kingdom or the Managing Director of the Fund, the policies are not producing the desired improvement in the balance of payments, the Government of the United Kingdom will consult with the Fund during the period of the stand-by arrangement . . . to find appropriate solutions' (Callaghan 1967: para. 16).

Although the impression was created among certain 'spending' Cabinet ministers that the IMF was exerting 'direct control' over the Government's expenditure decisions (see Crossman 1976, 2: 587, 589), the Government took pains to give the opposite impression in Parliament. The new Chancellor Roy Jenkins when making the letter public stated that 'in spite of misleading reports to the contrary, the Fund has not attached conditions to this credit. . . . This letter sets out the policies already announced to the House that the Government are following' (UK Jenkins 1967a: 643–4). In response to questioning, Jenkins added that the letter 'does not in any way restrict my freedom of manoeuvre in arriving at the Budget next spring. . . . What we have to face at the present are not conditions of the International Monetary Fund, but the realities of the situation' (UK Jenkins 1967a: 646–7). Responding to a sharp attack from Labour backbencher Michael Foot, Jenkins told Parliament that:

> we have lived too long, under successive Governments, within an economic straitjacket. But [critics of the IMF stand-by] are wrong in seeing the essence of that straitjacket as being the decision to take a stand-by credit or the terms of the letter of intent. The straitjacket arises not out of that, but out of the facts that we have been spending abroad more than we have been earning, that 1967 will be our fifth successive year with a balance of payments deficit, that as a result we are heavily in debt, and that, again, under successive Governments, we have suffered eight major balance of payments crises in the past 20 years. Those are the stark facts of the situation.
>
> (UK Jenkins 1967b: 1197)

When asked by the Conservative Shadow Chancellor Iain Macleod about the final paragraph of the letter (quoted above) and specifically about whether the initiative for consultations between the Fund and the Government could come solely from the Fund – i.e., irrespective of the wishes of the Government – the Chancellor responded that 'the paragraph . . . means exactly what it says; but it is consultation and certainly not instruction' (UK Jenkins 1967b: 1201).

In introducing the letter to Parliament, Jenkins had asserted that a 'common view' existed between the Fund and Government about British economic policy which was expressed through the letter of intent, adding that 'we shall, of course, continue to consult with the Fund about the working out of this policy, but that is a normal international arrangement for all countries' (UK Jenkins 1967a: 644). However, when the British arrangement was discussed by the IMF Executive Board in Washington in late November 1967, it was just this question that certain IMF Executive Directors raised – whether the terms of the British stand-by were in fact a 'normal international arrangement for all countries.' There was a widespread view expressed by Executive Directors from developing countries that the British loan had been extended on 'less stringent' terms (Dell 1981: 13). IMF Managing Director Pierre-

Paul Schweitzer had anticipated approval difficulties from developing country Executive Directors, given that phasing and the accompanying possibility that drawings could be suspended were absent from the UK arrangement. Accordingly, Schweitzer

> took pains to explain the reasoning behind the proposed terms of the UK stand-by arrangement. Action was necessary to forestall or cope with an impairment of the international monetary system. There was a devaluation of a major currency, the need to support a return to confidence in that currency with maximum speed, and the need to maintain that confidence in the future. In these circumstances, it seemed to him that all of the financial support which the Fund could make available to the member ought to be forthcoming en masse whenever needed. This reasoning explained why no phasing . . . had been included.
>
> (De Vries 1976, 1: 341)

Schweitzer assured the Executive Board that the UK arrangement was not without qualifications. The IMF 'had made maximum and, Mr. Schweitzer thought, successful efforts to reach understandings on a program and had endeavored to find effective procedures other than phasing' for monitoring British progress. 'The Chancellor of the Exchequer had agreed to consult the Fund on a quarterly basis to review the UK economy and the balance of payments. If necessary, there would be more formal consultations . . . on any further action that might be required should the given policies not be producing the desired improvement in the balance of payments' (De Vries 1976, 1: 341).

While all Executive Directors ultimately supported the UK request, the Executive Director from Brazil Alexandre Kafka directly raised the comparison between the terms set for the UK and the terms that had become common for developing borrowers. Kafka noted that the British arrangement 'contained no provisions for phasing, no performance clauses, and relatively few ceilings on variables, such as credit expansion, that were often subject to ceilings under the terms of stand-by arrangements (i.e., performance criteria). In other words, although this stand-by was in the highest credit tranches, it lacked both a quantitatively defined program and the usual clauses contained in stand-by arrangements. Instead, it included unusually far-reaching provisions for consultations' (De Vries 1976, 1: 342). There was a substantive difference between quantitative stipulations for other IMF borrowers and mere consultations for the UK, and Kafka noted that 'the UK stand-by arrangement would certainly be studied with great interest by members, and . . . many might wish the stand-by arrangements that were approved for them to be modeled on the same lines, unless it could be demonstrated that their situations differed substantially' (De Vries 1976, 1: 342).

The Managing Director's position was that the British situation was indeed different – sterling was a major international currency, the devaluation had threatened the stability of the entire international monetary system, and the loan was extended in part in order to restore confidence (De Vries 1976, 1: 341). But Kafka's views on the Executive Board were not isolated: 'nearly all of the Executive Directors for the developing members supported Mr. Kafka's position.' The Mexican Executive Director 'hoped that this type of stand-by arrangement would be more widely used in the Fund's operations, thus ensuring uniform standards for all members,' while other developing-member Executive Directors 'hoped that the emphasis in the UK stand-by arrangement on general policy measures and consultations, rather than on quantitative targets and ceilings, signaled a departure from what they called the more rigid form of stand-by arrangement that had been customary' (De Vries 1976, 1: 343).

The issues raised in these deliberations led to a general review of IMF policies to determine if in fact industrial countries were subject to less severe terms when using Fund financing than were developing countries. The Executive Board undertook this review in August and September 1968, beginning with a paper written by the IMF staff that evaluated existing policies and recommended that they be continued (De Vries 1976, 1: 343–4). The staff argued that, except in three types of situation, the Fund's conditionality practices – including clauses inserted into stand-by agreements providing for consultation, phasing, and performance criteria – should be maintained. The first two exceptions dealt with 'low conditionality' drawings in the first credit tranche (see De Vries 1976, 1: 344); the third exception, however, was directly relevant to the recently negotiated UK stand-by. The staff view was that:

> phasing should not be stipulated when the stand-by arrangement had been requested to maintain confidence in the member's currency, ready availability of the full amount of the arrangement was considered essential as a deterrent to speculation, and maintenance of the value of the currency was important for the stability of several other currencies. In this . . . situation, the performance clauses would provide for consultation with the Fund.
>
> (De Vries 1976, 1: 344)

According to the IMF historian (De Vries 1976, 1: 345–6), the Executive Board divided into 'the familiar dichotomy of view' between industrial members who largely supported the continuation of the status quo, and developing members who had much greater difficulty with existing policy. Although Executive Directors from industrial countries 'recognized the importance of policies that gave equitable treatment to all members, . . . in their opinion the policies that the Fund had been following were in the right direction and were for the benefit of all members.' Executive Directors from developing countries, however, pointed 'to the detailed figures in the staff paper which showed that the number of performance criteria in the stand-by arrangements for members in the Western Hemisphere and in Asia was on average much greater than for members in Europe.' The 1967 British stand-by came up directly in the deliberations. The UK Executive Director defended the absence of specific safeguards in the arrangement, arguing that 'the UK economy was the subject of close examination by the Fund' and that 'therefore, the form of the stand-by arrangement did not mean that the United Kingdom could make use of the Fund's resources on terms that were any less stringent than those for other members.' Conditionality *vis-à-vis* the UK 'had been expressed largely in qualitative rather than in quantitative terms because the difficulties of accurate forecasting were particularly marked in the case of the United Kingdom. The letter of intent had included certain precise figures as goals, and the staff had frequently expressed their views in quantitative terms. But quantitative performance criteria would not have been effective and would have lessened the confidence-building effect of the stand-by arrangement, the key reason for having the arrangement' (De Vries 1976, 1: 345). But the fact that the quantitative elements in the British stand-by were 'goals' rather than 'conditions' and that there was no phasing to ensure the fulfillment of these goals was precisely the point of contention within the Executive Board.

According to the IMF historian (De Vries 1976, 1: 346), there did exist some common ground between industrialized country and developing country views. Industrial members agreed that equality of treatment was essential, while developing members conceded the point that 'equality of treatment did not mean identity of treatment.' The policy issues ultimately 'came down to reconciling the need for flexibility with the requirement that all members be treated uniformly.' As a result of the review, a decision that outlined the Fund's conditionality policies was taken in September 1968. The decision stipulated that phasing and performance clauses would be included in all stand-by arrangements beyond the first credit tranche, except in 'exceptional cases . . . when the Fund considers it essential that the full amount of the stand-by arrangement be promptly available. In these stand-by arrangements, the performance clauses will be so drafted as to require the member to consult the Fund in order to reach understandings, if needed, on new or amended performance criteria' (De Vries 1976, 2: 197). With respect to performance clauses, the divergent views of industrial and developing country members were reflected in the decision. *Vis-à-vis* developing members that had sought to limit the extent of the domestic policy conditions, the decision stipulated that 'performance clauses will cover those performance criteria necessary to evaluate implementation of the program with a view to ensuring the achievement of its objectives, but no others' (De Vries 1976, 2: 197). However, *vis-à-vis* industrial countries that had argued for a continuation of current policies, the decision acknowledged that 'no general rule as to the number and content of performance criteria can be adopted in view of the diversity of problems and institutional arrangements of members' (De Vries 1976, 2: 197). Nonetheless, IMF staff member David Finch (1989: 10) recounts that as a result of the decision Managing Director Schweitzer 'insisted that the next financing arrangement for an industrial country include for the first time provisions releasing IMF resources over time in association with performance undertakings similar to those used in developing countries.'

As part of the 1967 arrangement, IMF staff teams visited London at three-month intervals through 1968. Contrary to expectations, the British balance of payments situation did not dramatically improve following devaluation, despite additional deflationary measures in January and March 1968 (De Vries 1976, 1: 441; Jenkins 1991: 219–20). In Cabinet, the possibility was raised that if the March 1968 Budget was not sufficient to restore confidence in sterling, a second devaluation could occur (Crossman 1976, 2: 695; Castle 1984: 393; Browning 1986: 21; Jenkins 1991: 232–47). The British did, however, meet the quantitative 'goals' of the 1967 letter: the 1968–69 borrowing requirement was well under target at £500 million, while M3 grew at the slightly slower rate in 1968 of 7.5 per cent versus 9.8 per cent in 1967 (Browning 1986: 360, 363; Crawford 1983: 424). Nevertheless, the UK's current account deficit actually rose slightly in 1968, and it was in this context that the British drew the entire $1.4 billion amount of their stand-by in June 1968 (De Vries 1976, 1: 332, 440; IMF 1989b: 718, row 77).

From the IMF's perspective, the consultative arrangements of quarterly staff visits as stipulated in the 1967 letter of intent were not entirely satisfactory (see De Vries 1976, 1: 440–3). The Fund's view was that improvement in the British economy and particularly in the British payments situation had been 'disappointingly slow' following the devaluation: 'by mid-1968 the staff and several Executive Directors had come to believe that the measures taken were not fully effective and that, while the authorities had imposed strong fiscal measures, they had not made enough use of monetary and credit restraints' (De Vries 1976, 1: 441–2). The Fund 'urge[d] more stringent policies' in its quarterly staff visits, but as the Fund historian diplomatically notes, 'consultations revealed differences of view about the effectiveness of aggregate monetary restraints' (De Vries 1976, 1: 442–3). An informal seminar was held in London in October 1968 at a technical level between UK and IMF officials:[11] 'the seminar did not entirely resolve these differences of view, but a much greater tightening of UK credit policy nevertheless did occur, and . . . the situation of the United Kingdom began to improve' (De Vries 1976, 1: 443).

The 'much greater tightening' of credit in Britain was reflected in Chancellor of the Exchequer Roy Jenkins' April 1969 Budget Speech in which he stated that he attached 'the greatest importance to monetary policy.' Jenkins introduced the rate of credit expansion in the public and private sectors as a policy target in the Budget (although he did not publicly attach a precise figure); he acknowledged that the volume of credit in the British economy in 1968 had been 'a great deal more than we could afford' and pledged that the Government 'cannot allow credit to be supplied on anything like this scale in the coming year' (UK Jenkins 1969a: 1007–8). It is probable that this pledge to limit credit expansion was in part the product of external pressure. Through 1968, British and Fund officials had disagreed at a technical level regarding the effectiveness of monetary targets. However, 'early in 1969,' UK officials had informally indicated to the IMF that they would like to negotiate another one-year stand-by (De Vries 1976, 1: 348). Given Britain's external position, 'it appeared unlikely that debt repayments due on the 1964–65 drawings could be made' (Crawford 1983: 424; Jenkins 1991: 274). Certainly, the 1969 Budget was formulated with the knowledge that a letter of intent would need to be written to the IMF in the near future, and the inclusion in the Budget of a reduction in monetary growth as a policy target allowed the Chancellor to respond to subsequent criticism. When the Conservative Shadow Chancellor charged that the Government's 1969 commitments to the IMF 'make quite clear [Jenkins'] capitulation to the monetary policy doctrines of the IMF,' Jenkins was able to reply, 'it is rather odd to describe as capitulation a policy which I clearly announced in my Budget speech two-and-a-half months ago' (UK Jenkins 1969b: 1003; see also Browning 1986: 270; Benn 1988: 125).

Jenkins comments cavalierly in his memoirs (1991: 274) that in applying for the 1969 loan, 'some new regulations for the surveillance of those in our position had been agreed during the previous summer without our greatly noticing.' He visited Washington in April 1969 'to make a largely unavailing attempt to get Pierre-Paul Schweitzer soften the IMF terms. . . . My appeal was essentially based on bogus dignity. "We will in fact obey the rules," I said in effect, "but, please, don't make them nominally apply to us because we are such an important country".' Of the conditionality accompanying the 1969 British arrangement with the Fund, Jenkins (1991: 274) recounts that 'no major country (New Zealand was the nearest relevant approach to one) had hitherto accepted such a degree of surveillance.'

It is instructive to compare the stipulations of the 1967 UK–IMF arrangement with the stricter conditionality contained in the 1969 letter. Whereas the 1967 stand-by had contained a 'governing paragraph' listing 'a high rate of economic growth which will make for full employment' as one of the 'main objectives of policy' (UK Jenkins 1967a: 645; Callaghan 1967: para. 3), the 1969 letter made no mention of either full employment or high growth. Rather, the letter pledged that 'it is the Government's policy to do everything necessary to put the United Kingdom balance of payments on a secure and healthy basis, as an essential means to sustained growth and prosperity. . . . The objective is to obtain a substantial and continuing balance of payments surplus' (Jenkins 1969: para. 4). Whereas the 1967 stand-by of $1.4 billion was available immediately, the $1 billion 1969 arrangement was phased: $500 million was available for immediate drawing, but 'before making a request for a further purchase [of the remaining $500 million], the Government will consult with the Fund and reach understanding regarding the circumstances in which such purchases may be made' (Jenkins 1969: para. 1). Although both the 1967 and 1969 agreements stipulated quarterly consultations, the 1969 consultations, accompanied by phasing and the commitment to 'reach understanding' prior to additional drawings, were of a more stringent character (Callaghan 1967: paras 9, 16; Jenkins 1969: paras 1, 13).

With respect to the quantitative policy stipulations, the Government in the 1969 letter stated its 'intentions' and 'objectives.' While the 1967 arrangement had included 'expectations' of lower money growth and 'so far as can be seen at present' a borrowing requirement under

£1 billion (Callaghan 1967: paras 10, 11), the 1969 performance clauses covered a wider scope and were more specifically defined. The 1969 letter stated that the Government's objective for the financial year 1969–70 was 'to obtain a surplus of at least £300 million on the current and long-term capital account of the balance of payments' (Jenkins 1969: para. 5). To reach this external surplus, the letter outlined the Government's commitment to limit the growth of public expenditure and private consumption 'so that there is room for the desired substantial and continuing balance of payments surplus to develop. . . . For 1969–70 public expenditure will . . . be held within the totals announced . . . which allowed for an increase of 1 per cent in real terms. . . . In 1969–70 the Central Government's accounts . . . are intended to be in surplus by at least £850 million' (Jenkins 1969: paras 5–7). With respect to monetary policy, which had been an area of disagreement in 1968, the letter repeated the commitments Jenkins had made in his 1969 Budget statement that 'the Government attaches the greatest importance to monetary policy' and that 'the increase in credit in the economy was too high, and the Government intends not to permit credit to be supplied to the economy on anything like this scale in 1969–70' (Jenkins 1969: para. 8). The letter went further, however, by affixing specific Domestic Credit Expansion (DCE) targets and by pledging that the Government would monitor the achievement of these targets quarterly.

> The Government's objectives and policies imply a domestic credit expansion for the private and public sectors in [1969–70] of not more than £400 million, compared with some £1,225 million in 1968–69. It is the Government's policy to ensure that the course quarter by quarter of domestic credit expansion . . . is consistent with the intended result for the year as a whole, and to take action as appropriate to this end.
>
> (Jenkins 1969: paras 8–9)

When the IMF Executive Board considered the UK arrangement in June 1969, Managing Director Schweitzer told the Board that he was satisfied that the arrangement was consistent with the Fund's new policy regarding stand-bys (De Vries 1976, 1: 348). The elements that had been criticized within the Executive Board in 1967 – the lack of phasing and the operationalization of conditionality as consultation – were rectified with the 1969 arrangement, and it was 'readily accepted' by the Board (De Vries 1976, 1: 349). The British drew $500 million from the stand-by in late June 1969. In September 1969, December 1969, and March 1970, the Executive Board agreed that the UK had consulted with the Fund on its fiscal and monetary policies and that the British could make further drawings: the British drew $175 million, $175 million, and $150 million respectively (De Vries 1976, 1: 349–51, 321).

Beginning in late 1969, the British balance of payments moved into substantial surplus with continued improvement through 1970 and 1971. The British were able to repay entirely their June 1968 drawings by August 1971 (repayment was not scheduled to be complete until June 1973). By the end of 1971, the UK had 'virtually eliminated its short-term and medium-term obligations,' and in 1972, it completed repayment of the last of the IMF drawings from the 1960s (De Vries 1976, 1: 351, 396; De Vries 1985, 1: 34, 569; Crawford 1983: 425). When outlining British intentions to repay its IMF borrowings early, UK Executive Director Derek Mitchell in March 1972 'emphasized to the Fund management that the 1969 stand-by arrangement and the Fund's subsequent close surveillance of the UK economic situation had received adverse comments in the UK press and in the UK Parliament. Hence, for domestic political reasons the UK authorities were especially eager to repay all their outstanding indebtedness to the Fund and to announce the repayment publicly as soon as possible . . . in order to present it as voluntary' (De Vries 1985, 1: 32–3).

With respect to monetary policy, further discussions were held between IMF and UK officials in April 1970: 'there was a much greater harmony of opinions than at the earlier seminar, and very few areas of difference now remained' (De Vries 1976, 1: 445; see also Browning 1986: 273–4). The British Treasury had begun internal intermediate monetary targeting at the behest of the IMF following the 1967 devaluation and stand-by (Fforde 1982: 66), and the Chancellor had publicly announced a DCE target in the 1969 letter of intent. But despite the 'greater harmony of opinions,' public announcement of monetary targets was not continued. Although internal intermediate monetary targeting continued through the early 1970s and 'constituted an internal aim' of policy (Richardson 1978: 53), monetary targeting during this period can hardly be regarded as effective at containing monetary growth, given the explosive M3 growth rates of over 25 per cent in 1972 and 1973 (Browning 1986: 360). In fact, UK officials by 1972 had adopted a macroeconomic policy posture that de-emphasized monetary control: during the annual UK–IMF consultations in July 1972 (when the British were no longer subject to Fund conditionality because of the early repayment), 'UK authorities . . . seemed convinced that wage demands were more a cause of the rise in domestic prices than were increases in domestic money supply' (De Vries 1985, 1: 49). The monetary control emphases imposed upon the British by the IMF in the late 1960s had clearly receded once the loans were repaid.

CONCLUSION

This chapter has reviewed the imposition and institutionalization of conditionality within the IMF's lending policies, and its extension to cover the UK's borrowings from the Fund. Although neither the institutionalization of conditionality nor its extension was without controversy, by the late 1960s the process was largely complete. The Fund historian comments that 'as the membership of the Fund grew and as stand-by arrangements became commonly used by members in all regions, the working out of a financial program as a prelude to a stand-by arrangement became almost a standard practice. . . . The Fund tried to make certain that the programs set up for different members were as consistent and uniform as possible' (De Vries 1976, 1: 364–5).

The various elements of the institutionalization of IMF conditionality can be summarized into four points. First, by the late 1950s, a stand-by available for a fixed period rather than a direct and immediate loan was the framework by which the IMF provided financing for borrowing members. Second, the process of arranging a stand-by was highly standardized. Low conditionality in the first credit tranche became an established practice, and if a member stated its intention to borrow in the upper tranches, a staff visit would occur to discuss the accompanying economic program, and a letter of intent would be written that would include stipulations regarding government borrowing, monetary policy, trade, credit, etc. In some ways, this standardization tended to make the arrangement of an IMF stand-by a technical rather than political matter, and during the 1950s, the IMF staff developed close working relations on a technical level with the economic authorities from a host of developing countries (De Vries 1976, 1: 364–5; De Vries 1987: 64–70, 102–9). Third, a 'principle of uniformity' that stipulated formal equality between all Fund members and similar treatment of all borrowers was operationally incorporated into the IMF's borrowing practices over time (Gold 1979: 489–94). When in 1967 and 1968 developing members charged that they were not being treated fairly, industrial members conceded the point that 'equality of treatment for all members was essential and that such treatment should explicitly be seen as being equal' (De Vries 1976, 1: 346). In practice, the principle of uniformity had a 'leading role' in the evolution of the mechanisms by which members made use of IMF resources (Gold 1979: 489) and was an important factor leading to the extension of stricter forms of conditionality to developed members like the UK in the late 1960s. Fourth, there was no symmetry between surplus and deficit countries in the balance of payments adjustment burdens. Fund-supervised balance of payments stabilization programs applied only to deficit countries seeking the use of IMF resources; the early conception of the Fund as 'a financial cooperative, with a pool of resources available for use on a revolving basis as differences in the phasing of the business cycle in each country created rotating temporary financing needs' (Finch 1989: 8) did not endure.

Up through the early 1970s, a clear trend can be observed in the extension of IMF conditionality over British economic and monetary policy, from the near no-conditionality drawings of 1956 and 1961 to the considerably stiffer terms that were associated with the stand-bys and drawings of the late 1960s. It is perhaps in the field of monetary policy that the IMF's influence on British economic affairs during the 1960s can be most clearly observed. In 1959, the Government published the Radcliffe Report concerning monetary policy and financial institutions that, according to the 1973–83 Governor of the Bank of England Gordon Richardson, illustrated the general tone of British Governments during the late 1950s and early 1960s towards the issue of monetary control; the report stated that the authorities 'regard the structure of interest rates rather than the supply of money as the centrepiece of the monetary mechanism. This does not mean that the supply of money is unimportant, but that its control is incidental to interest rate policy' (quoted by Richardson 1978: 51). By contrast, monetary growth constraints and Domestic Credit Expansion ceilings were central to Fund stand-by arrangements: 'the view of the staff and of the Executive Directors [was] that changes in the money supply and credit in an economy had a strong impact on aggregate domestic demand and a related effect on the balance of payments'[12] (De Vries 1976, 1: 363). The British authorities, however, were reluctant to accept the importance ascribed by Fund officials to the control of the money supply, and as late as October 1968, UK and Fund officials were disagreeing at a technical level over monetary control.

IMF staff-member C. David Finch (1989: 10) argues that it was weakness in monetary policy that was responsible for the persistent UK payments difficulties in 1968. Finch recounts that 'the political authorities found it hard to make the decision to allow higher interest

rates by removing support from bonds in times of market pressure. . . .
Linking further IMF financing to a crucial decision became a key to
action.' It was in anticipation of applying for an additional IMF stand-
by that Chancellor of the Exchequer Roy Jenkins declared in April
1969 that 'I attach the greatest importance to monetary policy' and
pledged a reduction in the money supply and domestic credit levels
(UK Jenkins 1969a: 1007–8); when the Government published its 1969
letter of intent, a specific credit ceiling figure was included, to be further specified to the IMF in terms of quarterly targets (Jenkins 1969:
para. 9). As IMF staff-member Finch (1989: 10) recounts, 'since the
limits on bank credit could be met only if the Bank of England cur-
tailed its support of the bond market, the Government agreed to the
crucial tightening of monetary policy.' The instruments of monetary
policy in Britain had thus reversed themselves in the ten years between the 1959 Radcliffe Report and the 1969 IMF stand-by: UK
monetary policy had moved from interest rate management in which
control of the money supply was 'incidental to interest rate policy' to
publicly announced credit targets in which interest rates on government bonds had to be free to rise. IMF conditionality was a crucial
element of the process by which this shift occurred.

3 New Directions for Labour, 1970–74:
'We Must in the Future Alter the Priorities in Favour of Economic Growth'[1]

The Labour Party came to power in the February 1974 general election upon a campaign manifesto pledging 'a fundamental and irreversible shift in the balance of wealth and power in favour of working people and their families' (Labour Party 1974a: 15). In this chapter, the experiences and 'lessons' of Labour's 1964–70 period in government as well as the party's policy development during the 1970–74 opposition period are selectively reviewed in order to understand the origins of the policy emphases that were curbed in 1975 and 1976. The evolution of Labour policy in two critical areas up to 1974 are examined – sterling's exchange rate and relations with the trade unions. Problems that emerged in each of these policy domains came to exert decisive influences upon both the 1964–70 and the 1974–79 Labour Governments.

EXCHANGE RATE POLICY AND THE 1967 DEVALUATION

The United Kingdom between 1945 and 1972 experienced two politically traumatic devaluations, both under Labour Governments. In 1949, sterling was devalued by over 30 per cent, from $4.03 to $2.80, and the Government's capitulation to devaluation pressures in the late 1940s made senior ministers of the next Labour Government in 1964 extremely unwilling to bear the stigma of another postwar devaluation. Both Prime Minister Harold Wilson and Chancellor of the Exchequer James Callaghan saw the 1949 devaluation as one of the factors leading to Labour's 1951 electoral defeat (Ponting 1989: 65; Callaghan 1987: 159–60). As Callaghan recounts in his memoirs (1987: 159), 'it is difficult to recreate at this distance of time how violently public and international sentiment opposed any idea of devaluing the second most important reserve currency in the world. It was almost a moral issue.' Avoiding devaluation, however, proved difficult and ultimately impossible for Harold Wilson's 1964–70 Government, and the futility of maintaining sterling's exchange rate at $2.80 was a searing experience. When Labour came to power in October 1964, senior ministers were told that Britain was running an unprecedented balance of payments deficit of £750–£800 million for the year and that the Bank of England's foreign currency reserves were inadequate to defend the pound without a change in policies (Callaghan 1987: 169, 174–5). Devaluation was briefly considered at the highest levels of the Government and was immediately rejected (Burk et al. 1988: 47–50; MacDougall 1987: 152–6). As Callaghan (1987: 159–60) recounts, 'if we had devalued on coming to power in October 1964, the Tory Opposition as well as the press would have hammered home day after day that devaluation was always Labour's soft option, and took place whenever a Labour Government was elected' (see also Wilson 1971; Crosland 1982: 125–6; Ponting 1989: 65–6). Instead, the new Government imposed an import surcharge of 15 per cent on manufactured products, accompanied by a mildly deflationary mini-budget (Ponting 1989: 66–9; Callaghan 1987: 170–3).

Complicating the exchange rate difficulties was the Government's weak five-seat parliamentary majority that quickly narrowed to three after a surprising by-election loss in early 1965. A second election was expected soon. When one of Prime Minister Wilson's Cabinet colleagues argued for the necessity of devaluation, Wilson responded, 'you're talking nonsense. Devaluation would sweep us away. We would have to go to the country defeated. We can't have it' (Crossman 1975, 1: 71; Ponting 1989: 71). The Chancellor too felt that Labour's slim majority and the expectation of a second election made devaluation impossible; 'given our minute majority, I did not see how we could hope to win the second general election that was bound to follow within a short time, with a sterling devaluation hanging around the Government's neck' (Callaghan 1987: 160).

Given that the Bank of England's currency reserves were insufficient and that the Government had decided against devaluation, the British turned to the United States for assistance, having kept the United States fully apprised of economic developments in the UK (Callaghan 1987: 159; Ponting 1989: 46). In mid-1965, the US Government under President Lyndon Johnson began internal discussions about the terms upon which financial support would be made available to London. By autumn, a secret *quid pro quo* with the British had been worked out: if the UK pledged to continue its strategic defense commitments in Germany and east of Suez, to deflate the domestic economy, and to abstain from stimulatory economic policy measures in the future, the US would assist in holding sterling at $2.80 and devaluation would be avoided (Ponting 1989: 80–1). When the pound came under pressure in late July 1965, a deflationary package was approved by the Cabinet in an emergency atmosphere; devaluation as an alternative was not considered (Ponting 1989: 78–9). The United States delivered on the *quid pro quo* in September 1965 when the New York Federal Reserve Bank and the Bank of England coordinated a counter-attack on international currency exchanges in support of sterling, following the British Trades Union Congress' formal acceptance of the Government's statutory pay policies (Callaghan 1987: 190; Solomon 1977: 90–1). Coordinated central bank action combined with the Government's domestic deflation efforts kept sterling stable into 1966.

The Government called and decisively won a general election in March 1966, increasing its parliamentary majority to 97. If devaluation had previously been undesirable because of the Government's parliamentary weakness and the anticipation of a second election, both of these factors ceased to be issues after March 1966 (Ponting 1989: 167). The Government did not have to wait long for pressure to re-emerge on sterling. In July 1966, following some imprudent public comments of visiting French Prime Minister Georges Pompidou that France had had a successful devaluation in 1958 and that Harold Wilson should act to straighten out the British economy, devaluation was suddenly and unexpectedly an issue again as sterling weakened on foreign exchange markets. The Bank of England reported to the Prime Minister and the Chancellor that British reserves were dropping sharply and that major action was again needed to restrain domestic demand (Ponting 1989: 189–90; Callaghan 1987: 196–7). In crucial Cabinet meetings on 19 and 20 July 1966, the Government formally considered and rejected devaluation by a vote of 17:6 in favor of an emergency budget that cut £500 million from the Government's expenditure plans; additionally, a six-month statutory wage freeze was approved, to be followed by six months of 'severe restraint' on wage increases. The July 1966 measures were the most extensive deflationary package from the Government yet and belied Labour's policy promise upon coming to power in 1964 that it would overcome the 'stop' phase of British 'stop-go' macroeconomic policy (Ponting 1989: 190–200; Crossman 1975, 1: 576–8; Callaghan 1987: 198–9; MacDougall 1987: 168–70; Castle 1984: 149–50; Benn 1987: 457–8). Nonetheless, sterling was held at $2.80.

In February 1967, the United States proposed that the secret *quid pro quo* of 1965 be put on a permanent basis, that a joint sterling–dollar area be created that would protect both currencies as well as the position of gold, and that a 25-year multi-billion dollar loan be arranged to fund all sterling debts at the $2.80 parity. In return, the United Kingdom would commit to maintaining its strategic position in the Far East as well as the continuation of its policy orientation of demand suppression (Ponting 1989: 288–9; Callaghan 1987: 185, 211–12). The American proposal was rejected by the British for two reasons. First, the deal would have made the contemplated UK entry into the European Economic Community impossible because of French President Charles De Gaulle's certain objections to it. Second, unlike the secret *quid pro quo* of 1965, the 1967 deal would have been a public arrangement in which the British exchanged a significant degree of macroeconomic autonomy and a costly geo-strategic commitment in return for financial support; a public deal was not acceptable (Ponting 1989: 288–9; Callaghan 1987: 212). Instead, the Prime Minister and the Chancellor hoped that by running the domestic economy beneath full capacity and by gradually curtailing Britain's east of Suez geo-strategic positions, a payments surplus would be possible in 1967 and 1968. While the Government still wished to avoid devaluation, Wilson considered the 1965 deal with the United States to be terminated, having rejected the offer to put it on a more permanent basis (Ponting 1989: 103–4, 288–9).

In October 1967, sterling once again came under exchange market pressure due to a variety of factors.[2] By this time, the Prime Minister himself had come around to the necessity of reconsidering devaluation (Crossman 1976, 2: 437; Shore 1988: 53), having consistently and autocratically forbidden even its mention for the previous three years (see Crosland 1982: 136, 152–3, 184–9; Whitehead 1985: 6; MacDougall 1987: 156, 1988: 52; Sheldon 1988: 51; Jay 1988: 52; Benn 1989: 510). As pressure on sterling mounted, the Head of the Government Economic Service Alec Cairncross met with the Chancellor to tell him that devaluation was unavoidable. Cairncross (1988: 53) recounts that Callaghan 'was not easily persuaded that devaluation was inevitable. . . . I put it to him that we were in for a very large external deficit for the next year and that he would be asked repeatedly through the winter "what are you doing about it?" And he would have no answer' (see also Callaghan 1987: 218). The Prime Minister concurred a few days later, and on 13 November 1967, Wilson, Callaghan, the Bank of England Governor Leslie O'Brien, and two senior officials fixed the new sterling rate at $2.40 (Callaghan 1987: 221). A public announcement was made five days later.

Devaluation was a major setback for the Government. Successively subordinating virtually all other economic policy aims to the maintenance of sterling at $2.80, the sense of defeat when devaluation finally occurred was crushing. In holding off devaluation for three years, the Government had largely surrendered control over the broader direction of both its domestic macroeconomic policy and its strategic defense posture, a sizeable external debt had been incurred defending sterling, and much of the domestic macroeconomic agenda upon which the Government had been elected was repudiated. The Government had squandered the goodwill of the Trades Union Congress (TUC) on incomes policies that had proved unable in the end to avoid devaluation, and trade union antagonism was rising sharply (see Coates 1989: 37–67). When the Government finally did devalue, it was clearly not a policy that had been chosen willingly; as Chancellor of the Exchequer Callaghan bluntly told the Cabinet, 'this is the most agonizing reappraisal I have ever had to do and I will not pretend that it is anything but a failure of our policies' (Castle 1984: 325; Ponting 1989: 292).

Devaluation notwithstanding, the Government's ability to maintain the new sterling parity of $2.40 continued to be a worry through 1968 and 1969 for Callaghan's successor as Chancellor, Roy Jenkins (see Jenkins 1991: 219–20, 234–45, 255–6, 271–2). After Labour lost the 1970 general election and went into opposition, reassessment of its policy on sterling began almost immediately. Fabian Socialists in the party held a seminar attended by ex-Ministers that discussed the Government's record. As one participant described it, the seminar concluded that 'the decision not to devalue in 1964 did dictate the whole pattern of the Government and yet it was never collectively discussed by Ministers' (Benn 1988: 305). When Harold Wilson published his memoirs in 1971, he noted in the first sentence of the preface (1971: xvii) that 'this book is the record of a Government all but a year of whose life was dominated by an inherited balance of payments problem which was nearing a crisis at the moment we took office; we lived and governed during a period when that problem made frenetic speculative attack on Britain both easy and profitable.' Within the party's policy-making organs, a rethinking of exchange rate policy commenced. In June 1971, the Labour Party Industrial Committee in a paper on domestic unemployment questioned the commitment to a fixed external value for sterling, arguing that 'to ensure that the balance of payments does not again become a major obstacle of growth . . . direct action will be needed, as necessary, on our terms of trade. [This means] . . . a deliberate policy of adjusting the parity of the pound to accord with the basic facts of our trade balance, instead, as in the past, of waiting for a massive balance of payments crisis to force change upon us' (Hatfield 1978: 62). Shadow Chancellor of the Exchequer Roy Jenkins was equivocal about exchange rate policy in his speech at the 1971 Labour Party Conference, arguing on the one hand that 'we should never again allow ourselves to be a prisoner of a rigid over-valued exchange rate, and a currency which is a national status symbol and not an instrument of economic management,' but adding, however, that 'we should not swing away from this into thinking that an easy series of devaluations, or a chaotic world monetary system, are the answer to our problems' (Hatfield 1978: 63).

Other important figures in the party were publicly rethinking exchange rate policy. Former minister Tony Crosland while in opposition published two books in which he argued that the central problem of the 1964–70 Labour Government had been the absence of sufficient economic growth, and that the lack of growth was directly related to balance of payments problems and the exchange rate.

> Growth was consistently sacrificed to the balance of payments, notably to the defence of a fixed and unrealistic rate of exchange. This central failure bedeviled all the efforts and good intentions of the Labour Government. It constrained public expenditure. It antagonized the Trade Unions and alienated large groups of workers. It killed the National Plan and frustrated policies for improving the industrial structure. . . . And it has made it hard for Labour to claim in future . . . that we can manage things more efficiently than [the Conservatives] can.
>
> (Crosland 1974: 18)

But the problem was not simply that economic growth had failed to occur, but rather that the Government had deliberately chosen to suppress growth in an effort to achieve external balance with an overvalued currency. 'Changes in home demand – crudely, stop-go and deflation – have been used as the main instruments for controlling (or attempting to control) the balance of payments and the level of inflation,' Crosland (1971: 81) argued:

> One can see why this happened. Alternative instruments, such as devaluation or incomes policy, seemed fraught with difficulties. . . . On existing policies, growth will continue to be sacrificed to one or

other of these two objectives. A future Labour Government must therefore consciously alter the priorities. This requires a *political* decision. . . . We must in the future alter the priorities in favour of economic growth.

(emphasis in original)

What was needed was a firm commitment by Labour to strong economic growth; Labour must articulate its economic and social priorities – of which sustained economic growth was the linchpin – and must then demonstrate its determination to stick with its priorities in the face of external constraints. 'If the Labour Government is to achieve more next time than we did in 1964–70, certain crucial decisions need to be taken and ratified *in advance*; for otherwise our objectives will be lost in the confused hurly-burly and day-to-day crisis of government' (Crosland 1974: 44, original emphasis).

Labour while in opposition published extensive policy documents outlining its economic and social priorities (see Labour Party 1972, 1973a, 1973c; Labour Party Study Group 1973). With respect to the constraint that the exchange rate posed, Labour's position by 1974 was clear: if it were again to form a government, it would prioritize domestic growth and employment objectives ahead of exchange rate stability. But this policy shift occurred only gradually over the 1970–74 opposition period. The 1972 *Labour's Programme for Britain* was equivocal. It stated that a future Labour Government 'would reject any kind of international agreement which compelled us to accept increased unemployment for the sake of maintaining a fixed parity' (Labour Party 1972: 70); however, it scornfully condemned the Conservative Government for 'devaluing' (i.e., floating) sterling in June 1972: 'Devaluation is never an easy way out. It puts up prices and hits the living standards of every family in the land. It reduces the prices of our exports abroad, and increases the prices of all our imports. We have to sell more to pay for the same volume of imports' (Labour Party 1972: 14). By 1973, however, this equivocation had largely been eliminated. The 1973 *Labour's Programme for Britain* argued that:

> the surest guarantee of full employment is the resolute pursuit of policies for sound and steady economic growth. . . . The next Labour Government will therefore keep the twin objectives of economic growth and full employment uppermost in its considerations in the day-to-day management of the economy. . . . We cannot escape from the reality that for a major trading nation such as Britain, events in the outside world can sometimes work to the detriment of our own stan-

dards of living. But Labour will refuse to distort the domestic economy
in order to maintain an unrealistic exchange rate.

(Labour Party 1973a: 16)

Although the 1973 *Programme* acknowledged that there were negative
inflationary effects accompanying a depreciating currency, 'our exports
must not be allowed to become uncompetitive against those of our
leading competitors among the industrial countries of the world. This
means that Britain must avoid international commitments which might
hamper growth' (Labour Party 1973a: 16). The disavowal of an exchange rate commitment also appeared in Labour's February 1974 election
manifesto: 'we would reject any kind of international agreement which
compelled us to accept increased unemployment for the sake of maintaining a fixed [sterling] parity' (Labour Party 1974a: 6). Labour con-
tested both 1974 election campaigns with a commitment to de-emphasize
the exchange rate while other more important economic goals were
pursued.

THE TRADE UNIONS AND THE SOCIAL CONTRACT

In 1974, many Labour Party leaders felt that a major lesson to be
learned from their 1970 electoral defeat was that they must never again
allow an adversarial relationship to develop between a Labour Government and the trade unions over industrial relations and broader economic policy. The 1974–79 head of the Policy Unit Bernard Donoughue
(1989: 42) has argued that Labour's approach towards the trade unions
in 1974 'goes back to *In Place of Strife* when Callaghan and Wilson
were involved in that terrible experience of trying to impose reforms
on the trade unions.'[3] According to 1968–70 Minister for Employment
Barbara Castle (1980: 9), Labour's difficulties with industrial relations
reform in the late 1960s along with the problems the Conservative
Government had experienced with the unions during 1972–74 'had driven
home the lesson that there could be no future for a Labour Government which set itself at odds with the trade unions. . . . All [Labour
leaders] realized that the next Labour Government must carry the trade
unions with it in its policies.'

Accordingly, Labour while in opposition sought out a new relationship with the trade unions, pledging that upon a return to power, it
would repeal the Conservative Government's Industrial Relations Act
and would avoid any kind of statutory pay policy. In early 1972, the

party and the TUC formed the TUC–Labour Party Liaison Committee as a new policy-making link between the party and the unions. The TUC regarded itself as a partner with Labour, not just during elections, but also in economic policy formulation; the TUC's terms of reference for the Liaison Committee stipulated that the Committee 'would ensure that agreement on policy would extend to the parliamentary [Labour] party' (Middlemas 1990: 372). But discussion of certain topics in the Liaison Committee was problematic; incomes policy – even the mention of a 'voluntary' (i.e., non-statutory) policy – was initially taboo. When the topic was brought up, head of the Transport and General Workers Union Jack Jones ended the discussion by interjecting that 'it would be disastrous if any word went from the meeting that we had been discussing prices and incomes policy' (Castle 1980: 10). Labour's anti-inflation strategy that relied upon the cooperation of the trade unions through what became known as the Social Contract evolved only gradually over the 1970–74 opposition period.

The foundation of the Social Contract as it emerged in 1973 and 1974 was a *quid pro quo* commitment between a future Labour Government and its trade unions allies in which the Government through its progressive economic, social, and industrial policies would create an appropriate 'climate' to which the trade unions would respond with wage restraint (Castle 1980: 10–11). In February 1973, these commitments were reflected in the joint TUC–Labour Party Liaison Committee statement *Economic Policy and the Cost of Living*, which was a public agreement between the Labour Party and the TUC on a wide range of sensitive and important economic matters, including price controls, housing and rents, transportation, public works, economic redistribution through progressive taxation, welfare expansion, expansion of public ownership, state supervision of private investment, and the extension of 'industrial democracy' (TUC–Labour Party Liaison Committee 1973: 313–14; Coates 1980: 4–5; Taylor 1987: 22–3). In the document, the Labour Party with appropriate qualifiers pledged to consult and include the TUC in the formulation of its economic policy when it took power: 'It will be the first task of that Labour Government on taking office, and having due regard to the circumstances at that time, to conclude with the TUC, on the basis of the understandings being reached on the Liaison Committee, a wide-ranging agreement on the policies to be pursued in all these aspects of our economic life and to discuss with them the order of priorities of their fulfilment' (TUC–Labour Party Liaison Committee 1973: 315). With respect to the delicate issues of wage restraint and incomes policies, however,

Economic Policy and the Cost of Living was elliptical: a 'wide ranging and permanent system of price controls' was to be established, so
that 'in deciding to permit or refuse particular price increases, or whether
or not to order price reductions, the system will have to concern itself
deeply with profits, profit margins, and productivity. In this way, the
next Labour Government will prevent the erosion of real wages – and
thus influence the whole climate of collective bargaining' (TUC-Labour
Party Liaison Committee 1973: 313). The agreement noted that good
relations between the Government and the trade unions would of themselves enable a successful anti-inflationary policy to function: 'the
approach set out in this statement . . . will further engender the strong
feeling of mutual confidence which alone will make it possible to reach
the wide-ranging agreement which is necessary to control inflation and
achieve sustained growth in the standard of living' (TUC–Labour Party
Liaison Committee 1973: 315). Although some Labour politicians were
uneasy with this approach, Barbara Castle (1980: 10) notes that the
'strong feeling of mutual confidence' was as close as Labour could get
to a pledge from the trade unions on a voluntary incomes policy; as
TUC General Secretary Len Murray told Shadow Labour Ministers in
January 1974, 'if you are relying on some commitment by the TUC to
some kind of incomes policy, you have got to think again. There ain't
going to be any statement like that' (Castle 1980: 19–20).

Over 1973 and into 1974, the so-called Social Contract became an
increasingly important, if muddled, part of Labour's electoral strategy.
When Conservative Prime Minister Edward Heath called a snap election in February 1974 in the context of an impending coal miners'
strike and a direct challenge to his Government's pay policy, Labour
was well situated to make the claim that it could manage relations
with the trade unions more successfully than could the Conservatives
(Hatfield 1978: 228; Coates 1989: 72). However, it became evident
during the February 1974 election campaign that the term 'Social Contract' had different meanings depending upon who was speaking. Harold
Wilson during the campaign spoke of the need for a tripartist Social
Contract with each partner willing to make sacrifices to fight inflation,
adding that 'we have agreed such a new contract with the TUC;' however, TUC General Council member Hugh Scanlon directly contradicted
Wilson in a televised interview by stating that 'we are not agreed on
any specific policy as of now' (Butler and Kavanagh 1974: 98). Wilson asserts in his memoirs (1979: 43) that the 'strong feeling of mutual confidence' passage from *Economic Policy and the Cost of Living*
'was widely interpreted as a voluntary agreement [by the TUC] to accept

restraint in pay demands as part of a wider social agreement. Indeed [TUC General Secretary] Len Murray in a television programme in which he and I appeared together confirmed this interpretation in answer to a question by the interviewer.'

Labour's February 1974 election manifesto made use of some of the same phrasing from *Economic Policy and the Cost of Living*, including the necessity of creating an appropriate 'climate' through the Social Contract (Labour Party 1974a: 8). But the manifesto went further by raising the delicate subject of incomes policies explicitly.

> After so many failures in the field of incomes policy – under the Labour Government but even more seriously under the Tory Government's compulsory wage controls – only deeds can persuade. Only practical action by the Government to create a much fairer distribution of the national wealth can convince the worker and his family and his trade union that 'an incomes policy' is not some kind of trick to force him, particularly if he works in a public service or nationalised industry, to bear the brunt of the national burden. But as it is provided that the Government is ready to act – against high prices, rents and other impositions falling most heavily on the low paid and on pensioners – so we believe that the trade unions *voluntarily* (which is the only way it can be done for any period in a free society) will co-operate to make the whole policy successful. We believe that the action we propose on prices, together with an understanding with the TUC on the lines which we have already agreed, will create the right economic climate for money incomes to grow in line with production. That is the essence of the new Social Contract which the Labour Party has discussed at length and agreed with the TUC and which must take its place as a central feature of the new economic policy of a Labour Government.[4]
>
> (Labour Party 1974a: 9–10, emphasis in original)

It was implicit that in order to obtain wage restraint from the trade unions, any new Labour Government had to be seen delivering its side of the Social Contract *quid pro quo* as soon as possible (Whitehead 1985: 123).

More generally, Labour's 1970–74 period in opposition saw a marked leftward drift in the party's broader policy orientation (see Hatfield 1978; Coates 1980). Labour policy documents from this period were ambitious and wide-ranging. Social welfare programs were to be sharply expanded. The party was committed to increasing pensions by 28 per cent within its first parliamentary session, and thereafter, basic pensions 'would be updated each year in relation to average earnings, not just to the cost of living' (TUC–Labour Party Liaison Committee 1973: 314; Labour Party 1974a: 7; Castle 1980: 38, fn 1). The National Health Service was to be revised and expanded, and education spending was also to be increased (TUC–Labour Party Liaison Committee 1973: 313; Labour Party 1974a: 8, 12). Price controls and state subsidies would stabilize food prices and the price of other essential consumer goods in order 'to prevent the erosion of real wages' (TUC–Labour Party Liaison Committee 1973a: 313; Labour Party 1974a: 8). With respect to housing, land would be taken into public ownership so that it would be 'freely and cheaply available,' subsidies for local authority house building would be expanded, and the 'aim' of the next Labour Government was at least 400 000 new homes by the Government's last year (TUC–Labour Party Liaison Committee 1973a: 313; Labour Party 1974a: 8–9).

Labour's macroeconomic policy planning was centered around a full employment commitment. Labour's 1972 *Programme* pledged that:

> the achievement of full employment will . . . be the most urgent task facing the next Labour Government. We do not accept the excuse that the present level of unemployment is the result of some fundamental change in the way the economy operates, and that unemployment can never again be reduced to the level which was regarded as normal ten or twenty years ago. We see no evidence for this. Given the right economic, regional and industrial policies, and the necessary development of the public services, unemployment can be dramatically reduced.
>
> (Labour Party 1972: 13)

It was in this context that Labour's industrial policy plans in 1972 and 1973 came to be premised upon an extensive expansion of the public sector. Within Labour's policy-making committees, it was proposed that Labour create a state holding company, the National Enterprise Board (NEB), with the purpose of 'introduc[ing] public ownership into the strongholds of private industry' (Labour Party Study Group 1973: 12; Forester 1979: 77–8; Foote 1985: 318–21; Middlemas 1990: 370–2). The NEB would not only hold shares of existing nationalized industries and joint public-private firms; it would also hold shares that the Government would acquire in the future in return for the conditional financial assistance provided to individual firms and industries (Labour Party Study Group 1973: 12). The NEB 'must be represented in the commanding heights of the modern capitalist economy – manufacturing and services – to ensure that the planning strategy of the Government will be matched by operational instruments for its policies;' representation in the 'commanding heights' was quantitatively defined as 'the takeover of some twenty to twenty-five companies' (Labour Party Study Group 1973: 14, 21).

Although the NEB or some variation of it had been proposed within the party as early as 1969 (Labour Party Study Group 1973: 12), a commitment to such wide-scale nationalizations went far beyond what Harold Wilson and others on Labour's front bench had in mind. A confrontation ensued when the Labour Party National Executive Committee (NEC) in May 1973 voted to include in *Labour's Programme 1973* the commitment to nationalize 'some twenty-five of our largest manufacturers' (Hatfield 1978: 196; Labour Party 1973a: 34). The day following the NEC vote, Harold Wilson issued a statement as Labour's parliamentary leader that repudiated the commitment, stating that 'it was inconceivable that the party would go into a general election on this proposal, nor could any incoming Labour government be so committed' (Hatfield 1978: 198–9).

Throughout the controversy, Wilson made it clear that he had no conflict with the other policy commitments in *Programme 1973* (Hatfield 1978: 201, 214). It is important therefore not to let the nationalization controversy obscure the leftward tilt of the other policy areas upon which the party, including the parliamentary leadership, was publicly agreed. Labour's 'priorities' were summarized in *Programme 1973* into eleven points: (1) price controls extended to the retail level, combined with food subsidies; (2) immediate increases in pensions; (3) housing measures with an emphasis on public housing; (4) education expenditure increases; (5) social services expenditure increases; (6) industrial relations and industrial democracy reforms; (7) full employment; (8) the redistribution of income and wealth; (9) greater accountability of economic power; (10) citizens' rights towards greater democratization in central and local government, and the outlawing of discrimination based on gender and religion; and (11) renegotiation of the Treaty of Accession to the Common Market (Labour Party 1973a: 11–12). With the significant exceptions of the nationalization commitment and the UK's continued membership in the Common Market,[5] there was broad public agreement within the party upon the other policy commitments undertaken in the context of the Social Contract and Labour's *Programme*.

CONCLUSION

Labour's *1973 Programme* stated clearly its intention to break with the past: 'Labour's aim is no less than a new social order. The people must determine the nation's destiny, and only by economic liberation can they have the collective social strength to decide that destiny' (Labour Party 1973a: 12; Hatfield 1978: 174). Perhaps the high-water mark of the Labour left's influence on policy was when soon-to-be Minister of Industry Tony Benn concluded the 1973 Party Conference debate on public ownership by pledging that 'the crisis we inherit when we come to power will be the occasion for fundamental change and not the excuse for postponing it' (Labour Party 1973b: 187; Middlemas 1990: 372). This chapter has reviewed the leftward drift of Labour policy during the early 1970s in order to provide a context for the external constraints that emerged after Labour came to power in March 1974. Special attention was paid to two key policy areas: Labour's approach *vis-à-vis* sterling and the trade unions. Both sterling and the unions were crucial and determining policy domains during the 1964–70 Government; both would be crucial and determining after 1974 as well.

4 Burden-Sharing and Loosened Conditionality, 1974–75:
'The Nature of What Constitutes a Sustainable Balance of Payments has been Radically Changed'[1]

Benjamin Cohen (1983: 315–17) has argued that the major transformations that occurred in the international monetary system during the 1970s – floating exchange rates, the suspension of gold convertibility, the expansion of the role of private banking institutions for payments financing – were 'norm-governed changes.' With respect to the provision of official balance of payments financing, he identifies an international regime encompassing 'the set of implicit or explicit principles, norms, rules, and decision-making procedures governing access to external credit for balance of payments purposes' and argues that 'no matter how profound the [balance of payments financing] regime's recent change may appear, it does not in fact add up to a transformation in kind. . . . At the level of principles and norms, the regime remains very much as it was' (Cohen 1983: 317, 333). The penultimate principle of the regime – that countries should enjoy 'adequate but not unlimited' access to financing – remains intact, Cohen argues (1983: 323).

This is an overview characterization of the period, however. A more detailed examination reveals that following the 1973–74 petroleum producers' price shock, both the extent of official payments financing as well as the nature of the accompanying conditionality emerged as highly contentious points of debate among advanced industrialized countries, and that the availability of low-conditionality and no-conditionality financing facilities increased. The massive financing needs resulting from the Organization of Petroleum Exporting Countries (OPEC) price shock called into question the adequacy and appropriateness of the arrangements and policies that had evolved heretofore within the IMF, and norms and policies did change in response to the changed international economic circumstances. In this chapter the adaptation of official payments financing mechanisms within the IMF to the new circumstances of the mid-1970s are outlined to show that, in light of the higher costs of imported energy and the dangers of global recession that could result from simultaneous deflation across advanced industrialized countries, there was a new emphasis that held that deficits were to be financed rather than rapidly adjusted to. If the purpose of conditionality as it had emerged within the postwar international monetary system had been to prod deficit countries towards policy changes that would facilitate sustainable payments positions in the near term, the easing of conditionality in response to the 1973–74 OPEC price shock constituted a significant shift in approach.

THE COLLAPSE OF BRETTON WOODS AND THE OPEC PRICE SHOCK

On 15 August 1971, the international monetary system became a 'non-system' when US President Richard Nixon, faced with the prospect of a run on US gold reserves, suspended the American dollar's convertibility into gold and thereby unilaterally put international monetary relations on a pure dollar standard (see among others Gilpin 1987: 134–51). Although the German and Dutch currencies had been floated as early as May 1971, it was not until the United States 'closed the gold window' that generalized floating was begun. Although there were repeated efforts in the early 1970s to return to fixed exchange rates, by 1974 the Committee of Twenty (formally entitled the *ad hoc* Committee of the Board of Governors on Reform of the International Monetary System and Related Issues) conceded that floating rates were more than a temporary development (Dam 1982: 216–21).

At the time, it was widely expected that the shift to floating would allow governments greater economic policy freedom (OECD 1985: 7). Bank of England official Kit McMahon (1986: 2) recounts that 'the idea was that if a country had inflationary policies it would no longer be able to export its inflation to a trading partner forced to buy its currency . . . . Now it was hoped that well-run nations would be able to enjoy the fruits of their virtue unaffected by others' mistakes.' However, exchange rates in the new environment of the float were proving to be unexpectedly volatile: as early as January 1974 IMF Managing Director Johannes Witteveen (1974a: 20) was commenting publicly how 10 per cent swings in the value of the dollar *vis-à-vis* European currencies were occurring 'in a remarkably short space of time.'

The difficulties of re-establishing exchange rate stability intensified when Arab petroleum producers in the context of the October 1973

Arab–Israeli war announced a selective embargo of crude oil exports along with a substantial price increase. While the embargo did not persist, the price increase did, and between mid-October 1973 and January 1974, the world market price of crude oil quadrupled. The price shock was forecast to have a devastating impact upon the already difficult world payments situation of the early 1970s, and the IMF Managing Director became alarmed about the global financing situation almost immediately (De Vries 1985, 1: 305–6). OPEC countries because of their increased oil revenues were projected to accrue huge payments surpluses (*OECD Economic Outlook*, July 1975, p. 7, Table 33). 'The Fund staff estimated in January 1974 that the combined current account surpluses of the nine major oil exporting countries would increase in 1974 to perhaps $65 billion .... This anticipated increase would have its counterpart in a deterioration of similar magnitude for all other countries combined' (De Vries 1985, 1: 309). Moreover, given the price inelasticity of the demand for imported oil and the low import propensities of oil-exporting countries, the OPEC surpluses were not projected to be temporary; accordingly, oil-importers were forecast to experience sharp and sustained structural deficits. In July 1974, the OECD forecast a $17 billion deficit for the entire OECD area during the first half of 1974, worsening to $21.5 billion in the second half, and improving only marginally thereafter (*OECD Economic Outlook*, July 1974, p. 46).

Johannes Witteveen saw his role as IMF Managing Director as an activist one: he was 'quick to spot troubles in the world economy, eager to find solutions, and prepared to speak out forcefully and candidly' (De Vries 1985, 2: 1004). In public speeches during the first half of 1974, Witteveen (1974a: 17) warned that the combination of the 'staggering disequilibrium in the global balance of payments ... coming at a time when there is not yet agreement on international monetary reform ... will place strains on the monetary system far in excess of any that have been experienced since the war.' The new situation demanded innovative solutions, Witteveen (1974d: 129) asserted: 'Orthodox textbook responses cannot in present circumstances be applied to many of the problems policy-makers face. The nature of what constitutes a sustainable balance of payments has been radically changed by the rise in oil prices.'

EASING THE RULES: THE JANUARY 1974 COMMITTEE OF
TWENTY MEETING AND THE 1974 OIL FACILITY

Witteveen (1974d: 133) argued forcefully that, given the new situation, balance of payments disequilibria could not

> be eliminated by any of the traditional policy responses which the
> Fund and its members have come to regard as normal over the past
> twenty-five years . . . . In the past, the accepted remedies for bal-
> ance of payments deficits have been currency devaluation, internal
> deflation, or import restraint. In response to an oil-induced deficit,
> however, it seems clear that each of these policies would be wrong.

The Fund staff regarded the payments deficits of oil-importers as structural
and long-term problems; their current account imbalances 'did not lie
in inappropriate macroeconomic policies or in unrealistic exchange rates'
nor could they be eliminated 'by the usual changes in monetary or
fiscal policy or in exchange rates.' More basic structural changes were
required 'in the patterns of consumption and production of both oil
exporting and oil importing countries . . . . These changes would take
several years, possibly a decade or two, to accomplish' (De Vries 1985,
1: 310). Economists in the OECD largely concurred. In July 1975, the
OECD forecast continuing substantial (although declining) OPEC surpluses totaling some $200–250 billion over 1974–80, suggesting that
as a whole 'the OECD current account *may* be back in surplus by
1980' (*OECD Economic Outlook*, July 1975, p. 78, my emphasis).

Managing Director Witteveen (1974a: 20) publicly set forth his assessment of the situation in a January 1974 speech and called upon
'oil importing countries as a group to accept a substantial deterioration in their current account.' The prospective surpluses of oil exporters
were beyond their capacity to absorb, Witteveen argued, and 'the counterpart of these surpluses will be a substantial and continuing collective
deficit for the oil consuming countries. This much is clear.' But how
would this deficit be distributed and financed among oil consumers,
Witteveen asked. 'It is vitally important that a broad measure of agreement
be reached on the answers to these questions. If countries follow
contractionary paths or inconsistent policies, there is a strong risk of
generating a more serious slowdown in world trade and economic growth
than would otherwise occur.'

It was with these concerns as a background that Committee of Twenty
Finance Ministers met in Rome in January 1974. In a note to the assembled ministers, Witteveen cautioned that 'attempts to eliminate the

additional current deficit caused by higher oil prices through deflation-ary demand policies, import restrictions, and general resort to exchange rate depreciation would serve only to shift the payments problem from one oil importing country to another and to damage world trade and economic activity' (Dell 1981: 22). The warning was well-received and in the communiqué released after the meeting, ministers pledged that

> in managing their international payments, countries must not adopt policies which would merely aggravate the problems of other coun-tries. Accordingly, [ministers] stressed the importance of avoiding competitive depreciation and the escalation of restrictions on trade and payments. They further resolved to pursue policies that would sustain appropriate levels of economic activity and employment, while minimizing inflation . . . .
>
> The Committee agreed that there should be the closest international cooperation and consultation in pursuit of these objectives. They noted that the International Monetary Fund, the World Bank, and other international organizations are concerned to find orderly means by which the changes in current account positions may be financed, and they urged that these organizations should cooperate in finding an early solution to these questions.
>
> (Committee of Twenty 1974: 17, 22–3)

British Chancellor of the Exchequer Anthony Barber subsequently characterized the consensus achieved at Rome as one of 'fundamental importance.' according to Barber:

> There was near unanimity that we should reject the orthodox solu-tion of reliance on domestic deflation associated with external measures such as depreciation of the exchange rate. And we reached this con-clusion for a reason which, when clearly stated and perceived, may seem self-evident – that given the inability of major oil suppliers in the short run at least to spend all of their receipts, there is simply no possibility of restoring the imbalance of current earnings.
>
> (*Financial Times*, 5 February 1974, 'Overseas Banker's Club,' p. 9)

The Rome consensus spread. The OECD commented in July 1974 that 'it is by now a commonplace that OECD countries will, at least for the next year or so, have a large current deficit which needs to be "accepted" and "financed"' (*OECD Economic Outlook*, July 1974, p. 94). As a team of independent economists appointed by the OECD subsequently noted, 'the notion that a deficit on current account of some size should be accepted was subscribed to quite widely . . . . While a precise criterion for apportioning the total current-account deficit of OECD countries was never agreed on, there was widespread agreement that it should be shared out in some sense "fairly"' (McCracken et al. 1977: 72).

Managing Director Witteveen's idea for financing the current account deficits centered upon the creation of what came to be called the 'oil facilities' – new official borrowing arrangements administered by the Fund with looser conditionality policies that reflected the new situation. Witteveen argued that the means to finance the deficits existed in the surpluses of the oil exporting countries and advocated that the Fund play a leadership role by 'recycling' the OPEC surpluses to be used by oil importers (De Vries 1985, 1: 305, 314–15). Following the Managing Director's lead and after considerable informal discussion among themselves, ministers at the Rome Committee of Twenty meeting agreed that the proposal for a new oil facility 'should be urgently explored [although] it is recognized that such a facility poses operational problems which must be resolved and would . . . be only a partial measure, in view of the nature and the magnitude of the balance of payments problems created' (Committee of Twenty 1974: 23; De Vries 1985, 1: 314).

There was not, however, complete consensus upon the desirability of the oil facility; the Americans and Germans in particular resisted Witteveen's idea. US officials believed that forceful international pressure ought to be exerted on the oil-exporting countries for them to 'roll back' some of the recent price increases and that if oil-consuming countries worked together to cut oil imports and increase energy alternatives, crude oil prices were bound to fall. According to the IMF historian (De Vries 1985, 1: 315–16), 'US officials viewed Mr. Witteveen's proposal for helping to finance the anticipated large deficits as an acceptance by the international community of the new higher oil prices and as tantamount to underwriting these prices.' German Finance Minister Helmut Schmidt also expressed reservations, based largely upon a concern about the inflationary effects of the IMF introducing more liquidity into an already inflation-prone international economy (De Vries 1985, 1: 316). Nevertheless, the Managing Director remained determined on the need for a new Fund-administered oil facility; he 'did not want the Fund to remain inactive while the payments problems of members grew inordinately large' (De Vries 1985, 1: 317). Witteveen (1974c: 44) sought to counter some of the US objections at a press conference following the Rome meeting, pointing out that 'it is not a very effective weapon against the oil producing countries to refuse to

Table 4.1   IMF borrowing for the 1974 and 1975 oil facilities (SDR millions)

OECD countries	1974	1975	Oil-exporting countries	1974	1975
Austria	—	100	Abu Dhabi	100	—
Belgium	—	200	Iran	580	410
Canada	247	—	Kuwait	400	285
Germany	—	600	Nigeria	100	200
Netherlands	150	200	Oman	20	0.5
Norway	—	100	Saudi Arabia	1000	1250
Sweden	—	50	Trinidad and Tobago	—	10
Switzerland	—	250	Venezuela	450	200
Total OECD	397	1500	Total oil exporters	2650	2355.5

Source: De Vries (1985, 1: 346).

finance [the deficits] .... What you would do then is push a number of countries into most serious difficulties, while the oil producing countries themselves are not hurt very much. That's the problem .... It would be the weapon which would hurt the oil consumers much more than the oil producers' (see also De Vries 1985, 1: 317–18).

During the spring of 1974, the IMF Executive Board discussed the specific features of the oil facility and decided that it would be underwritten through Fund borrowing from both OPEC and OECD surplus countries. Witteveen traveled extensively in the Middle East and Europe to obtain assurances that the Fund would be able to borrow from surplus countries for the new facility (De Vries 1985, 1: 325–6). While several OPEC states participated, Canada and the Netherlands were the only OECD states persuaded to loan funds (see Table 4.1). West Germany, which was one of the handful of industrialized countries in payments surplus in 1974, was also asked by Witteveen to lend to the Fund for the oil facility; the Germans declined (De Vries 1985, 1: 326). US Treasury Secretary George Shultz informally assured Witteveen that, while the United States would not loan money to the Fund for the facility, neither would the US seek to draw on it once it was established (De Vries 1985, 1: 321).

The nature of the conditionality to be associated with oil facility drawings was deliberated through the spring of 1974 within the IMF Executive Board. It was decided that the oil facility would be kept separate from the Fund's normal borrowing facilities, in part 'to preserve the Fund's established policy on conditionality when its regular resources were used' (De Vries 1985, 1: 319–20). Witteveen (1974d:

136) pressed for quick action; for many deficit countries, he argued, 'the situation is too urgent to require the prior formulation of a comprehensive adjustment program. Following a drawing, however, there will be consultations between the Fund and the member on the policies needed for adjustment. Members drawing on the facility would be expected to pursue balance of payments policies that would lead to a viable medium-term outcome.' The Fund historian has commented that in her view there was 'virtually no conditionality attached to the 1974 oil facility' (De Vries 1985, 1: 322). By contrast, borrowers from the Fund's 'normal' facilities were required to formulate a comprehensive adjustment program in consultation with Fund officials prior to receiving Fund financing. The Managing Director's advocacy of after-the-fact consultations for oil facility drawings constituted a significant departure from the norms and practices governing conditionality that had evolved heretofore within the IMF.

In June 1974, the Executive Board formally established the new oil facility, albeit later and with a total amount of available funds that was less than Witteveen had originally hoped; the facility was open for business in September 1974 (De Vries 1985, 1: 328, 331, 3: 496–7). Witteveen (1974d: 135) 'made it quite clear that the new facility [was] not intended to provide a permanent solution for financing the extra foreign exchange costs of oil. And it certainly [could] not begin to solve the problems of internal adjustment resulting from the need to pay for, or reduce dependence on, imported oil.' Although it was apparent that the time frame for adjustment under oil facility was meant to be longer than that associated with the Fund's normal borrowing arrangements, it was not clearly specified in Witteveen's public statements (see Witteveen 1974b: 41). However, IMF staff were suggesting that it would take 'several years, possibly a decade or more' to accomplish the structural changes necessary for the payments imbalances to be corrected (De Vries 1985, 1: 310).

RENEWING THE OIL FACILITY, 1975

There were 38 borrowers from the 1974 oil facility, including several OECD members (Greece, Iceland, Italy, New Zealand, Spain, Turkey, and Yugoslavia). Following several years of low use during the early 1970s, member drawings on the Fund reached record levels in fiscal year 1974–75 (De Vries 1985 1: 331, 347–8; IMF 1976a: 87; *IMF Survey*, 9 July 1975, p. 170). But many oil-consumers found themselves able to finance their deficits by turning to private commercial banks 'which for the first time began to lend directly to the governments of many developing members. Readily available credit from private commercial banks, at low or even negative real rates of interest . . . helped induce members to borrow. And steadily rising deposits, particularly as oil exporting members banked their vastly enlarged oil revenues, induced creditors to lend' (De Vries 1987: 121–2). By the mid-1970s, international commercial bank financing was more widely available than it had been before, partially displacing the IMF's role as the primary provider of balance of payments financing.

Despite the expansion of commercial bank lending, when Finance Ministers met in September 1974 for the IMF's annual meeting, Managing Director Witteveen made a case for another 'substantially larger' oil facility for 1975 (De Vries 1985, 1: 333–4; Witteveen 1974e: 27). 'The role of official recycling will have to be larger in 1975 than in 1974,' Witteveen (1974e: 26) argued, 'mainly because of the increasing difficulties that have become evident with respect to financing through short-term money markets.' Relegating the financing task to the Euro-currency markets carried dangers of instability; 'oil exporting countries . . . might well be faced with certain problems and risks in channeling their growing volume of funds through private money markets. On the other hand, oil importing countries could find it increasingly difficult to finance their current account deficits by borrowing in these markets. Consequently, there is an urgent need to develop other channels of finance' (Witteveen 1974e: 23). The Managing Director publicly stated his expectation that payments financing difficulties were likely to get worse (Witteveen 1974e: 26); privately, he anticipated that 'at least Italy and the United Kingdom among industrial members might need financial assistance from the Fund' in 1975 (De Vries 1985, 1: 335).

British, French, and Italian Finance Ministers were all enthusiastic supporters of a renewed and enlarged oil facility. British Chancellor of the Exchequer Denis Healey (1974a: 79–80) led the charge, noting that although the $3.5 billion 1974 oil facility was proving useful for developing countries, industrial countries were also facing payments difficulties that were 'very much larger in scale' and 'may constitute a more urgent threat to the stability of the international economy. . . . Industrial countries are at present incurring some $50–65 billion a year [in deficits].' Healey suggested a 'more permanent arrangement' for recycling (De Vries 1985, 1: 335), arguing that 'there is a powerful case for establishing a much larger facility through which a significant proportion of the petro-dollar surplus can be firmly invested in an international organization so that we have a basis on which we may co-operate over the distribution of finance among the consuming countries . . . . We should see this operation as a continuing process, not simply a once-for-all transfer'[2] (Healey 1974a: 80). French Finance Minister Jean-Pierre Fourcade (1974: 95) explicitly endorsed Healey's recommendations at the meeting, while Italian Finance Minister Emilio Colombo (1974: 104) pointed out that the 1974 oil facility was recycling only about 5 per cent of the 1974 oil surplus and commented 'surely it would be most desirable for all concerned to expand greatly the oil facility.'

The new US Treasury Secretary William Simon, however, was not an enthusiastic supporter of a renewed and expanded oil facility. Simon (1974: 85) assured his counterparts that the American attitude was not one of 'laissez-faire, come what may. If there is a clear need for additional international lending mechanisms, the United States will support their establishment.' But Simon called for further study: 'the range of possible future problems is a wide one, and many problems can be envisaged that will never come to pass . . . . We must recognize that no recycling mechanism will ensure that every country can borrow unlimited amounts.' Healey in his speech (1974a: 76) had argued that:

> However successful we may be in reducing our demand for oil by conservation, if we were to limit our imports of oil to what we can pay for year to year by exports, we would create bankruptcy and unemployment on an unprecedented scale. So we must accept deficits on our balance of payments of a magnitude hitherto unthinkable, and we must finance those deficits by borrowing.

By contrast, Simon (1974: 85, 82–3) made the case for more orthodox policies of adjustment, noting that 'countries continue to have the responsibility to follow monetary, fiscal, and other policies such that their requirements for foreign borrowing are limited' and that 'in today's circumstances, in most countries, there is in my view no alternative to policies of balanced fiscal and monetary restraint . . . . Some are concerned that a determined international attack on inflation by fiscal and monetary restraint might push the world into a deep recession, even depression. I recognize this concern, but I do not believe we should let it distort our judgment.' Nor was the United States alone in expressing equivocations about the emerging financing-over-adjustment emphasis. German Finance Minister Hans Apel (1974: 117) told his counterparts that, while he approved of the limited 1974 oil facility and he agreed that excessive reliance on private sector recycling had limits, he also had reservations about a renewed and expanded oil facility in 1975. Although he saw 'merit in the creation of a specialized investment institution, operated jointly by oil producing and oil consuming nations, that would facilitate the placement of oil revenues in a stable and mutually advantageous manner,' his endorsement was qualified: 'I see no ... need for a general increase in international liquidity. The Fund as the guardian of the international monetary system should not, by its own action, engender new inflationary pressures' (Apel 1974: 119).

In light of the unenthusiastic response to his proposals among certain leading Fund members, Witteveen (1974e: 26–7) made it clear that he foresaw a greater degree of conditionality being applied to any renewed oil facility: 'as recycling enters its second year, it will be even more important than in the first year to ensure that this activity is organized in such a manner as to encourage the necessary adjustment in individual countries and in the world payments situation as a whole.' But although the terms were to be tighter, the broader logic offered by the Managing Director for a renewed facility was essentially still the same: 'It is well understood that ... the oil importing countries as a group cannot eliminate their overall current account deficit in the short run, and that attempts to do so would only reallocate the deficit among the oil importing countries and might have seriously constrictive effects on world trade and economic activity' (Witteveen 1974e: 21). Renewing the oil facility was especially important, Witteveen (1974e: 27) argued, because 'the oil-importing countries need to be given confidence that reasonable solutions will be found to their financing problems, and thus to be supported in pursuing policies that are appropriate in an international context.' Despite the Managing Director's appeal, oil-importers did not obtain this needed confidence at the 1974 IMF Annual Meeting, which ended with both the size and even the existence of a renewed facility very much in question (De Vries 1985, 1: 336).

The IMF Executive Board took up the question of renewal in late 1974, starting the discussion with a staff paper that reviewed anticipated financing needs for 1975 and recommended a facility of SDR 6–8 billion ($7–9.5 billion). There were 'intense debates' on the Executive Board between the American and other Executive Directors, with most non-American Executive Directors supporting the proposal for a renewed and larger facility and with the British Executive Director in particular pressing for a sizeable facility that would be available to both industrial and developing members (De Vries 1985, 1: 339–42). The Americans were opposed for three reasons. First, financing the oil price increases would in some way signify acceptance of them, and the American position continued to prefer coordinated action to reduce oil imports. 'The emphasis of US officials on adjustment was unusually strong since the Managing Director and officials of the United Kingdom were advocating a large facility that would accommodate some of the financing needs of industrial and developed members of the Fund, including those of the United Kingdom itself. It was these countries especially that US officials believed ought to curb their imports of crude oil, since they were among the world's largest consumers.' Second, the US authorities disliked the distinction between the 'oil-related' portion of a country's payments deficit and the rest of its deficit, arguing that 'the Fund's assessment of a member's need for financing should rather be related to the member's overall financial and balance of payments position.' Third, there was a preference among US authorities for private over public financing channels (De Vries 1985, 1: 340–1; see also Healey 1989: 423). As US Under-Secretary for Monetary Affairs Jack Bennett commented to the press, 'such short-cut new procedures' like the oil facility 'may have been justifiable as a crisis response to a new situation, but I fear the IMF's future would be damaged if it didn't take large steps in 1975 to more responsible and normal procedures' (*Wall Street Journal*, 18 December 1974, 'US Has Doubts,' p. 12). American opposition was not well-received, and some Executive Directors charged that the US was reneging on previous commitments by obstructing a renewed facility: as the French Executive Director pointed out, 'an identifiable oil-related problem certainly remained and posed difficulties with which the normal facilities of the Fund were not designed to deal' (De Vries 1985, 1: 342).

Partly as a counter to the renewal of the IMF oil facility, the United States in November 1974 proposed that a $25 billion Financial Support Fund (FSF) be set up through the OECD for balance of payments financing (*IMF Survey*, 18 November 1974, p. 365). Tentatively agreed upon in January 1975, the FSF would be distinct from the IMF oil facility in that it would only be available to OECD members, there would be no seeking of financing from OPEC countries, and it would be 'a safety net to be used as a last resort.' In addition, the terms upon which financing would be provided were to be at a tougher level of conditionality than existed under the IMF oil facility: 'the borrower [from the FSF] will undertake to carry out the policies needed to redress its external financial situation over an appropriate period . . . . The decision to grant the loan will be based on . . . the conditions related to the borrower's economic policies' (Group of Ten 1975: 19;

IMF Survey, 14 April 1975, p. 104).

British Chancellor of the Exchequer Denis Healey caucused his European counterparts in response to the US proposal of the FSF as a high-conditionality alternative to the renewal of the low-conditionality IMF oil facility and obtained 'total solidarity' on the need to insist upon the renewal of the oil facility (Healey 1989: 425). He met with US Treasury Secretary Simon and Chairman of the Federal Reserve Arthur Burns in Washington in January 1975 'for the show-down' and recounts the discussion in his memoirs (1989: 425–6):

> [William Simon] and Arthur Burns said that the President was personally committed to make it the OECD Support Fund or nothing. In that case, I said, we must insist on seeing the President ourselves. [Simon] wobbled, and after several angry hours he at last agreed to a Witteveen [oil] facility of $6 billion, on condition that we would support the OECD Support Fund as well.

With this agreement between the Americans and Europeans, the IMF's Interim Committee agreed to establish an SDR 5 billion oil facility for 1975. However, as the Fund historian has pointed out (De Vries 1985, 1: 430), the IMF staff's initial proposal of a somewhat larger SDR 6–8 billion facility had in fact been quite modest relative to the size of the potential payments financing problem, as it 'did not allow for drawings by the five [largest] members . . . . Should any of these five members draw, a facility of SDR 10 billion or larger would be needed' (De Vries 1985, 1: 340). But the more modest SDR 5 billion facility reflected a compromise that made agreement in the face of US opposition possible (De Vries 1985, 1: 340–1, 344; Healey 1989: 425–6). UK Chancellor of the Exchequer Healey (1989: 426) notes that in the event the renewed oil facility

> was soon used up, and not extended. But the OECD Support Fund never came into existence at all; though we Europeans all supported it as we had promised, the American Congress refused to ratify the agreement. It was fortunate that we persuaded Washington to agree to [a renewed oil facility], even on a reduced scale; otherwise there would have been nothing at all.

Managing Director Witteveen, however, had difficulty in raising the full SDR 5 billion authorization for the renewed facility. In his address at the September 1975 IMF annual meeting, Witteveen (1975a: 26) reminded assembled ministers that financing problems for many primary producing countries continued to be 'especially acute' and that 'a few industrial countries also face difficulties. In this situation, I am particularly concerned that the resources available for the Fund's oil facility are still inadequate. I believe that creditor countries should cooperate with the Fund to secure the full amount of new borrowing – SDR 5 billion – that was originally agreed on.' Despite his appeals, Witteveen was able to raise only SDR 3.86 billion for the renewed facility (see Table 4.1 above). Combined with SDR 464 million that remained unused from 1974, the total size of the 1975 facility was SDR 4.32 billion (De Vries 1985, 1: 344–5).

Forty-five borrowers took advantage of the 1975 facility and drew the full available amount; all of the OECD members that had used the facility in 1974 did so again in 1975, in addition to OECD member drawings from Finland, Portugal, and the United Kingdom (De Vries 1985, 1: 347–8; IMF 1976a: 87). The Fund historian has described the 'stricter conditionality . . . reflecting the position taken by US officials' that was applied to borrowers from the 1975 facility (De Vries 1985, 1: 343):

> The member making a drawing was to describe to the Fund its policies to achieve medium-term solutions to its balance of payments problems and to have the Fund assess the adequacy of these policies. The Fund was also to judge the extent to which reserves could be used to meet the member's payments deficit. The member was to describe the measures it had taken, or proposed to take, to conserve oil or to develop alternative sources of energy, although these measures were not subject to the Fund's assessment. As in the 1974 facility, access to the 1975 facility was also to depend on a member's avoidance of the introduction or intensification of restrictions on trade and capital.
>
> (See De Vries 1985, 1: 343, fn 12 for more detail.)

The effort to tighten oil facility conditionality in 1975 also reflected a compromise: 'The management and staff had favored even stricter conditions in the form of quantitative targets for monetary and fiscal policies, as was done when the Fund approved stand-by arrangements. Most Executive Directors did not want to go so far, however' (De Vries 1985, 1: 343). In the event, according to the Fund historian, the 1975 facility had 'almost no conditionality.' Although governments presented adjustment programs to the IMF, 'the Fund did not seriously attempt to see that these programs were implemented . . . . For the most part the oil facility proved to be an unconditional arrangement' (De Vries 1985, 1: 349; see also De Vries 1987: 119).

CONCLUSION

Both the extent of official payments financing as well as the nature of the conditionality that accompanied such financing were transformed following the 1973–74 OPEC price shock. The international emphasis on 'sharing the deficit' and the creation of the oil facilities signified the emergence of an alternative approach to the problem of payments imbalances that emphasized, tolerated, and even encouraged strategies of medium-term financing over rapid adjustment.[3] Managing Director Witteveen when making the case for the oil facility in 1974 emphasized the new dynamic for oil-importing deficit countries presented by the global economic situation. 'Trade restrictions or excessive demand deflation,' Witteveen (1974d: 133) argued, 'could only succeed in improving one country's balance of payments by worsening the position of other oil importing countries. If these other countries were to respond by adopting similar policies, the result would be a distortion in the allocation of resources, and possibly a cumulative deflationary effect on the world economy.' It is clear that Witteveen's conception of the financing problem facing oil-importers in 1974 and 1975 was comparable to a Prisoners' Dilemma game:[4] only through a mutual willingness to 'accept' and finance payments deficits could the cumulative deflationary effects of the OPEC price shock be contained. Any individual oil-importer's efforts to adjust rapidly would merely shift the payments burdens to other oil-importers. While individual deficit countries might be able to better their particular payments position, the improvement would only occur at the expense of others in similar situations. As Witteveen (1974g: 380–1) emphasized, 'an attempt by oil importing countries as a group to eliminate the deficit arising from higher oil prices too quickly through excessively deflationary demand policies, restrictions on trade and payments, or general resort to exchange rate depreciation, would be extremely dangerous. Such measures could only shift the payment problems from one country to another and would damage world trade and economic activity.'

Witteveen (1974d: 136) articulated a leadership role for the IMF in the new situation, arguing that 'an interruption in the growth of world trade, brought about by mutually incompatible policies, would have disastrous consequences . . . . The Fund has the duty and the responsibility to help prevent this.' It was for this reason, Witteveen (1974d: 134) noted, that the Committee of Twenty's January 1974 'agreement on the general principle that the oil importing countries should be prepared to accept sizeable current account deficits' was so important. 'In the present situation, it is uncommonly difficult for oil importing countries – both those in relatively strong positions and those in relatively weak positions – to judge their respective responsibilities in the adjustment process, and it is not apparent that they see eye to eye on this matter' (Witteveen 1974e: 23). But with the agreed Committee of Twenty communiqué, 'we now have an internationally agreed and accepted standard of conduct against which we can judge the actions of individual countries' (Witteveen 1974d: 134). Non-cooperative burden-shifting behavior, defined as 'excessively deflationary demand policies, restrictions on trade and payments, or general resort to exchange rate depreciation' (Witteveen 1974g: 380–1), was to be avoided. Although Witteveen acknowledged (1974d: 134) that 'the [Rome] communiqué is a joint declaration of intent . . . . [and] it does not, of course, indicate what policies will in fact be adopted,' he nonetheless referred to the Rome communiqué repeatedly in 1974 (1974d: 134, 1974f: 272–3, 1974g: 381) as a formal acknowledgement that oil-importing countries must avoid shifting their deficit problems to one another.

Although 'the slogan "accept the oil deficit" gradually came into vogue among financial officials' in 1974 (De Vries 1985, 1: 314), the current account balances of the leading OECD countries reacted quite differently to the OPEC price shock and not all of the leading OECD countries were in deficit or stayed in deficit for very long. Between 1973 and 1974, West Germany more than doubled its current account surplus from $5.2 billion to $10.6 billion; the United States transformed a $1.9 billion surplus in 1974 into a whopping $18.1 billion surplus in 1975; and Japan improved its current account position from a $4.7 billion deficit in 1974, to near balance in 1975, to a $3.7 billion surplus in 1976 (IMF 1989: 142). Together, West Germany, the United States, and Japan ran a cumulative current account surplus of some $25 billion over 1974–76 (McCracken et al. 1977: 68–9). These figures suggest that, 'accept the oil deficit' slogans notwithstanding, the three largest OECD states did not much follow the burden-sharing Committee of Twenty guidelines.[5]

Other OECD countries had different experiences, however. The United Kingdom ran an unprecedented current account deficit in 1974 of $7.5 billion, improving to a $3.4 billion deficit in 1975 and $1.7 billion in 1976. Italy, like Britain, also experienced a massive deficit in 1974 of $8.0 billion, came close to surplus in 1975, only to fall back into a deficit of $2.9 billion in 1976. France was more erratic and saw its current account position swing back and forth by approximately $6.0 billion over 1974–76, starting from a 1974 deficit of $3.9 billion. The smaller OECD countries as a group were also in substantial deficit (IMF 1989: 142; McCracken et al. 1977: 69). If West Germany, the United States, and Japan are excluded, the remaining OECD countries ran a cumulative 1974–76 current account deficit of almost $90 billion (McCracken et al. 1977: 68–9). As a team of independent economists appointed by the OECD concluded, 'there was a strong tendency for the current deficit to be shifted from the early "deflators" to the slower "deflators"' (McCracken et al. 1977: 74).

It was the British in 1974 and 1975 who most fully subscribed to the burden-sharing logic of the Committee of Twenty commitments made in Rome. As Chancellor of the Exchequer Denis Healey argues in his memoirs (1989: 423), 'Britain and Italy were the only countries to fulfil this undertaking [from Rome]. The United States, Japan, and West Germany did the opposite; they deflated their economies so as to reduce their deficits at our expense' (see also Healey 1989: 393). It was not until well into 1975 that Healey, citing foreign confidence and his concern about Britain's future ability to finance its deficits, reluctantly moved towards tougher fiscal and monetary deflation to address the UK's payments weaknesses.

5 Labour Economic Policy, March 1974–May 1975:
'A Phoney Phase'[1]

This chapter outlines the economic policy strategy during the first year of the 1974–79 Labour Government. I argue that the domestic political imperatives that guided and limited the Government's policy choices during this period stemmed from its arrival in power in the midst of a worldwide recession with a minority position in Parliament, an ideologically divided Cabinet, a left-of-center Manifesto, and a Social Contract partnership with the trade unions. However, the financing-over-adjustment emphases in the international political economy (discussed in Chapter 4) proved to be a relatively favorable environment, given the Government's domestic constraints. Conditions changed, however, in June 1975 with the first sustained run on sterling and the emergence and intensification of external pressure on the Government for policy retrenchment.

EXTERNAL BORROWING AND AVOIDING PROBLEMS, MARCH–DECEMBER 1974

Conservative British Prime Minister Ted Heath called the February 1974 general election in the context of a challenge by the National Union of Mineworkers (NUM) to the Government's Prices and Incomes Policy. The October 1973 OPEC price shock had strengthened the coal miners' collective bargaining position; when in November 1973 the NUM imposed an overtime ban, coal production fell by 22 per cent within a week (Foote 1988: 174). The Government responded by announcing in December 1973 that Britain would go on a three-day work week to conserve energy. In early February 1974, the NUM conducted a strike vote that showed 81 per cent of its membership in favor; the Government on 7 February called a general election on the theme 'Who Governs Britain?' (see Whitehead 1985: 99–115; Fay and Young 1976). The election was not desired by Labour leader Harold Wilson; senior party officials had not yet finalized Labour's campaign manifesto (Wilson

Table 5.1   General election results, February 1974

	Votes	Vote %	Seats
Labour	11 646 391	37.1	301
Conservatives	11 872 180	37.8	297
Liberal	6 058 744	19.3	14
Scottish/Welsh Nationalist	804 554	2.6	9
Others (mainly Ulster Unionists)	958 293	3.1	14
Total (78.1% turnout)	31 340 162	100	635

Source: Butler and Kavanagh (1974: 275–6).

1979: 5; Middlemas 1991: 44). Nevertheless, Labour in the election won slightly more seats in Parliament than did the Conservatives, with slightly fewer votes, and it formed the next, albeit minority, Government (see Table 5.1).

It was not an auspicious time to come to power. The new Chancellor of the Exchequer Denis Healey in his first budget speech quoted the National Institute of Economic and Social Research's commentary on the Conservative Government's economic legacy: 'It is not often that a Government finds itself confronted with the possibility of a simultaneous failure to achieve all four main policy objectives – adequate economic growth, full employment, a satisfactory balance of payments, and reasonably stable prices' (*National Institute Economic Review*, February 1974, p. 4; UK Healey 1974a: 282; Middlemas 1991: 21; Dell 1991: 10). By virtually every indicator, the economic situation in the UK in early 1974 was deteriorating. Inflation was sharply accelerating, rising from 9.2 per cent in 1973 to 15.9 per cent in 1974, as the economy reacted to the quadrupling of oil prices on top of the Conservative Government's 1972–73 expansionary drive (IMF 1989b: 116–17; Browning 1986: 31–58). Moreover, British inflation was strongly reinforced by the indexation mechanisms in the Conservative Government's pay policy, and basic hourly wage rates increased by 24 per cent between November 1973 and July 1974[2] (OECD 1975: 11). The balance of payments, which had been in surplus during 1971 and 1972, had moved into deficit in 1973 and would be in extreme deficit in 1974 due to the oil price shock. The M3 money supply had expanded by over 25 per cent in 1972 and again in 1973. Only unemployment, which had fallen somewhat during 1972–73, seemed reasonably stable (Browning 1986: 357–60, 364).

In putting together the Cabinet in March 1974, Prime Minister Harold

Wilson had to accommodate a Labour Party in which the ideological center had moved to the left (see Chapter 3). Accordingly, he incorporated the left within the Cabinet by putting them in important economic posts – Tony Benn at Industry, Michael Foot at Employment, Peter Shore at Trade, and Barbara Castle at Social Services (Castle 1980: 30). Although the Party's social democratic wing was given the more prominent Cabinet portfolios – Roy Jenkins at the Home Office, James Callaghan at the Foreign Office, Denis Healey at the Treasury, and Tony Crosland at Environment – Labour moderates were nonetheless on the defensive. As future Minister of Industry Tony Benn expressed in his diary (1989: 94) a month before the election, 'one of the great arguments of the right is that you can't win an election with a left-wing programme. If you have a left-wing programme and you win an election, then the right will have lost that argument.'

The new Government held a minority position in Parliament. Governing decisions had to be made with the knowledge that the Government would be unable to prevent defeat should the opposition parties unite against it and that a second general election could not be far away. Accordingly unpleasant and difficult measures tended to be avoided or postponed. On 18 September, the Government called a second general election, with Harold Wilson claiming grandly in Labour's election Manifesto that 'no post-war British Government has achieved more in six months' than Labour had from March to September 1974 (Labour Party 1974b). Although the Government won the October 1974 election somewhat more decisively (see Table 5.2), its overall majority (allowing for the Speaker) was only four, and as was immediately apparent to the Prime Minister 'would clearly not long survive the erosion of by-elections and possible defections' (Wilson 1979: 85).

Denis Healey (1980: 11) has recounted that within an hour of first entering the Treasury building as Chancellor in March 1974 he was told by officials that he had to produce a budget in exactly three weeks. Extensive discussions ensued within the Treasury about the so-called budget judgement, which was 'an estimate of the degree to which demand should be increased or reduced by government action so as to produce the best mix of growth and price stability' (Healey 1980: 11; Barnett 1982: 23–5; Dell 1991: 30–3). The budget Healey presented to Parliament three weeks later was characterized by the Chancellor as 'broadly neutral on demand, with the bias if any on the side of caution' (UK Healey 1974a: 294; Dell 1991: 31). Healey forecast that demand at year-end 'may be running at about £200 million lower than would otherwise have been the case' because of the budget's impact

Table 5.2   General election results, October 1974

	Votes	Vote %	Seats
Labour	11 457 079	39.2	319
Conservatives	10 464 817	35.8	277
Liberal	5 346 754	18.3	13
Scottish/Welsh Nationalist	1 005 938	3.5	14
Others (mainly Ulster Unionists)	897 164	3.1	12
Total (72.8% turnout)	29 189 178	100	635

Source: Butler and Kavanagh (1975: 293–4).

(UK Healey 1974a: 327; Castle 1980: 50–1). The Chancellor stated his intention to improve Britain's external payments situation by exporting more and devoting more resources to export production. In what was to become an increasingly prominent theme in his speeches over the next three years, Healey argued

> my Budget must ensure that there is enough room fully to exploit the opportunities for exports . . . and also for the industrial investment needed for export-oriented growth . . . . Some hon. Members may argue that I should not leave room for the expansion of exports and investment until the [external] demand is clearly there. But there is all the evidence we need that [external] demand is waiting to be met.[3]

(UK Healey 1974a: 293).

Some of Healey's Cabinet colleagues were in favor of a more expansionary budget; as Chancellor of the Duchy of Lancaster Harold Lever argued, "'this ought above all to have been a reflationary Budget." The essence of our policy was the Social Contract, which, above all, was based on reducing unemployment and going for growth. [Lever] thought the Budget would inevitably increase unemployment and we should be in trouble with the trade unions' (Castle 1980: 51; Dell 1991: 34; see also Benn 1989: 127).

Healey in his memoirs (1989:393) retrospectively views the March 1974 Budget as a 'mistake.' Conceived within the framework of a 'broadly neutral' budget judgement, it turned out to be inadvertently stimulatory and reflationary. According to Healey (1989: 380–1), the Budget was formulated with a Public Sector Borrowing Requirement (PSBR) forecast that was underestimated by £4 billion, an amount equivalent to 5.4 per cent of GDP for 1974. This 'hidden' PSBR underestimate resulted in substantial additional stimulus to domestic demand. As Healey declares in his memoirs (1989: 380–1), 'the magnitude of that one forecasting error was greater than any fiscal change made by any Chancellor in British history.' In the view of Chief Secretary to the Treasury Joel Barnett (1982: 24), 'there can be little doubt that different decisions would have been reached had the forecasts been less wide of the mark . . . . Indeed, the whole course of the next five years might have been changed had we decided we could not plan for such a high PSBR and therefore not increased public expenditure to the extent we did.' Thus, a budget intended to be broadly neutral and to shift resources into exports turned out to be strongly stimulatory, thereby exacerbating the UK's external financing needs (see also Holmes 1985: 9; Middlemas 1991: 102; Ham 1981: 104–5).

Consistent with the emphases outlined at the January 1974 Committee of Twenty meeting (see Chapter 4), Healey announced in the Budget that he had made arrangements to finance Britain's external deficit through borrowing. On his authority, the Bank of England had secured a $2.5 billion foreign currency loan through the British clearing banks 'to make it clear to the world that we can finance the deficit that lies ahead' (UK Healey 1974a: 286). Although he acknowledged that 'our balance of payments deficit must be reduced,' he also noted that 'a good part [of the deficit] is due to the high price of oil, and we accept the view of the OECD and of the IMF that it would be wrong for the industrial oil-importing countries to seek to eliminate that part of their deficits in the near future' (UK Healey 1974a: 292). *Vis-à-vis* the 'non-oil' part of the deficit, Healey argued, 'we cannot hope to eliminate the whole of the underlying deficit this year; nor would it be right to do so' (UK Healey 1974a: 285). Echoing themes from the IMF Managing Director and the Committee of Twenty communiqué, Healey told Parliament that 'borrowing is more sensible in economic and human terms than trying to cut imports by massive deflation. But no one should imagine that it is a soft option. The interest has to be paid each year . . . . Later on instalments of the capital will have to be repaid as well' (UK Healey 1974a: 286).

Healey acknowledged to Parliament that the external dimension had influenced the budget judgement. 'If I were concerned only with managing the domestic aspects of our economy, I should prefer to risk having a bit too much demand rather than too little . . . . But we cannot shut our eyes to external economic problems . . . . Taking our total situation into account, I believe that given our present external problems, a reflationary Budget at this moment would involve us in unacceptable risks' (UK Healey 1974a: 293). In Cabinet, Healey was more specific about the external dangers. At one of the Government's first Cabinet meetings, he expressed his surprise that 'there had been no run on sterling' (Castle 1980: 50). *Vis-à-vis* the UK's external financing needs, he told Cabinet that he wanted to steer clear of loan conditionality: the $2.5 billion borrowing from the clearing banks was on the best possible terms and was 'without recourse to the International Monetary Fund, which he wanted to avoid, "with its strings"' (Castle 1980: 50). In July 1974, the Chancellor announced an additional $1.2 billion foreign currency loan from Iran to Britain (Browning 1986: 61; UK Healey 1974b: 1050); in his memoirs, Healey (1989: 423) reveals that he also raised an additional loan from Saudi Arabia during this period.[4]

The UK was in a particularly advantageous position in 1974 and early 1975 in terms of its ability to finance its current account deficit. Sterling in 1974 was still the world's second largest reserve currency (IMF 1975a: 39; Healey 1989: 411). When the foreign exchange holdings of OPEC countries ballooned as the result of the oil price hike, a significant portion of their accumulated surplus reserves were held in the UK. The Bank of England estimated in March 1975 that nearly 40 per cent of OPEC countries' current account surpluses was held in Britain, almost double the amount in the United States at the time, and in the more narrow terms of official sterling reserves, the Bank reported strong growth in the size of oil exporters' official sterling balances (*Bank of England Quarterly Bulletin*, March 1975, p. 24, March 1976, p. 23; see also Howard 1976b). As one informed source recounts:

> Although the balance of payments was desperately weak, quite a lot of the oil countries had had some historical tradition and connection of investing a proportion of their reserves in sterling. And after the oil shock, their reserves suddenly went ahead by leaps and bounds, and if they had had N per cent in sterling before, for quite a time they went on investing N per cent in sterling .... Although N was quite low, the actual amount of the reserves accruing was so vast that really quite a large amount was flowing almost automatically into sterling investments. And that held the sterling position – the in-flow from the OPEC countries. It was kind of automatic and a not-very-well-considered in-flow.
>
> (Interview material; see also Pliatzky 1982: 132;
> Burk and Cairncross 1992: 29, fn 26)

But sterling's reserve status gave the Government breathing room; as

Healey explained (1974b) in a November 1974 letter to US Treasury Secretary Simon, 'we have had a substantial inflow of investment in sterling assets of many kinds, as well as public sector borrowing, and there should be no difficulty in financing the current account deficit' (see also Burk and Cairncross 1992: 174).

However, the situation was not without risk. As former head of the Government Economic Service Alec Cairncross (1975: 19–20) presciently commented in March 1975, 'the danger of running a deficit covered by short-term borrowing is precisely that of having to revise policy abruptly when loans are not renewed or no fresh loans can be raised' (see also Bernstein 1983: 268–9). Given that OPEC countries' preferences for sterling were based largely upon 'inertia in their cash management' (OECD 1985: 70), capital inflows could quickly and unexpectedly become capital outflows. Although there were *ad hoc* discussions through 1974 about external financing and the current account deficit, it is unclear whether Cabinet ministers were fully aware of the risks (see Castle 1980: 81, 126, 141; Donoughue 1985: 55–6, 1987: 51–6). Within the Treasury, however, there was extensive discussion about the risks of the Government's strategy (Barnett 1982: 24–5; Donoughue 1985: 56). As early as the miners' strike, the Industrial Strategy Steering Group had begun to explore how economic recovery might occur, but its agenda 'was limited by Treasury acceptance that despite the very heavy deficit and the constant threat to sterling, the [new Labour] Government could not abandon its policy of borrowing to 'tunnel through' . . . for fear of losing either its slender majority or trade union cooperation, or both' (Middlemas 1991: 86). Chief Secretary of the Treasury Joel Barnett (1982: 31, 23) characterizes the period as 'a phoney phase' during which the Government resisted external adjustment and continued to spend money 'which in the event we did not have.'

In anticipation of the second 1974 election, the Chancellor in July brought forward a set of mildly reflationary measures by announcing a 2 per cent cut in the general rate of the Value Added Tax (VAT) as well as an increase in food subsidies. Healey estimated that the measures would increase total demand by less than £200 million and add 'a relatively small amount – some £340 million' to the PSBR (UK Healey 1974b: 1051–3; Dell 1991: 76–81). The reception the package received in Cabinet was mixed. Minister for Social Services Barbara Castle expressed regret that social spending had not been increased (Castle 1980: 150); on the other hand, Chancellor of the Duchy of Lancaster Harold Lever praised Healey for the stimulation that a tax cut would give to the economy: 'when I look at what other countries are doing, I have to congratulate the Chancellor on his courage' (Castle 1980: 150). The dampening effect on inflation of the VAT cut and the increased food subsidies allowed the Government to claim a substantial (if short-lived) victory over inflation during the October election campaign (Barnett 1982: 31–2; Dell 1991: 81).

In the run-up to the election, Healey in his public speeches began to relate Britain's domestic economic problems with the policy actions other states were taking, voicing his concern that if governments fought inflation

> through massive reductions in demand beyond the reductions already imposed by the increases in oil prices, the current decline in economic activity could lead within two years to a world slump on the scale of the 'thirties. Although the signs of this danger are already mounting, I do not believe we will be so foolish. Indeed I was greatly encouraged in meeting some of my European and American colleagues ... by the universal recognition that it would be fatal to seek an answer to the problem of world inflation by creating a world slump. Mass unemployment is not regarded by any Government as an answer to our current problems. We must therefore take account of the deflationary impact of the petro-dollar surplus and accept the inevitability of massive payments deficits on oil account for some years to come.
>
> (Ham 1981: 106–7)

Vis-à-vis unemployment, Healey noted that it was

> likely to rise ... unless I do something about it. There is a problem for a country which has the inheritance which I incurred leading the world in reflation. And this is why I spent so much time ... trying to persuade some of my colleagues abroad that the cut in world demand of $90 billion – $80 billion this year, produced by the petro-dollar surplus – should not be multiplied and aggravated by domestic policies of deflation.
>
> (Ham 1981: 107–8)

Harold Wilson recounts in his memoirs (1979: 85) that because the Government held only a narrow majority in Parliament following the October 1974 election, 'I pressed the Cabinet at our first post-election meeting to push on fast with our declared legislative programme, particularly with Bills likely to prove controversial, and/or complicated and lengthy.' But the foremost controversial, and/or complicated and lengthy issue confronting the Government in late 1974 and early 1975 was not its external payments position, but rather the deeply divisive referendum on the 'renegotiated' terms of Britain's entry into the European Community (see among others Butler and Kitzinger 1976; Silkin 1977; Newman 1983: 235–58; Featherstone 1988: 41–75; George 1990: 76–99; Jenkins 1991: 399–418). Economic policy issues were secondary to the Government's internal difficulties over Europe, and thus it was on behalf of a deeply divided Government that Healey introduced a new Budget to Parliament following the October elections (UK Healey 1974c).

The main aim of the new Budget was to provide assistance in the form of price code relaxation and corporate tax relief to British companies that were experiencing difficulties.[5] Healey told Parliament that he expected that the provision of corporate tax relief would result in an £800 million increase in the borrowing requirement and that the borrowing requirement forecast for 1974–75, which had been estimated at £2.7 billion in the spring, had more than doubled to £6.3 billion (UK Healey 1974c: 250–1, 279; *National Institute Economic Review*, November 1974, pp. 7–8). When previewed to Cabinet, the £6.3 billion PSBR brought 'whistles through the teeth' (Castle 1980: 213). The Chancellor, however, expressed caution about attaching too much importance to economic forecasts:

> Their origin lies in the extrapolation from a partially known past, through an unknown present, to an unknowable future, according to theories about the causal relationships between certain economic variables which are hotly disputed by academic economists and may well in fact change from country to country or from decade to decade. The current state of our economic knowledge allows of nothing better, but I hope no one will rely on it too much.
> (UK Healey 1974c: 252–3)

With respect to the current account deficit (which was forecast to be 'below £4000 million'), Healey told Parliament that, while he foresaw 'no difficulty' in financing the deficit, 'I want to make it quite clear that this does not mean that I contemplate borrowing indefinitely on anything like the present scale. I am determined that the balance of payments shall show a continuing and sustained improvement, and this will be a crucial objective of my strategy' (UK Healey 1974c: 247, 249–50). The heart of Healey's strategy – 'my first priority in economic management' – continued to be the shift of resources into exports and investment and away from domestic consumption, and he acknowledged that the shift would be painful: 'At least in the next few years, the great majority of us cannot expect any appreciable increase in our living standards, and increases in public expenditure will have to be held below the average increases in national output' (UK Healey 1974c: 254). Although 'in other circumstances the massive deflationary effect of the oil price increase and the fall-off in world trade might have made more reflation desirable,' under the circumstances any scope for reflation in Britain depended 'critically on the policies of the US and Germany' (UK Healey 1974c: 280, 244). The Chancellor conceded that a £6.3 billion PSBR was 'disturbingly large,' a figure that 'one would never accept in normal circumstances. But in present circumstances, if I had made an attempt to close it . . . the result could only have been a large fall in our national output and a massive increase in unemployment' (UK Healey 1974c: 279). Healey noted that the inflow of sterling from abroad was helping to address Britain's financing needs, but he did not raise the more troubling question of how a now doubled PSBR forecast might affect external confidence (UK Healey 1974c: 248).

The first sustained downward pressure on sterling since Labour came to power occurred in December 1974 following a news report that Saudi Arabia had decided that henceforth it would accept oil revenues exclusively in dollars as opposed to the roughly 75 per cent dollars– 25 per cent sterling balance it had accepted previously (Browning 1986: 64; *Bank of England Quarterly Bulletin*, March 1975, p. 6; *Bank of England: Report and Accounts for the Year Ended 28 February 1975*, pp. 18–19; *National Institute Economic Review*, February 1975, p. 99). Coincidentally, when the report appeared, Healey was in Saudi Arabia seeking to secure financing for the renewed IMF oil facility; he recounts in his memoirs (1989: 425) that 'I was woken up in the middle of the night with the news that there was a serious run on the pound. My hosts knew nothing of [Saudi Oil Minister Sheik] Yamani's decision [to no longer accept payment in sterling]; when I told them, they bought £200 million of [British] gilts in the next two days, so the trouble died down. They were men of honour and integrity.' Upon his return to the UK, Healey made a reassuring statement in Parliament that 'the Saudi Ministers made it clear that they intend not only to maintain but to increase their holdings of currency in this country. . . . The decision [to accept only dollars] was purely in order to simplify matters. . . . The important thing is that the Saudi authorities plan to maintain and increase their investment in this country' (UK Healey 1974d: 984).

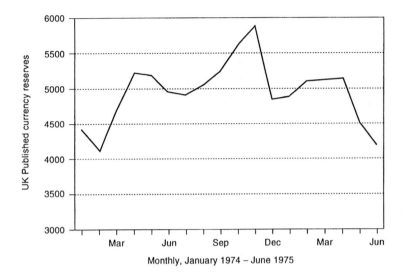

Figure 5.1 UK currency reserves 1974–75

Source: *Bank of England Quarterly Bulletin*, March 1976, Statistical Annex, table 23

But Saudi commitments of support notwithstanding, sterling fell by 4.5 per cent in value against other currencies during the fourth quarter of 1974, and despite the drawing of $1.5 billion on the $2.5 billion clearing bank loan and considerable additional external borrowing by British public sector bodies, the UK's published foreign currency reserves fell by over $1 billion in December 1974 (see Figure 5.1;[6] *Bank of England Quarterly Bulletin*, March 1975, p. 6, and *Bank of England Quarterly Bulletin*, March 1976, Statistical Annex, Table 23; Castle 1980: 284). Private figures compiled by American central bank officials on the magnitude of the Bank of England's intervention on foreign exchange markets show a sharply heavier drain during the fourth quarter of 1974 (see Figure 5.2; McCormick 1976).

BLOCKED ALTERNATIVES, JANUARY–MAY 1975

Through 1974 and into 1975, proposals for economic retrenchment were largely kept off the agenda, initially because of the Government's minority position in Parliament, and later because of the run-up to the

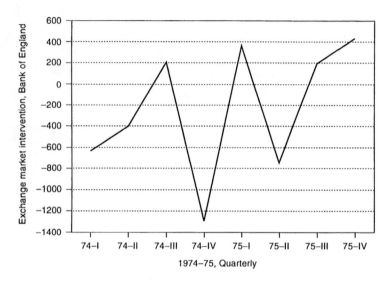

Figure 5.2   Bank of England exchange market intervention 1974–75

Source: McCormick (1976)

June 1975 referendum on the Common Market (Donoughue 1987: 57; Whitehead 1985: 147). Given the Government's parliamentary weakness and its internal divisions, continued external financing was probably the most politically viable economic strategy for it to pursue. Fortunately, it was also a strategy that was compatible with the developments and emphases emerging in the global economy during this period.

Nevertheless, increasing attention was being focused on the problem of wage-push inflation in the UK. The National Institute for Economic and Social Research observed in November 1974 that many of the current wage settlements occurring at around 20 per cent were '*in anticipation* of further price rises of this order. . . . 20 per cent inflation thus becomes a self-fulfilling prophecy' (*National Institute Economic Review*, November 1974, p. 4, original emphasis; Browning 1986: 63, fn 4). As early as April 1974, the Chancellor had begun talking 'in semi-private conditions' that he believed wage restraint was going to be necessary to bring inflation under control, but he accepted that, given the Government's minority position, only a 'voluntary' (as opposed to statutory) policy was feasible or possible (Middlemas 1991: 90–1). In June 1974, the TUC General Council as its part of the Social Contract had issued advisory 'guidelines' on wage bargaining that acknowledged that 'the scope for real increases in consumption at present is limited.' The General Council asked union negotiators 'to take account of the general economic and industrial situation and of the economic and social policies being pursued by the Government. The current circumstances . . . impose limits on what can be achieved at this time' (TUC 1974a: 289–90; Coates 1980: 62). It was with the TUC guidelines that the Government hoped to reduce British inflation. Healey (1974b) wrote to US Treasury Secretary Simon in November 1974 that the UK was 'having some success' *vis-à-vis* inflation, and that 'the most important factor in maintaining this improvement will be the rate at which earnings rise: if settlements can be confined to what is needed to cover the increase in prices, then we can reasonably expect to see a decrease in the rate of inflation in [1975].'

This expectation proved to be unfounded. In February 1975, the rate of inflation on an annual basis reached 20 per cent, with wage rates rising at an annual rate of 29 per cent (Browning 1986: 65). The TUC's guidelines and the changed 'climate' that the Government had sought to create with the Social Contract were ineffective at inducing wage restraint (Healey 1989: 394; TUC–Labour Party Liaison Committee 1973: 313; Labour Party 1974a: 8). By early 1975, Healey was no longer 'semi-private' in making the case for wage restraint. In a January speech, the Chancellor explicitly linked wage restraint with continued full employment, arguing publicly that 'it is far better that more people should be in work, even if that means accepting lower wages on average, than that those lucky enough to keep their jobs should scoop the pool while millions are living on the dole. That is what the Social Contract is about.' The press interpreted the speech as a warning that 'Britain must now except lower average wages or face mounting unemployment,' noting that this was 'the first time that the Chancellor or any member of the Wilson Government has given the Social Contract this interpretation' (*Sunday Times*, 12 January 1975, 'Unions Wary,' p. 1). At a TUC–Labour Party Liaison Committee meeting, Healey bluntly told the assembled union leaders that because of Britain's financing requirements, something had to be done about inflation.

The oil producers were simply not prepared to put their money into a country where its value could be undermined. 'The flurry last December [1974] cost us $1,000 million of our reserves.' If inflation undermined commercial borrowing . . . one of two things would happen: either we should have to reduce the standard of living . . . or we should have to start borrowing from institutions which would impose terms, like a statutory incomes policy, which a Labour Government would find unacceptable. 'There have been no conditions on our borrowing so far.' He didn't want to have to face conditions. . . . We simply had to get wage settlements down.

(Castle 1980: 284–5)

Healey's comments were not well received. General Secretary of the Transport and General Workers' Union Jack Jones recounts in his memoirs (1986: 295) that 'sometimes I felt that political leaders did not appreciate the hard work involved in influencing rank-and-file opinion. . . . [General Secretary of the TUC] Len Murray was constrained to say [to the Government Ministers] that wage restraint was not the 'be all and end all' . . . in solving the economic problems of the country.'

Inside the Government, the Prime Minister was adamantly opposed to even the suggestion of an incomes policy. When the Prime Minister's Policy Unit wrote a paper arguing the necessity of some form of pay policy before the end of 1974, Wilson's comment was 'analysis fine, except any mention of incomes policy is out' (Whitehead 1987: 251). The Prime Minister had told Denis Healey directly 'you know, Denis, I'll support you in everything you want to do except incomes policy' (Whitehead 1985: 148; Healey 1989: 394), but communication between Chancellor and Prime Minister about economic policy was not frequent (Donoughue 1987: 56–7, 1989: 42; Barnett 1982: 63). As Policy Unit head Bernard Donoughue (1989: 42) recounts, 'Wilson seemed on the whole curiously uninterested in economics.'

It was in this context that the Chancellor in the winter and spring of 1975 brought forward the first of what was to become a succession of expenditure cuts packages. Spending had increased sharply after Labour came to power in March 1974. Measured in nominal prices, public expenditure increased by 29 per cent in 1974; in inflation-adjusted prices, it increased by 12.4 per cent in fiscal year 1974–75 (Pliatzky 1982: 212–13). Chief Secretary of the Treasury Joel Barnett recounts that 'we just took the [election] manifesto . . . and my ministerial colleagues started spending in accordance with that manifesto' (Whitehead 1985: 127). In Barnett's view (1982: 189), the Government's economic problems had been made 'impossible by pledges foolishly made without any serious thought as to where the money would come from. You name it, we were pledged to increase it.' The Treasury official with responsibility for overseeing the Government's public expenditure has characterized 1974–75 as a period of both 'frenetic activity' and 'collective madness' (Pliatzky 1982: 130).

Within the Treasury, 'long Budget strategy meetings' were occurring between Ministers, officials, and advisers, including economic advisers Nicholas Kaldor and Wynne Godley who argued for import controls rather than public expenditure cuts as a means of reducing the UK's external deficits (Barnett 1982: 62, 24–5). The TUC (1975: 264–5) at about this time also began to press for action on imports, arguing in its 1975 *Economic Review* that 'the Government should not seek to correct the serious trade deficit by holding back demand because this would reduce employment, damage industrial confidence, and impede rather than promote the structural changes needed in the economy. Temporary import controls should be imposed and the Government should act resolutely to stop investment and employment from falling further.' When the TUC's Economic Committee met with Healey in March 1975 to discuss TUC recommendations, it emphasized 'the need for the Government to take measures to improve the employment situation' (TUC 1975: 266). *Vis-à-vis* the 1975 budget, the TUC recommended that 'priority had to be given to the maintenance of living standards and full employment. . . . The economy should be encouraged to grow at a rate of 2.9 per cent. . . . [and] selective import controls should be imposed to protect the balance of payments' (TUC 1975: 266).

Discussions of a more reflationary economic strategy that would include import controls were also occurring among non-Treasury ministers. In the Ministerial Committee on Economic Strategy in February 1975, Minister of Industry Tony Benn circulated a paper entitled 'The Alternative Economic Strategy in Outline' in which he set forward two broad policy alternatives for the Government – Strategy A and Strategy B (Benn 1989: 324–6, 725–7). As Minister for Social Services Barbara Castle (1980: 353, fn 1) has described Benn's paper:

> Strategy A embodied the conventional economic approach of cutting living standards and increasing unemployment to wipe out the balance of payments deficit and reduce inflation. Strategy B put the preservation of jobs and industrial capacity first. It involved large-scale selective assistance to industry . . ., selective import restrictions, rationing and allocation of some imported materials and fuel, work sharing, more egalitarian taxation, control of capital outflows and acceptance of a further downward float in sterling to make us more competitive.
>
>   (See also Benn 1989: 302; Dell 1991: 124)

Benn's argument was that 'Strategy A and its variants entails as a deliberate act of policy a relatively sharp cut in living standards and employment achieved by traditional, indirect, macro-economic measures of a broadly indiscriminate nature,' and that it would ultimately involve 'the withdrawal of support from the Government by the TUC and the Labour movement.' By contrast, Strategy B was 'intended to operate more slowly and more selectively by direct action at particular points of weakness and with greater emphasis on the preservation of employment and manufacturing capacity' (Benn 1989: 726–7). The paper was not well received. Foreign Secretary Jim Callaghan's view was that 'this business about export/import controls is like devaluation. It doesn't solve the problem.' The Chancellor argued that Strategy B was a 'caricature; it oversimplifies to the point of distortion.' For Healey, 'the key question is can we go on borrowing? We are living 5 per cent to 6 per cent above our earnings. It will be very much harder to borrow £3 billion [in 1975]; maybe we will have to go to the IMF or the OECD and suffer supervision' (Benn 1989: 325).

Chief Secretary to the Treasury Joel Barnett (1982: 62) recounts that 'after many meetings . . . it became clear that [quota restrictions] and other fundamentally new ways of dealing with our economic problems did not offer a satisfactory solution. So we were back with tax and expenditure cuts.' In late March 1975, the Chancellor presented the Cabinet with a proposal for over £1 billion in cuts in planned public expenditure for 1976–77, emphasizing the problems of external financing and wage-push inflation. Britain's credit was 'low and falling,' Healey argued.

> Inflation was running at 20 per cent. The borrowing requirement was much too high for comfort and we might get a sudden collapse of confidence. The main source of inflation was wage inflation. He hoped he would be able to work out tougher [wage] guidelines with the TUC, 'but we can't take credit for that now.' He didn't want to be 'too nasty' in this year's Budget, because the level of world trade was falling. . . . But the figure [of £1 billion in public expenditure cuts] was the minimum necessary.
>
> (Castle 1980: 352)

There was spirited resistance from certain ministers, however. Minister for the Environment Tony Crosland delivered 'the most powerful criticism,' arguing that 'he was against a decision now, what was the object of it? It couldn't improve the balance of payments this year, it couldn't moderate wage claims, there was enough slack in the economy to provide the shift [to exports]. . . . The political effects would be traumatic and half the Manifesto would go down the drain' (Barnett 1982:

64; Benn 1989: 356). The view of Chief Secretary Barnett (1982: 64) was that Crosland 'had no coherent alternative strategy. He just didn't like public expenditure cuts – but who did?. . . . I felt he basically knew there was no alternative, but he had to go through the motions.' Minister of Trade Peter Shore argued that the proposals would not work on their own terms, as they would not of themselves directly address the external imbalance: 'if we *just* have a deflationary package, we won't be in a better position at the end of the year to seize our [export] opportunities. There is a missing component in Denis's proposals: an effective element for increasing exports or reducing imports this year' (Castle 1980: 352–3, original emphasis). Minister of Social Services Barbara Castle, Minister of Industry Tony Benn, and Minister of Employment Michael Foot also opposed the expenditure cuts, with Foot emphasizing the negative impact it could have on the Government's relations with the trade unions: '"We are in danger of drifting into a conventional Treasury package with no light at the end of the tunnel." We should face the trade unions with a direct choice: tougher [wage] guidelines or disastrous [expenditure] cuts.' By cutting public expenditure, Foot argued, the Government would be jeopardizing the chance of obtaining tougher wage restraint (Castle 1980: 352–3; Benn 1989: 356–7; Barnett 1982: 64).

But opposition to the cuts was a minority position in Cabinet. Healey received strong support from former Chancellors Jim Callaghan and Roy Jenkins and 'acquiescent' support from other ministers. As Home Secretary Jenkins warned, 'if Denis could not say something publicly about the borrowing requirement, there might be a collapse of confidence' (Castle 1980: 353; Benn 1989: 357). At the end of the discussion, Healey summed up his position by telling his colleagues that circumstances had changed and that the Government had to react. 'The things we counted on haven't happened: [wage restraint through] the Social Contract and reflation by other countries' (Castle 1980: 353–4).

Expenditure cuts of £1 billion were announced in the Government's April 1975 Budget (UK Healey 1975a: 273–322) and constituted a turning point. Rather than taking action that would 'improve the employment situation' as the TUC (1975: 266) had recommended, the Chancellor announced measures that would dampen domestic demand at a time when unemployment was already moving upward (Gardner 1987: 56). Healey forecast in the Budget that 'the pressure of demand in the United Kingdom will continue easing and unemployment will continue to rise for the remainder of [1975]. I must warn the House that it could be touching a million, or 4 per cent by the end of the year' (UK Healey

1975a: 320). Healey told Parliament that the situation 'has given me great concern, since I absolutely reject the use of mass unemployment as an instrument of policy' (UK Healey 1975a: 320). Nonetheless, as the National Institute for Economic and Social Research perceptively commented:

> The last time unemployment reached 3/4 million on an upward trend in mid-1971, policy was already moving towards stimulation of demand, and this was the tendency on all previous occasions when the unemployment figures had been rising for any length of time.... Demand management policy is evidently now being used not to maintain a high and stable level of employment but as a bargaining weapon in an attempt to get some effective tightening of the Social Contract.
>
> (*National Institute Economic Review*, May 1975, p. 9; Ham 1981: 123)

Healey hinted at some of the concerns within the Treasury about the linkages between the domestic economic situation, confidence, and Britain's financing needs. 'In 1974 we had little difficulty in borrowing sufficient money to cover this enormous [current account] deficit on commercial terms, from sources which imposed no policy conditions on their lending.... If we are to go on attracting such funds, their owners must believe that the value of the money they have placed with us is not threatened by the consequences of our policy actions or inactions' (UK Healey 1975a: 274). On unchanged policies, Healey argued, the 1975–76 PSBR would have been over £10 billion – 'too high by any standards' – and would have involved 'unacceptable risks' (UK Healey 1975a: 285–6). The measures in the Budget would reduce the estimated size of the PSBR by over £1 billion in 1975–76 and by over £3 billion in 1976–77, and the current account deficit for 1975 was expected to be 'at least a billion pounds lower than in 1974' (UK Healey 1975a: 286, 274). The Chancellor clearly and presciently outlined the dangers if borrowing continued on such a large scale:

> We in Britain must keep control of our own policy. We must keep ahead of events. It would be disastrous if we were forced, as some times in the past, into running desperately after events which we could not control. By relying unduly on borrowing we would run the risk of being forced to accept political and economic conditions imposed by the will of others. This would represent an absolute and unequivocal loss of sovereignty. (UK Healey 1975a: 284; Browning 1986: 98).

Healey also took aim at the TUC in the Budget Statement. He first outlined the Government's record regarding social expenditures, asserting 'we in the Government have honoured our side of the Social Contract. . . . Total Government expenditure on items which make up the social wage increased 34 per cent last year – or about 12 per cent in real terms. In fact the social wage now amounts to about £1,000 a year for every member of the working population' (UK Healey 1975a: 280; Browning 1986: 66). But the Social Contract was not having a restraining effect on wage settlements.

> Pay has been running about 8 per cent or 9 per cent above prices. . . . As I have warned the House and the country on many occasions . . . settlements so far beyond the increase in the cost of living are bound severely to restrict my room for manoeuvre in this Budget and to limit the pace at which the Government can carry out their remaining commitments under the Social Contract. . . . Unless . . . the [TUC's] voluntary policy achieves stricter adherence to guidelines laid down by the trade unions of their own free will, the consequences can only be rising unemployment, cuts in public expenditure, lower living standards for the country as a whole, and growing tension throughout society.
>
> (UK Healey 1975a: 280–2; Dell 1991: 153)

At a meeting of the TUC–Labour Party Liaison Committee the following week, the TUC told the Government that the Budget was a disappointment in that 'it did nothing to prevent the emergence of higher unemployment towards the end of 1975' (TUC 1975: 268). Healey, however, reiterated that something had to be done about wages: 'The level of settlements has been well above the spirit of the [TUC voluntary wage] guidelines and I hope we can discuss how we can prevent this from happening again' (Castle 1980: 372). TUC General Secretary Len Murray responded with ambivalence, telling the Chancellor that '"history repeats itself, sometimes as tragedy and sometimes as farce,"'. . . . Unemployment wouldn't bring down wage demands. However, Murray acknowledged that regarding wages, the TUC was '"less than satisfied with our performance."' But then again [the Government] mustn't press . . . too much. At the coming [TUC] Congress there was a danger of a coalition against the Social Contract' (Castle 1980: 372).

There was some effort to tighten wage restraint in May 1975 with a TUC review of collective bargaining developments (TUC 1975: 270–1). There had been many 'special factors,' 'special case increases,' and 'complications,' the TUC defensively argued, and when these were taken into account, 'the underlying rate of increase in wages was closer to movements in retail prices than was suggested by much uninformed comment.'[7] The TUC acknowledged, however, that 'there had been undesirable gaps in the observance of the [TUC's wage] guidelines, and . . . if settlements in the next round of negotiations were pitched at the [same] level, . . . the prospect of reducing inflation towards the end of [1975] and during [1976] would be seriously threatened' (TUC 1975: 271). The TUC sent a circular to union pay negotiators, reminding them that 'there was nothing in the present situation that reduced the need for the Social Contract or the need to reach agreements on the basis of guidelines' (TUC 1975: 271; Taylor 1987: 52–3), but it had little effect.

In May 1975, Healey presented the Cabinet with an additional £3 billion expenditure cuts package spread out over 1975–79, arguing that the economic situation was dire. 'If we are able to get the inflation rate down, the prospects for public expenditure will be better,' Healey argued, 'but we have no policy for this at present' (Castle 1980: 398). In other words, the Government had no effective policy for wage restraint. The Chancellor's proposal encountered bitter and intense resistance from his colleagues, however, (see Castle 1980: 397–401; Donoughue 1987: 62–3; Benn 1989: 379–81). Minister for the Environment Tony Crosland argued that there must be a proper economic assessment before any decision on further public expenditure cuts was reached: 'Why are we discussing this? Why has the balance of payments situation worsened since the Budget? The Chancellor's paper hasn't proved the need to create more spare capacity' (Castle 1980: 399). With different emphases, Minister of Social Services Barbara Castle, Minister of Industry Tony Benn, and Minister of Employment Michael Foot were strongly opposed. They argued that public expenditure cuts of this depth 'would destroy any hope of getting a voluntary incomes policy' and advocated import controls as an alternative (Castle 1980: 399–400; Benn 1989: 379–80). Even the Chancellor's Cabinet supporters – Foreign Secretary Jim Callaghan, Home Secretary Roy Jenkins, and Minister of Education Reg Prentice – argued that the Government should be looking not just at expenditure cuts but at other policy alternatives (i.e., wage controls) as well (Castle 1980: 400). The Prime Minister summed up by saying that the discussion would be resumed after the upcoming parliamentary recess, but that officials should start 'exploratory work' on expenditure cuts (Castle 1980: 400–1). In the Prime Minister's Policy Unit, this was deemed to be a rejection of Healey's expenditure cuts proposals; in the view of Policy Unit head Bernard

Donoughue (1987: 62), 'it was evident that Cabinet Ministers still would not confront the problem unless they had no alternative.'

The situation on wages continued to deteriorate. In May and June 1975, the National Union of Railwaymen (NUR) put in a wage claim for an up-to-35 per cent increase; British Rail counter-offered at 21 per cent. Arbitration came out with 27.5 per cent, but the NUR turned this down and voted for strike action instead (Whitehead 1985: 149; Haines 1977: 46–7; Dell 1991: 151–2, 157–8). There had been selling pressure on sterling since early June. On 12 June Healey told Cabinet that 'if the railways strike materializes – or worse still, if we give in to the NUR – the position would be untenable' (Castle 1980: 417–18). On 20 June, a railway strike was narrowly averted when the Government opted to settle at 30 per cent (Foote 1988: 188; Whitehead 1985: 149; Wilson 1979: 113). As the NUR leader noted after agreement had been reached, 30 per cent was less than what the miners and the power workers had received, and thus the NUR was 'within the interpretation of the Social Contract laid down by other public sector unions' (Whitehead 1985: 149). In Policy Unit head Bernard Donoughue's view (1989: 41), the NUR settlement was 'so ludicrous that even ministers with trade union affiliations had to say this cannot go on,' and it contributed to the Government's decision 'to come to grips with the income situation.' Privately, the Prime Minister told Donoughue that he now felt that 'something must be done about wages,' and he asked for suggestions (Donoughue 1985: 57). With the Cabinet divided and the TUC seemingly unable to curb wage settlements, external pressure on sterling mounted. The pound lost over three cents against the US dollar in one day (30 June 1975) before action was taken.

CONCLUSION

Rather than adjusting to the massive current account imbalances confronting Britain due to the quadrupling of the price of oil in 1973–74, the Labour Government during its first year in office pursued a borrowing strategy in an attempt to 'tunnel through' (Middlemas 1991: 86, 99). This strategy was possible because of the changed emphases in the international political economy that encouraged borrowing over adjustment as well as the inflow of OPEC current account surpluses to London. This strategy was necessary because of the domestic political circumstances of 1974 and early 1975. From March to October 1974, Labour was a minority Government; after October, its parliamentary majority was narrow and likely to erode. The Government was internally divided over a number of the important issues it faced (the Common Market, public expenditure, incomes policy), and its Social Contract partnership with the TUC was proving unable to bring about wage restraint and a reduction in inflation. It was in these circumstances that external pressures – starting with a run on sterling in June 1975 – began to push the Government toward policy change.

6 Labour Economic Policy, June 1975–March 1976:

'We Knew we were Riding a Crisis'[1]

This chapter reviews British economic policy during a period of intermittent 'structural' pressure for policy change upon the authorities. In June 1975, the IMF noted that 'balance of payments management was obviously becoming more difficult' for the British (De Vries 1985, 1: 464). OPEC countries with large current account surpluses were increasingly less willing to place them in London, and downward pressure on the pound had created a growing sense of urgency on the Government to take measures that would 'restore confidence.' After extensive and difficult negotiations between and among the Government and the Trades Union Congress (TUC), a tougher 'voluntary' incomes policy emerged in July 1975 that sharply limited wage increases. By early 1976, the Government's public expenditure plans had been substantially scaled back.

While structural pressures did not determine the specific features of the policy retrenchment that emerged during this period, the currency crisis of June 1975 effectively forced the Government into action by making the continuation of the status quo unviable. Nevertheless, there continued to be room for manoeuvre, and the confidence arguments deployed by the Chancellor of the Exchequer were not always definitive. As Denis Healey acknowledged to his Cabinet colleagues in July 1975, 'it is very difficult to know what is *essential* to maintain confidence' (Castle 1980: 462, original emphasis). Conditions changed, however, in March 1976 with the emergence of renewed and sustained selling pressure on sterling that ultimately led the Government to the IMF.

THE JUNE 1975 STERLING CRISIS AND THE £6 PAY POLICY

According to Harold Wilson's press secretary (Haines 1977: 44–5, 48), the Prime Minister by the spring of 1975 had come to the conclusion that some kind of action that would curb wage settlements was necessary, but a statutory incomes policy was ruled out because of the Government's Manifesto commitments. In any event, nothing could be done until after the 5 June referendum on Britain's Common Market membership (see also Wilson 1979: 111–14). According to head of the Policy Unit Brian Donoughue (1987: 65), the Prime Minister at about this time set up MISC 91, a secret committee of selected senior ministers, to discuss the question of incomes policy; because of the sensitivity of the issue, 'it could not be exposed too early to all colleagues. The Prime Minister did not want it to become immediately a left-right battle ground.' But with the June 1975 rate of inflation hitting 26 per cent and basic hourly wages up 32 per cent on the year (Browning 1986: 66–7), the currency markets forced the Government's hand.

At a Cabinet meeting on 12 June, the Chancellor warned his colleagues about the precarious state of the pound. 'This morning we have had the most severe attack on sterling we ever have had. It has cost us $500 million to hold the rate even here. *We have got to stop the slide.* I have been talking to the central bankers in Paris and the real reason for this run is the widespread feeling that we lack the will to deal with inflation' (Castle 1980: 417–18, original emphasis). With pressure on sterling mounting, one participant within Downing Street recalls that 'we moved from the very idea [of incomes policy] being taboo, or you can't talk about it, to all of a sudden the acceptance that an incomes policy was going to occur. And the argument became whether or not it would be statutory' (Whitehead 1987: 251; Castle 1980: 426).

The Policy Unit was suggesting a simple approach that would limit pay increases to £6 per week, to be enforced by a 'battery of sanctions' against any private employer breaking the policy (Donoughue 1987: 63–4). Minister of Employment Michael Foot, however, was adamantly opposed to any kind of statutory policy, dismissing it as 'only possible with a consent that does not exist' (Castle 1980: 426). Foot proposed that the Government try to persuade the TUC to accept a 15 per cent target for wage increases or a flat £9 weekly increase across the board (Castle 1980: 421; Benn 1989: 403–4). The Chancellor argued that a tighter figure of 10 per cent or a flat £5 would be necessary if inflation were to be reduced to single digits. Healey told Cabinet that the situation was 'more urgent than any of us realised. . . . Borrowing could stop "overnight." Anything could trigger off a disastrous run on the pound and force us into £1 billion's worth of public expenditure cuts *this year*.' There was not a minute to waste. '"We must have a credible [incomes] policy by the end of July"' (Castle 1980: 426, original emphasis; see also Benn 1989: 404). Further discussion in Cabinet, however, revealed the extent to which the Government continued to disagree. Home Secretary Roy Jenkins argued for a statutory policy coupled with expenditure cuts, Minister of the Environment Tony Crosland preferred higher unemployment to a statutory policy, and Minister of Trade Peter Shore and Minister for Social Services Barbara Castle argued for a voluntary policy that was premised upon the consent of the TUC (Castle 1980: 427–8; Benn 1989: 404; Middlemas 1991: 94; Dell 1991: 158–9). Healey responded by warning that 'we should announce a credible policy soon because the Arabs and the shop stewards are both threatening us. . . . The Government must tell the TUC that 10 per cent is the maximum for pay increases' (Benn 1989: 405). Disagreement among ministers notwithstanding, the Prime Minister summed up by noting a consensus that the Government should aim for a voluntary wage norm of 10 per cent and negotiate this figure with the unions (Castle 1980: 430; Benn 1989: 405; Dell 1991: 158).

Although the extent of the preliminary discussions among and between ministers and TUC officials regarding incomes policy is not clear,[2] the issue was exasperating for all sides. Head of the Transport and General Workers Union, Jack Jones, complained to the Prime Minister that although the TUC was 'anxious to help, . . . some speeches coming from members of the Government are not helping us to get acceptance of [a pay policy]. It is quite wrong to lay all the blame on wages, as if the unions were the only criminals in the community' (Castle 1980: 431; see also Jones 1986: 394). By contrast, Healey's view was that the unions through exorbitant wage demands had 'defaulted on their part of the [Social] Contract' (Healey 1989: 394). The TUC General Council for its part considered in late June a draft paper on pay policy entitled *The Development of the Social Contract* and 'generally agreed that there were strong grounds for developing the Social Contract approach on the basis of a clear, simple policy on which the trade union Movement could unite' (TUC 1975: 272; see also Taylor 1987: 55; MacDougall 1987: 219). With opinion on both sides moving towards the initiation of some form of incomes policy, Minister of Employment Michael Foot served as pragmatic mediator searching for a pay norm that the TUC would accept but that would also address the Government's confidence and credibility problems (Castle 1980: 431).

Pressure from the currency markets intensified. On 30 June, sterling fell by over three cents against the US dollar to reach a record low of $2.19. A meeting between the Prime Minister, the Chancellor, and the Governor of the Bank of England Gordon Richardson was quickly arranged, with the MISC 91 committee assembled to meet afterwards. According to Bernard Donoughue (1987: 67), Richardson revealed that sterling was 'collapsing. Apparently £0.5 billion had been lost from the official reserves in the last few days.' Healey (1989: 394–5) recounts that the Prime Minister finally told him that 'he would after all support a statutory pay policy, providing the legal sanctions were directed only against employers who conceded too much and not against workers who demanded too much.' In the MISC 91 committee meeting, the Chancellor sought approval for two White Papers: 'one to be published the very next day would propose a statutory incomes policy with a 10 per cent pay norm; the other to be produced the following week listing massive public expenditure cuts and price controls. The assembled Ministers in MISC 91 . . . did not explicitly support the Chancellor's proposals. Most just listened solemnly' (Donoughue 1987: 67; see also Haines 1977: 52–4; Wilson 1979: 115; Healey 1989: 395; Dell 1991: 163–4). That evening, a battle ensued within Downing Street over the content of the statement on pay policy the Chancellor would make in Parliament the following day. It was only after much argument with his staff that the Prime Minister came down firmly against the proposed statement from the Treasury announcing a statutory policy 'using the law in the pay bargaining process' (Haines 1977: 59; see also Wilson 1979: 115; Donoughue 1987: 67–9; Dell 1991: 164–6). The following morning, prior to a hastily called emergency Cabinet meeting, Wilson told Healey that he 'had changed his mind and that we were going for a voluntary rather than a statutory policy.' According to Bernard Donoughue (1987: 69), 'the Chancellor . . . was commendably agnostic and readily abandoned his officials' proposals. . . . Mr Wilson and Mr Healey therefore went together into Cabinet to support the voluntary approach'[3] (Donoughue 1987: 69).

The emergency Cabinet began with a bleak description from the Chancellor.

> The pound . . . had fallen 1 per cent yesterday and this morning it had reached its lowest devaluation ever. . . . We could face a disastrous withdrawal of funds at any time – just what he had kept warning us of. Nigeria, Kuwait and Saudi Arabia had all warned us that, though they were anxious to be friendly, there was a limit to the amount of devaluation they would stand. Nigeria, for instance, had told us she would withdraw her funds if the pound fell below $2.17, and we had now reached that point. We simply had to stop inflation in its tracks.
> (Castle 1980: 439; Dell 1991: 166–7)

Healey 'did not believe that heavy cuts in public expenditure this year would have any effect on inflation whatever. All they would do would be to create more unemployment' (Castle 1980: 439). Confidence demanded that the Government initiate steps towards a credible incomes policy that would reduce the level of wage settlements. Healey acknowledged that 'enormous progress' had been made with the TUC which was now ready to limit wage increases to the inflation target of 10 per cent or by £6 per week; the problem was making this commitment believable (Castle 1980: 439). 'Unless he, Denis, was able to make a statement that afternoon which carried conviction, the run on the pound would continue and the withdrawal of funds would start. . . . This is why he had been discussing with the PM, Shirley [Williams], and Mike [Foot] the need to impose a legal sanction on employers. . . . Nothing less would restore confidence' (Castle 1980: 439–40; see also Benn 1989: 411).

In the discussion that followed, however, Healey continued to encounter strong resistance from colleagues. In Minister of Employment Michael Foot's view, the 10 per cent legal limit was a statutory policy, and he doubted whether the TUC would accept 10 per cent. 'What Denis was proposing would put the whole burden of the crisis on wages and we should be trying to solve it by imposing a wage cut. We really must take more time to try and get an agreed policy' (Castle 1980: 440). Foreign Secretary Jim Callaghan argued that the Government 'shouldn't go into detail on wages and prices today: merely make a firm statement of our intention and determination to get inflation down and to take all the measures necessary to achieve it' (Castle 1980: 440–1). Minister for the Environment Tony Crosland also wanted delay, arguing that 'you cannot produce a workable incomes policy in one night's discussion' (Castle 1980: 440). Minister for Social Services Barbara Castle and Minister of Trade Peter Shore were suspicious of Healey's dire description of the economic situation. 'How could the rest of us possibly check how serious the situation was,' Castle (1980: 440) wondered. Shore directly questioned the Chancellor about the OPEC countries' warnings: 'How far is the threat of withdrawals of funds a real one? . . . There is always an element of bluff' (Castle 1980: 441). Healey responded that the sell-off was already occurring and that the oil producers had sold £130 million on 26 and 27 June (Castle 1980: 441). Wilson summed up the discussion in favor of an immediate statement in Parliament, but that 'it should be in such a form that it would help us to keep the TUC in play.' The Chancellor, however, 'insisted that we must spell out the wages target of 10 per cent. . . . If confidence was to be restored we must make it clear that we were determined to secure compliance and must spell out the sanctions we had in mind' (Castle 1980: 442–3). A committee was appointed to draft the Chancellor's statement (Castle 1980: 443).

That afternoon, Healey in an emergency House of Commons statement clarified the Government's policy intentions *vis-à-vis* wages. Although discussions between the Government, the TUC, and the Confederation of British Industry (CBI) were not yet concluded, Healey stated, 'I believe that it is necessary for the Government to state their intentions now. We are determined to bring the rate of domestic inflation down to 10 per cent by the end of the next pay round and to single figures by the end of 1976. This means the increase in wages and salaries during the next pay round cannot exceed 10 per cent' (UK Healey 1975b: 1189). Although the Government 'should much prefer to proceed on the basis of a voluntary policy agreed with the CBI and the TUC,' Healey told Parliament, 'a voluntary policy will not be acceptable to the Government unless it satisfies the targets . . . for reducing inflation and includes convincing arrangements for ensuring compliance. If . . . no agreement can be reached which meets these conditions,' he warned, 'the Government will be obliged to legislate to impose a legal requirement on both public and private sector employers to comply with the 10 per cent limit' (UK Healey 1975b: 1190).

Healey (1989: 395) recounts that he 'spent the next eight days in continual discussions with the TUC leaders on the details.' A flat-rate approach was agreed at a 'hard negotiating session' between Healey, Wilson and Jack Jones, Head of the Transport and General Workers Union; according to Jones (1986: 298), 'I had been pressing for £7 to £8. . . . I came down to £6, reluctantly but in order to get an agreement.' The TUC General Council by a vote of 19–13 approved a redraft of its paper *The Development of the Social Contract* that endorsed the £6 limit and stated clearly that 'the TUC will oppose any settlement in excess of this figure' (TUC 1975: 356, 273; Taylor 1987: 56–7). The TUC's endorsement both allowed the Government to claim the £6 policy was voluntary (UK Parliament 1975: 3–5) and helped to keep the Government together. As Minister of Employment Michael Foot told his like-minded colleagues, 'if the TUC was prepared to accept a tough pay policy, we should not complain. "We must not be more republican than the TUC"' (Castle 1980: 448).

The unions had accepted the Chancellor's confidence argument; when the TUC General Council reaffirmed its support for the £6 policy in late July, wage restraint 'was urged not because wage increases caused inflation, but because inflation was destroying foreign confidence' (Taylor 1987: 56; TUC 1975: 273, 347–8). The £6 policy was seen as a way to avoid IMF conditionality: 'the General Council recognised that unless the decline in the exchange rate and the consequent outflow of funds was stemmed, the UK would have been forced to borrow from international bodies such as the International Monetary Fund. The price of any such loans would have been an insistence on policies such as severe deflation, including sharp cuts in public expenditure and personal spending, producing a significant fall in living standards and an intolerable rise in unemployment' (TUC 1975: 355). Thus, the TUC supported and actively enforced the £6 policy both as a response to the confidence problem and as an alternative to further deflationary public expenditure cuts.

PUBLIC EXPENDITURE, IMPORT CONTROLS, IMF BORROWING, AND CURRENCY DEPRECIATION: AUTUMN 1975–WINTER 1976

Once the Cabinet had approved the £6 pay policy, the Chancellor circulated an additional paper to his colleagues seeking £2 billion in cuts in planned public expenditure through 1978–79 to be announced in the pay policy debate in Parliament (Castle 1980: 457). Minister for Social Services Barbara Castle was furious: in her view, the Chancellor had wrangled a tough pay policy 'as an *alternative* to public expenditure cuts, knowing all the while that . . . he was going to demand his full public expenditure cuts as well' (Castle 1980: 457, original emphasis). Indeed, the Chancellor in his emergency statement in Parliament had said that foreign confidence did not demand action on public expenditure: 'The problem in this country today is not excess demand. It is not pressure on capacity. We have a large number of unemployed and our factories are working below capacity. To increase unemployment by cutting public expenditure could in no sense help in that regard. That is well understood abroad' (UK Healey 1975b: 1195).

However, when his public expenditure proposal was discussed in Cabinet in mid-July, Healey pointed to the 'severe imbalance' in the British economy. 'We were spending 5 per cent more abroad than we earned. Internally, public expenditure and loans amounted to 19 pence in the pound more than we were getting in taxes, etc. We had met the gap so far by borrowing and saving, but that couldn't go on.' The balance of payments gap had to be closed by 1978, Healey argued:

'we couldn't go at the balance of payments more slowly because that would mean increasing borrowing' (Castle 1980: 460–1). The proposal came under sharp attack from the Chancellor's colleagues: Minister for the Environment Tony Crosland argued that Healey had not made the case for a 'savage change in strategy;' Minister for Trade Peter Shore demanded to know what had changed since the Government's previous public expenditure plans; Minister of Employment Michael Foot warned that announcing £2 billion in public expenditure cuts during the incomes policy debate 'would greatly add to the party's problems' (Castle 1980: 461). The Chancellor responded to the criticisms by arguing that '"if I don't say anything [on public expenditure] . . . it might have an effect on confidence". . . . Why had there been such a big change in outlook?. . . . "We did not expect so deep a recession." The Germans and Japanese hadn't done nearly enough reflating, but he still thought the world upturn should start next year' (Castle 1980: 462–3). The Prime Minister summed up by noting that the Government had 'no alternative but to support the Chancellor,' but added that Cabinet opinion was evenly divided as to whether Healey should specify the £2 billion figure to Parliament. Over Healey's protests – 'I must say to you, Prime Minister, that these matters cannot be decided by a majority in Cabinet' – Wilson suggested that a few ministers should work on the exact text and report back to Cabinet (Castle 1980: 463–4).

Although the Chancellor subsequently backed down on specifying the £2 billion figure (Castle 1980: 468), he was clear in his statement to Parliament that the Government in its annual review of public expenditure 'will be seeking further substantial economies in these programmes' (UK Healey 1975c: 70). Whereas in Cabinet his argument for public expenditure cuts centered on confidence, in Parliament he argued with different emphases. By 1977, 'world economic recovery should be well established and the British economy should be returning towards full capacity;' under these conditions it would be 'quite unrealistic' to stick to the Government's current public expenditure plans (UK Healey 1975c: 70). 'It is to an expansion in exports and investment that we must look for the extra demand needed to bring unemployment down, and this requires a continuing shift in the current balance of resources within the economy.' Public expenditure cuts were necessary as part of the continuing shift into exports (UK Healey 1975c: 70).

Measured in terms of unemployment and manufacturing output, the 1974–75 recession was not cutting as deeply in the UK as it was in other advanced industrialized states. The OECD noted that in the first quarter of 1975, 'industrial production had fallen from its last peak by some 20 per cent in Japan, 10–15 per cent in the United States, Germany, France and Italy, and 5 per cent in the United Kingdom;' British unemployment at the start of 1975 was lower than in the United States, France, and Canada (*OECD Economic Outlook*, July 1975, p. 5; July 1976, p. 32, Table 12). But a better performance on industrial production and unemployment was achieved at the cost of a worsening current account balance and inflation outlook. When the OECD revised downward its estimate of industrial countries' aggregate 1975 current account deficit as the positions of France, Italy, and the United States improved, *The Financial Times* noted how 'the United Kingdom would now seem to be about the only leading member of the OECD facing a seriously large current account deficit in 1975, estimated at about $7 billion' (*IMF Survey*, 26 May 1975, p. 159). *Vis-à-vis* inflation, Treasury Minister Edmund Dell (1991: 146–7) has commented that 'Britain was one of the few countries in which inflation continued to accelerate in 1975. In the USA inflation rose to 11 per cent in 1974 but then fell back. In Germany, the inflation rate was held at 6–7 per cent. In Japan, 1974 was a year of very high inflation, 25 per cent, but the rate halved in 1975. Britain [in 1975] seemed threatened with Latin American levels of inflation.' Given these conditions, the Chancellor promoted the Government's export-led strategy as the way to economic recovery in the UK. 'We in Britain foresaw [the depth and duration of the global recession] perhaps more clearly than some of our friends abroad,' Healey argued, but because of Britain's high inflation and weak current account position, the Government could not reflate demand in 1975 as it had in 1974. Rather, the UK had to look to other advanced industrialized countries with stronger payments positions to 'lead the way to world recovery' (UK Healey 1975c: 72–3).

However, Healey warned, 'if such countries do not pursue suitable reflationary policies, this will damage the flow of world trade just as directly as if they introduced physical controls on imports, and I shall then have to consider other measures for maintaining employment in Britain' (UK Healey 1975c: 72–3). Hints had already been given of what these 'other measures for maintaining employment' might be. When the Government in May 1975 renewed the General Agreement on Tariffs and Trade (GATT) pledge to refrain from imposing unilateral trade restrictions for balance of payments purposes, it did so 'on condition that financing to cover balance of payments deficits continues to be available and that economically stronger countries expand their economies to sustain international demand, increase imports, and alleviate the problem of the deficit countries' (*IMF Survey*, 9 June 1975, p. 161; see also *Financial Times*, 10 June 1976, 'Western countries,' p. 36; Dell 1991: 242).

Domestically, the Government was coming under growing pressure for direct action on imports; as unemployment climbed steadily during 1975 and into 1976 from 3 per cent to 5.5 per cent, 'selective' import controls became an increasingly central element of the TUC's representations to the Government (TUC 1975: 266–9; 1976a: 302–4; *Monthly Digest of Statistics*, December 1976, p. 24). Within the Labour Party, support for import controls as an employment preservation strategy was also growing. At the Labour Party Conference in September 1975, a National Executive Committee endorsed resolution was carried that criticized the Government for, among other things, its 'slowness in imposing selective import controls' (Labour Party 1975: 191, 205). The Labour Party Research Department was also pressing the Government for import controls, arguing that, the OPEC shock notwithstanding, other OECD countries (particularly Japan, Germany, and the US) were moving into or had remained in substantial current account surplus and that this was contrary to the commitments agreed at the January 1974 Committee of Twenty Finance Minister's meeting in Rome. The research staff advocated a 'temporary 15 per cent import surcharge, applied on a selective basis, initially to about two thirds of manufactured and semi-manufactured imports,' adding that 'we see no other way in which a continued increase in the already appalling level of unemployment can be averted' (Labour Party Research Department 1975a: 21–7; 1975b).

Within the Treasury, the balance of payments outlook continued to be gloomy. At a meeting of Treasury Ministers in October 1975, a short-term forecast was discussed that projected a balance of payments deficit in 1976 at the same level as in 1975, but substantially worsening in 1977, despite the coming on-line of North Sea oil: according to the forecast, the 1977 deficit 'could not be financed' (Dell 1991: 194). At a TUC–Labour Party Liaison Committee meeting in November 1975, Healey told union leaders that the Government was 'looking at import controls' (Castle 1980: 559). In December, the TUC Economic Committee met with Healey to press again the case for 'immediate selective measures ... to slow down the rise in unemployment and hasten an upturn in output.' Without action, the TUC warned, 'unemployment could well remain over the million mark for the next few years' (TUC 1976a: 301).

A week later, the Chancellor announced an extremely modest set of import quotas that would affect 0.16 per cent of the estimated total value of UK imports. There were to be quotas on textile imports from Spain and Portugal and an import licensing system to cover television sets and tubes; in addition, the Government would be seeking voluntary restraints on footwear imports from Eastern Europe (*IMF Survey*, 5 January 1976, p. 8; UK Healey 1975e: 1409–15). In announcing the measures, Healey reiterated that countries with stronger economies continued to have international reflation responsibilities. 'If they fail to act as necessary, countries with an adverse balance of payments will have to bring their foreign account into balance by restricting their imports, either through deflation or by other means,' Healey argued. 'Either would be damaging to world trade' (UK Healey 1975e: 1409–10). The UK's OECD trade partners were not at all pleased with the restrictions. The European Commission issued a statement expressing 'serious doubts about the justification for the urgent and unilateral procedure used by the British Government' and called the measures 'inopportune in view of the current international economic situation, where there is still the danger that even limited import controls could start a chain reaction' (*IMF Survey*, 5 January 1976, p. 8; Bernstein 1983: 300). The United States also issued a statement expressing American 'regret,' adding 'we assume that [the restrictions] will be temporary. . . . Protectionism is a serious danger in a world economy weakened by recession. No trade restrictions can therefore be taken lightly. . . . There can be no complacency even by those not directly affected' (*The Department of State Bulletin*, 2 February 1976, pp. 137–8).

The import controls were announced as part of a wider unemployment reduction package, involving employment subsidies, job training measures, and a relaxation of hire-purchase controls (UK Healey 1975e: 1404–8). However, with unemployment rising sharply to 5.1 per cent in December 1975 and 5.5 per cent in January 1976, the TUC was not at all satisfied. The TUC–Labour Party Liaison Committee in late January 1976 was highly strained. Head of the Transport and General Workers Union, Jack Jones, threatened to walk out unless unemployment was made the first item on the agenda; he told Healey that 'selective import controls was not just a question of colour TV tubes: "We've done damn all about Japan. . . . There must be a statement at the end of this meeting"' (Castle 1980: 630–1; private political diaries of Tony Benn, 26 January 1976). Head of the Amalgamated Union of Engineering Workers Hugh Scanlon was 'almost desperate,' asking ministers 'do you ever listen to us?. . . . Please tell us the truth. Are you afraid of

GATT, EEC or what?' (Castle 1980: 631; private political diaries of Tony Benn, 26 January 1976). The TUC leaders made it clear that 'if the Government did not take action in the short-term, its long-term credibility would be at stake' (TUC–Labour Party Liaison Committee Minutes, 26 January 1976). The Chancellor responded by noting that the economic situation was improving: 'The UK economy had already passed the trough of the recession. However, there would be a six-month lag before unemployment started levelling off' (TUC–Labour Party Liaison Committee Minutes, 26 January 1976). Jones, however, insisted that 'it was vital to give the impression of action,' and stressed the need to mention the employment proposals the TUC had made to ministers in the statement released after the meeting (private political diaries of Tony Benn, January 26, 1976). Thus, the Committee 'agreed a statement welcoming the Chancellor's undertaking to consider the [TUC's employment] suggestions . . . and to introduce at an early date measures which could affect the level of unemployment in the next few months' (TUC–Labour Party Liaison Committee Minutes, 26 January 1976). As Minister of Social Services Barbara Castle commented in her diary (1980: 631), 'in the end, the trade union boys were some-what mollified – and obviously deeply anxious to preserve our unity and the Government.'

Notwithstanding the worsening unemployment outlook, two other problems continued to have priority within the Treasury in the fall of 1975: the need for substantial additional cuts in public expenditure and the funding of the current account deficit (Dell 1991: 183). Healey (1989: 400) recounts that the two issues were closely linked: 'if we are not to become dependent on borrowing from . . . foreigners and from the IMF, we must try to eliminate our current account deficit within a few years. And we would be unable to reduce our external deficit if our internal fiscal deficit was still growing.' Following the July 1975 announcement of the Government's intention to seek further public expenditure savings (UK Healey 1975c: 71), senior ministers had met informally to discuss expenditure priorities (Castle 1980: 482–5; Crosland 1982: 306–7; Dell 1991: 186–7). In the view of Chief Secretary to the Treasury Joel Barnett (1982: 78–9), the meeting 'was wholly inconclusive. . . . I had the impression Cabinet was either not listening to Denis, or did not want to hear the unpalatable facts.'

In the fall, the Treasury generated its regular National Income Forecast which showed the PSBR rising from £9 billion to £12 billion for the current fiscal year (Donoughue 1987: 84; Dell 1991: 187). The Chancellor circulated a paper to Cabinet setting out £3.75 billion in public expenditure reductions, targeted for fiscal years 1977–78 and 1978–79. According to Barnett (1982: 80), 'we had convinced ourselves we could not make major cuts quickly. . . . We did not find it possible to make cuts in the year immediately ahead.' But Healey's paper argued that 'the situation beyond 1976 will be very different. . . . International and domestic demand should have recovered and the forward planning must be based on the assumption that unemployment will be falling very rapidly' (Castle 1980: 546).

The ensuing Cabinet discussion focused on the concept of 'resources' in the economy; Healey's reasoning centered around the idea that with world economic recovery, 'room would have to be made for investment and exports plus a modest improvement in living standards. To this end, the demands of public expenditure on resources had to be reduced' (Dell 1991: 188–9; see also Barnett 1982: 79–80). *Vis-à-vis* the current account deficit, the Chancellor told his colleagues that 'we *must* achieve a balance . . . by 1978, otherwise the burden of debt interest would wipe out the gains from North Sea oil and gas' (Castle 1980: 548, original emphasis). Healey directly linked expenditure cuts to Britain's ability to finance its deficits: 'we cannot escape these cuts. We cannot borrow unless we make the cuts now or within the next six months,' Healey argued (Benn 1989: 461). 'At present the public sector was borrowing 20 pence for every pound it spent, and the burden of debt was becoming crippling. We couldn't continue with a borrowing requirement of anything approaching the present £12 billion' (Castle 1980: 548).

As a counter to Healey's proposal, Minister for the Environment Tony Crosland suggested £2 billion in cuts with an additional £500 million held in reserve. Crosland argued that as the forecasts of an export- and investment-led economic upturn would probably not turn out, the anticipated pressure on resources therefore would not appear. 'The Chancellor would be digging a hole with nothing to fill it' (Castle 1980: 548; see also Dell 1991: 188). Crosland opposed the cuts on political grounds as well: 'what are we going to put in the shop window at the next election?' he reportedly asked (*Sunday Times*, 22 February 1976, 'How They Choose,' p. 61). According to Bernard Donoughue (1987: 85), Crosland served to 'knock down' the Treasury's resources argument; 'in the end most of the participants agreed that the real debate was over confidence in the currency and the unsustainable expansion of the public sector.' As Ministers spoke, Minister of Social Services Barbara Castle kept an informal tally of the votes. There were 'ten clearly in favour of Tony [Crosland]'s figure of £2½ billion; nine for the Chancellor's figure [of £3.75 billion], including Harold [Wilson], and two wobblers. . . . but Harold [Wilson] summed up that there was a "very slight" majority in favour of the £3.75 billion. . . . What interested me was how close a thing it had been' (Castle 1980: 549; see also Barnett 1982: 80).

The ensuing distribution of the cuts across departments was an agonizing and time-consuming process, with 'spending' Ministers fighting bitterly (Barnett 1982: 81–2; Crosland 1982: 308; *Sunday Times*, 22 February 1976, 'How They Choose,' p. 61). The final composition of the cuts was not completed until two long Cabinet meetings in December 1975, and given the determined resistance of his colleagues, the Chancellor in the end had to settle for £3 billion rather than £3.75 billion in total cuts (Barnett 1982: 81–2; Castle 1980: 593–7, 600–2; Benn 1989: 475–77, 478–9).

With respect to the financing of the current account deficit, the Government in December 1975 sent two formal letters of intent to the IMF, one to draw SDR 700 million (about £400 million) from Britain's first credit tranche, the other to draw SDR 1 billion (about £575 million) from the IMF's oil facility (De Vries 1985, 1: 464; Healey 1975a, 1975b). As early as August 1975, Treasury Ministers had been advised by officials to consider a confidential signal to the Fund that the UK would probably need to borrow from the oil facility (Dell 1991: 193). A low-conditionality drawing from the Fund was further discussed by Treasury Ministers in October and was put before Cabinet in early November (Dell 1991: 188, 193; Benn 1989: 459). On 10 November, the Chancellor made a statement in Parliament about the IMF borrowing, in which he outlined that 'the terms and conditions will be those normal for oil facility and first credit tranche drawings. . . . The Fund will require to be satisfied that United Kingdom policies are likely to achieve medium-term recovery of the balance of payments. I am confident that our existing policies will do this' (UK Healey 1975d: 920; see also Barnett 1982: 79).

The UK's published currency reserves had fallen sharply with the June–July 1975 run on sterling and continued to decline markedly through the end of the year (see Figure 6.1[4]). In its IMF letter of intent, the Government explained that it was 'undesirable to allow gross official reserves to decline significantly below present levels' (Healey 1975a: 5). The letter of intent made reference to the expenditure cuts that the Cabinet had agreed but that had not yet been announced, pledging that 'substantial reductions must be made' (Healey 1975a: 3). Notwithstanding pledges made during Labour's opposition period to avoid a repeat of

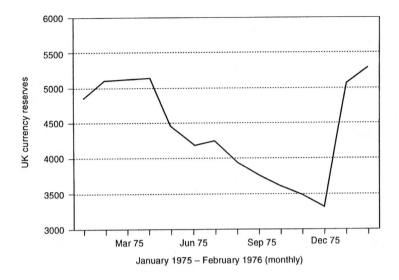

Figure 6.1 UK currency reserves, 1975–76

Source: Bank of England Quarterly Bulletin, June 1976, Statistical Annex, table 23

the demand suppression policies of the 1960s, the Chancellor stated baldly in the letter that 'although I have had to conclude that the present unemployment situation leaves little room for cutting the PSBR in 1976–77, it is my intention to restrain domestic demand in order to ensure that resources are available for net exports' (Healey 1975a: 4).

The IMF staff had been monitoring the British economic situation through the early and mid-1970s; according to the Fund historian, the staff considered Britain's economic problems 'basic and in need of resolution over the long term' (De Vries 1985, 1: 461). Despite extensive foreign currency borrowing, UK reserves had fallen in 1975 by over SDR 1 billion (see Figure 6.1) and the current account position continued to be vulnerable to OPEC governments and private entrepreneurs moving funds out of sterling (De Vries 1985, 1: 465). The staff was also dubious that the modest improvement in Britain's current account during 1975 (see Figure 6.2) would continue, as it was 'mainly attributable to a decline in domestic output and a drawing down of inventories of imported items' and these factors would likely be reversed with British economic recovery (De Vries 1985, 1: 465). Nevertheless, the staff acknowledged that 'the policies taken were

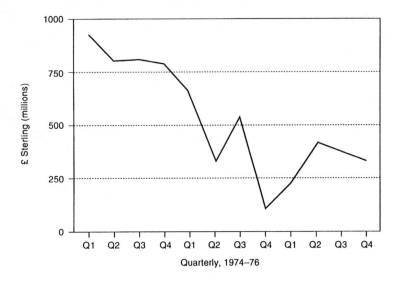

Figure 6.2   UK current account deficit 1974–76

Source: Monthly Digest of Statistics, May 1977, p. 131

appropriate to the United Kingdom's problems and were in fact already having some success,' and misgivings notwithstanding, it recommended to the IMF Executive Board that the British drawing be approved (De Vries 1985, 1: 465).

In light of the worsening current account and unemployment forecasts, officials in the Treasury suggested a 'substantial sterling depreciation' as a way to address both problems; the Chancellor, however, 'was scathing about this proposal. . . . Such a policy must take account of the effect on the holders of the sterling balances, notably Nigeria. It could turn into a rout' (Dell 1991: 195). Nevertheless, proposals regarding exchange rate depreciation continued to be circulated formally and informally within the Treasury and the Bank of England (Dell 1991: 195–6, 198; Britton 1991: 30). As the Treasury's senior economist Andrew Britton (1989: 40) recounts, 'by the beginning of 1976 the problem with inflation was reckoned to be abating and so the focus came back to unemployment. . . . But the feeling was that if we had reflationary measures which were needed to deal with unemployment, then the balance of payments would become a serious problem.' Sterling depreciation was a solution to the dilemma. According to Britton (1989: 40), 'the argument in the early months of 1976 was both about the possibility of using the exchange rate . . . as an instrument of policy, and the sort of movement that one would want if it proved possible. . . . There was considerable debate taking place within the Treasury as to quite what it should do.' Permanent Secretary to the Treasury Douglas Wass was a strong proponent of the 'controlled' depreciation strategy: according to one official, Wass and his pro-devaluation colleagues 'tried to persuade themselves that the devaluation strategy was the answer to everything. A fetish isn't too strong a word for one or two individuals. Douglas Wass was hypnotised that you could get out of it all by devaluation' (Holmes 1985: 81; Whitehead 1985: 183; Fay 1987: 73–4). At both the official and at the ministerial levels, however, there was strong skepticism about currency depreciation. Officials argued that the exchange markets were unstable and might not react as hoped. Chancellor of the Duchy of Lancaster Harold Lever was also opposed because of the domestic inflation effects and because of fears about the stability of the sterling balances held in London (Fay and Young 1978, 1: 34; Fay 1987: 74; Burk and Cairncross 1992: 22).

After falling sharply during the sterling crisis in the summer of 1975, the pound had more or less stabilized at just below $2.05 by late 1975 and early 1976 (see Figure 6.3). Harold Wilson (1979: 226–7) recounts that 'for months we had been told that $2.20 was the critical level. Below that the oil sheikhs would take their money out of Britain. . . . But the pound had steadily fallen from $2.17 on 1 July [1975] to . . . $2.04 on 1 October. It was held at about that level, sometimes with Bank of England help . . . until in January and February [1976] it hovered between $2.02 and $2.03.' While sterling 'hovered,' British interest rates as well as the differential between London rates and the rates prevailing abroad began to edge downward (see Figure 6.4; Crawford 1983: 427). With a $1/2$ per cent Minimum Lending Rate (MLR) cut in early February, *The Financial Times* reported that UK interest rates were now at their lowest level since 1973 and that the City of London's view was that rate cuts had gone as far as they would 'for the time being' because of the weak position of sterling (7 February 1976, 'Minimum lending,' p. 1). Nevertheless, the MLR was cut by a further $1/4$ per cent later in the month and yet again by $1/4$ per cent in early March.

The memoirs and public statements of the participants in the sterling depreciation discussions are near unanimous in the view that no decision on a depreciation strategy had been taken in late 1975 and early 1976. According to Treasury economist Andrew Britton (1991: 31), 'there was a suspicion in the markets that the British authorities

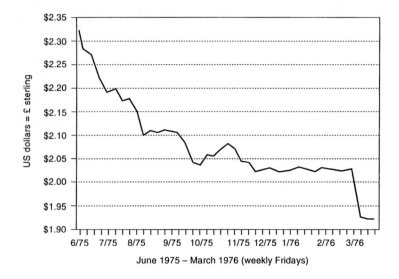

Figure 6.3   Sterling–dollar exchange rate 1975–76

Source: Bank of England Quarterly Bulletin, March 1976, Statistical Annex, table 26; June 1976, Statistical Annex, table 27

would welcome a ... depreciation of the pound. That suspicion was well-founded, although it would be wrong to say that a definite decision had been taken in the Treasury that the pound should be devalued.'[5] Denis Healey has been vague in recalling his attitude towards currency depreciation: 'Well, I think I'd come to the conclusion that the pound was a good deal too high and that it would be helpful if it were lower. But I learned from bitter experience later on what I think governments have sometimes learned, that once a trend changes it's very difficult to check it where you want it' (Whitehead 1985: 183–4; see also Healey 1989: 406, 426–7).

By early 1976, the Treasury's depreciation discussions were beginning to leak. *The Financial Times* reported on 17 January that 'there are those in Whitehall who manifest an almost embarrassing desire to talk the exchange rate down' ('UK cuts payments deficit,' p. 1). Economics editor for *The Sunday Times* Malcolm Crawford (1989: 173) recalls lunching with a senior Treasury official 'who talked openly about the [depreciation] policy and its supporters and opponents' (Burk and Cairncross 1992: 24, fn 10). Harold Wilson in his memoirs (1979: 227) recounts that early in March 1976, Foreign Secretary Callaghan

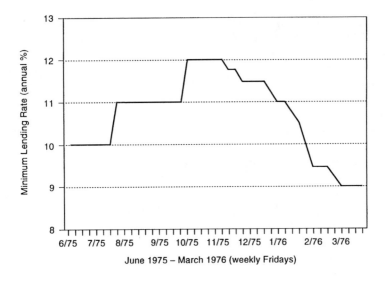

Figure 6.4   UK Minimum Lending Rate 1975–76

Source: Bank of England Quarterly Bulletin, June 1976, Statistical Annex, table 27

'voiced his anxieties to me. The Treasury weren't bent on forcing the pound down further, were they?. ... I told him that I too was carefully watching the decision. Certainly no decision had been taken, and the Treasury had given no hint of any move below the $2 market' (Holmes 1985: 81–2). On 4 March 1976, however, sterling fell beneath $2 for the first time. The following day, a ¹/₄ per cent MLR cut seemed to confirm market suspicion that the authorities did indeed want to push sterling down. Selling pressure on the currency suddenly became very heavy, setting off the run on sterling that ultimately led Britain to the IMF before the end of the year.

CONCLUSION

In light of subsequent events, it is perhaps easy to overlook the fact that on many measures important to 'confidence,' economic conditions in Britain were improving by early 1976. An effective incomes policy had been implemented in the summer with the TUC's consent and endorsement, and inflation had peaked in May 1975 (*Monthly Digest of Statistics*, June 1975, p. 156; June 1976, p. 156). Although the PSBR forecast had worsened, the Government published *Public Expenditure to 1979–80* in February 1976 outlining expenditure cuts that were 'intended broadly to stabilise the level of resources taken by expenditure programmes after 1976–77' (UK Parliament 1976: 2). Demands for reflation and import controls from the TUC and the Labour left-wing continued to be almost entirely put off.

However, in other policy domains regarded as important for confidence, it seemed that retrenchment had gone about as far as it could go politically. There continued to be deep divisions within the Government, ranging from those on the right who argued that the pay policy and expenditure cuts had not gone far enough, to those on the left who opposed and almost defeated the Chancellor's expenditure cuts package. The public expenditure cuts of late 1975 and early 1976 were obtained only after threats of resignation from the Chancellor and were approved with only the barest Cabinet majority (Barnett 1982: 80; Castle 1980: 549). Unemployment in early 1976 rose to the then unheard of level of 5.5 per cent, creating barely concealed tensions between the Government and its TUC partners in the Social Contract. As TUC General Council member Hugh Scanlon told ministers in February 1976, 'the trade union movement has taken policies from this Government we would never have taken from a Tory Government. I am deeply apprehensive, not only about the [public expenditure] cuts, but the level of unemployment.' Scanlon warned the Government that if its economic strategy did not start showing success, 'you are going to make our position almost impossible' (Castle 1980: 659–60). Labour's backbenches were also discontented; Chief Secretary to the Treasury Joel Barnett recounts (1982: 70) that he was 'finding it hard to educate even the more sympathetic backbenchers in the new realities of our situation.'

On 10 March 1976, the Government was rebuffed on its expenditure cuts plans when 37 Labour MPs abstained and thereby allowed the Opposition to defeat the Government. Only after the Government forced its supporters back into line through a vote of confidence were the cuts approved. Securing confidence on the exchange markets, however, would not be so easily achieved.

7 Burden-Shifting and Tightened Conditionality, 1975–76:

'The Practice of Financing the Status Quo is Coming to an End'[1]

As discussed in Chapter 4, there were indicators in 1975 suggesting growing differences of view among international financial officials over the appropriate mechanisms to address persisting current account deficits. In his remarks at the 1975 annual IMF meeting, IMF Managing Director Johannes Witteveen (1975b: 249) acknowledged that disagreements 'have naturally reflected differences among countries in economic priorities or objectives and in the assessment of evolving trends and prospects,' but he nonetheless hoped that the assembled officials would come to 'general agreement on two propositions. First countries must avoid policies that would achieve national objectives by shifting the burden to their trading partners. Second, given the strong interdependence of national economies, countries have international, as well as national, responsibilities.'

Witteveen's appeal, however, presumed a degree of consensus among the assembled officials, both on what was meant by policies that 'shifted the burden' and on the specific content and extent of countries' 'international responsibilities.' At the 1975 IMF meeting, the American, German, Japanese, and French representatives all seem to have conceived of the avoid-burden-shifting commitment as primarily a matter of avoiding trade restrictions (Simon 1975a: 108–9; Apel 1975: 46; Ohira 1975: 51–2; Fourcade 1975: 94). By contrast, the British and Italian representatives argued that to a large extent the burden had already been shifted when certain countries had reneged on their 1974 Committee of Twenty undertakings (Healey 1975c: 74; Colombo 1975: 38–9). These arguments were not well-received. This chapter reviews this conflict and the displacement of the low-conditionality, financing-over-adjustment emphases in the international economy of 1974–75 by the tougher and more conditional approach that was the context for the UK–IMF crisis of 1976.

THE MOVEMENT AWAY FROM BURDEN-SHARING, 1975

It is clear from the public addresses of the representatives from the major industrialized states that there was little agreement at the 1975 IMF Annual Meeting on the extent of members' burden-sharing responsibilities. British Chancellor of the Exchequer Denis Healey (1975c: 74) was sharply critical of his counterparts. 'Despite the warnings of the Managing Director, too few governments took account of the deflationary effect of the rise in oil prices. Too many attempted to achieve a balance in their current account too fast. . . . The result, as the Managing Director warned us [in 1974], was simply to redistribute the inevitable deficit among the [oil] consuming countries.' Italian Finance Minister Emilio Colombo (1975: 38) concurred. 'Had the international community acted more in accordance with the consensus reached . . . at the January 1974 Rome meeting of the Committee of Twenty,' the international recession could have been partly avoided. 'There was unanimous agreement at the time that in the short- to medium-term the oil deficit had to be financed and not corrected. It was recognized that corrective policies would only shift the imbalance from some oil importers to others, and that such policies would inevitably lead to a serious fall in world economic activity.'

Managing Director Witteveen (1975a: 21–2), although less critical, was largely in accord with the view that the accept-the-deficit emphases of 1974 had been disregarded. 'Most of the major industrial countries followed tight financial policies during 1974, notwithstanding the deflationary threat of higher oil prices. The main purpose in adopting these policies was to counter inflation, and this was understandable, but they had important consequences for the balance of payments of other countries.' The US, Germany, and Japan, Witteveen noted, had been 'particularly resolute' in fighting inflation 'and must be commended for their achievements in this field.' However, 'the impact of anti-inflation policies and other factors on their current account positions was quite dramatic. In these three countries, oil-related deficits totaling more than $30 billion were rapidly offset by positive changes elsewhere in the current account.' Denis Healey (1975c: 77) asserted that states with strong payments positions had 'a special responsibility to lead the world toward recovery.' Witteveen (1975a: 25) concurred and called attention to domestic demand policies in America, Germany, and Japan; 'these economies bulk large in the world economy. They are in relatively favorable balance of payments positions, have made considerable progress in reducing inflation, and have large amounts of economic slack. . . . It is reasonable – indeed, necessary – to ask these three countries to conduct their demand policies so as to take particular account of the international recession and of the serious constraints felt by many other countries in pursuing an expansionary course.'

US Treasury Secretary William Simon (1975a: 110), however, was wholly unreceptive to Healey's and Witteveen's arguments. 'Some have suggested that in order to help other nations out of recession, the United States should embark upon much more stimulative fiscal and monetary policies. We respectfully disagree. Too many of our current domestic troubles are rooted in such excesses in the past.' As to America's 'international responsibilities,' Simon argued, states had to assume a greater degree of individual responsibility for addressing their own economic problems: 'it would be unrealistic to expect that any single country could lead the rest of the world out of recession.' In contradiction of Witteveen's emphasis (1975a: 24) on a 'coordinated international approach' to recovery, Simon's view (1975a: 110) was that 'expanded world trade should not be regarded as the source, but as the product, of recovery. Indeed, let us recognize that the process of solving our economic troubles must begin at home, with each country acting on its own to make the tough decisions that are essential for sound, durable growth.'

By contrast, Denis Healey (1975c: 75–6) asserted that 'recovery is now the overriding priority facing the world economy' and questioned the reticence with which certain countries were approaching demand expansion. 'I imagine every finance minister here is continually asking himself the same question. Can I stimulate economic activity and employment without jeopardizing the progress I hope to make in checking inflation? It is a very real dilemma. But I cannot help feeling that its difficulties are sometimes overstated.' Healey singled out for criticism countries 'whose past growth has been based primarily on exports' (i.e., Germany and Japan), arguing that 'these are countries whose balance of payments position and moderate inflation rates enable them, and indeed require them, to lead the world to recovery. . . . If this has consequences for their balance of payments, they can well afford them.'

German Finance Minister Hans Apel's statement at the meeting (1975: 44) was understandably defensive.[2] Apel concurred with Healey that the current global recession 'fighting unemployment . . . must have the highest priority now,' and he outlined the 'strong measures to stimulate domestic activity' that the German government had taken. 'I am convinced that these measures are an appropriate contribution to the revival of the world economy' (see also *The Banker*, November 1975,

'Germany,' pp. 1232–3). But he added a clear and characteristically German warning about the ever-present dangers of inflation that echoed some of Simon's themes: 'let us not forget [that] inflationary pressures still persist in most countries, and this involves grave dangers. . . . We must be careful not to rekindle inflation while stimulating our economies.' It is clear that there was a growing divergence of views by late 1975 about the specific content of states' 'international responsibilities' and about what not 'shifting the burden' actually meant.

REASSERTING CONDITIONALITY, 1976

Most probably, it was apparent to Denis Healey that his earlier success in overcoming US opposition to the renewal of the oil facility (see Chapter 4) was not likely to be repeated. Indeed, Deputy Bundesbank Governor Otmar Emminger (1975: 327) was publicly hinting as early as January 1975 that the easy-financing period of the oil facilities was likely to end sooner than some would like. There was a 'general hardening of the attitudes of creditor countries towards debtors' in which 'both the US and Germany came to favor more rapid adjustment by deficit countries through IMF stabilization programs' (Bernstein 1983: 127–8). But with over half of the total IMF drawings in 1975 occurring through the low-conditionality oil facility (Dam 1982: 286), the terms accompanying IMF-provided financing were ineffective at pushing borrowers into the desired more rapid adjustment.

In addition, there was a predisposition within the US Government against *ad hoc* official IMF financing facilities. The US Treasury disliked the IMF assuming a financial intermediary role through the oil facilities, arguing that private financial markets could, should, and largely were fulfilling this role. As Managing Director Witteveen (1987: 33) recalls, 'the position of the industrial countries, but mainly the United States, has been . . . that [oil-induced current account] deficits should as far as possible be financed through the markets, and only in cases where they couldn't be completely financed through the market was there a role for the Fund;' the American attitude 'kept the oil facility limited and maximized the role of financing by the banks' (see also Healey 1989: 423).

In fundamental ways, however, American policy preferences – a desire to see more rapid deficit country adjustment as well as a dislike of the Fund supplanting the financial intermediary role of private markets – worked at cross purposes as there was no assurance that a reliance on private credit sources would promote adjustment. According to Witteveen (1987: 28), 'as long as countries ... don't have to come to the Fund for financial assistance, we really have no power, no sanctions.' Indeed Witteveen (1987: 35) has recounted one instance in which just the opposite was true.

> I'll never forget, I was visiting one of the poorest developing countries that was very much in need of some adjustment – it had very bad policies, really – and we were hoping to get them to accept some kind of an IMF program. At the same time, there were bankers visiting the capital offering big loans without *any* conditions. And I thought that was quite wrong.
>
> (Original emphasis)

The Managing Director became sufficiently concerned about the expansion of private non-conditional payments financing that he spoke publicly in April 1976 on the 'complementary roles' of the IMF and the international banking community. 'For private commercial banks,' Witteveen (1976a: 138–40) noted, 'balance of payments financing in some respects lies outside the mainstream of traditional banking operations,' and important 'questions' and 'concerns' were raised by the expansion of private bank lending for current account purposes. 'Balance of payments loans inevitably involve judgments that go beyond strictly commercial considerations into the field of national financial and economic policies. Competitive enlargement of this role of private banks might well foster a climate of all-too-easy borrowing by deficit countries, thus facilitating inflationary financing and delaying the adoption of needed adjustment policies.' For deficit countries relying heavily on shorter-term borrowings with high debt service, 'the question arises as to how much further the indebtedness can be pushed before the mounting debt burden becomes hazardous.' It was the IMF, he argued, that was best equipped for the 'crucial yet difficult judgments on the appropriateness of financial and foreign exchange policies. These matters are at the center of the Fund's concern.' And because drawings on the Fund since the OPEC shock had occurred mainly through the oil facilities, 'access to the regular resources of the Fund still remains largely unimpaired.' The underlying message of Witteveen's speech was clear, albeit unstated: drawings upon the Fund's 'regular resources' would necessarily be accompanied by greater conditionality. With this speech, the Managing Director's view on the desirability of more rapid deficit country adjustment moved closer to that of the United States. Henceforth there would be a greater emphasis on adjustment in the

Fund's lending activities than there had been during the previous two years.

In the eyes of US financial officials, chronic deficit countries began to be seen 'as a threat to the stability of the entire international economic, and especially monetary system' (Bernstein 1983: 129). In Secretary Simon's view, the lack of deficit country adjustment and the recurring exchange rate instability that deficit currencies were experiencing were closely related problems rooted essentially in domestic politics; Simon (1976) outlined his views in a confidential policy memo in the spring of 1976.

> Deep divisions on the distribution of income have in Italy and the United Kingdom, for example, been obscured by efforts to manufacture solutions through policies which would assure rapid economic expansion. Internally, highly expansionary fiscal and monetary policies have triggered strong and sustained inflationary pressures. These pressures have been augmented by 'external shocks,' the most important of which was the quadrupling in the prices of oil. The external manifestation of these underlying factors has been disequilibrium in balance of payments positions. The choice has been whether this disequilibrium should be financed or be permitted to reflect almost directly the exchange rate of the countries involved.
>
> On the premise that the underlying disequilibrium was of a transitory nature and that countries would over time effectively adjust, countries such as Italy opted to finance the imbalance in their external accounts. Unfortunately the basic premise has not been borne out by events. Adjustment has been almost nil and in fact heavy external borrowings (loans on international markets) have provided reserves which have been used to finance the status quo.

The 'financing of disequilibrium' should not and would not continue, Simon argued. Pressure on deficit countries to adjust should be and would be increasing. US bilateral assistance to Italy through currency swap drawings had 'been used judiciously in applying this pressure,' and the US Treasury was encouraging other official balance of payments lenders including the EC and the IMF 'to attach firm conditions to their credits' as well. 'The practice of financing the status quo is coming to an end. Italy no longer has access to private funds in the international money market and can no longer use this technique to avoid adjustment. The United Kingdom, while not in the same specific situation [as Italy], is in an overall sense in the same category.'

Simon (1976b) summarized US policy objectives *vis-à-vis* the problems presented by the British and Italian lack of adjustment into four points. The US sought to:

1. Discourage the use of import controls as a substitute for internal adjustment.
2. Create a climate both in terms of the legal content of the [IMF] Jamaica Agreements and in terms of world public opinion which makes competitive depreciation policies unacceptable.
3. Facilitate the provision of financing – through the IMF and the [OECD] Financial Support Fund – that would truly be conditional on tangible progress in the direction of domestic stabilization.
4. Keep the US from becoming involved either in a political sense or in a financial sense in the congestion produced by the Italian, British, and to a degree the French situations.

Thus, a reassertion of IMF loan conditionality in 1976 was a useful tool for the realization of American policy objectives *vis-à-vis* deficit countries. 'The US view was that only the IMF was in a position to force adjustment, because of its neutrality as a multilateral lending institution. It was felt that the Fund could "encourage those forces in deficit countries which favor adjustment via internationally responsible means"' (Bernstein 1983: 135, quoting US Treasury Under-Secretary for Monetary Affairs Edwin Yeo therein). There are indications that the view of German officials was similar. German Finance Ministry official Karl Otto Pöhl (1976: 108) at the October 1976 IMF annual meeting noted that Germany 'would very much welcome the IMF's assuming a larger role in future financing of balance of payments deficits. . . . To me, conditionality is not an irksome intrusion into the spheres of national autonomy, but a helpful guide to better stability performance and a useful instrument of improving the adjustment process.'

In July 1976, the IMF Managing Director added the topic of balance of payments financing to the Interim Committee's agenda at the Fund's upcoming 1976 annual meeting (De Vries 1987: 129). With the process of recovery in the industrial world now 'firmly established,' Witteveen (1976c: 219–20) declared, concerns about the deficits of oil-importers were no longer as pressing: 'as is well known, certain developed countries . . . are in serious balance of payments difficulties, but the general concern that arose about the external situation of these countries as a group immediately after the rise of oil prices has abated.' At the October 1976 IMF annual meeting, the burden-sharing emphasis that had been so prominent in the Managing Director's 1974 and 1975 annual meeting addresses was largely gone. In his 1976 address,

Witteveen (1976b: 16–17) asserted without qualification that 'the time has come to lay more stress on the adjustment of external positions and less emphasis on the mere financing of deficits.' The central theme of the speech was that the low-conditionality period of official financing was now over: 'the central principle of the Fund is the revolving character of its financial resources. It was never intended that these resources should be used to help perpetuate balance of payments disequilibria.' *Vis-à-vis* the British and Italian arguments from 1975 that much of their current account problems were traceable to the failures of other states to keep to their burden-sharing Committee of Twenty undertakings, Witteveen (1976b: 15) was markedly unsympathetic: the US, Germany, and Japan had embarked, not on deflationary burden-shifting to improve their external accounts, but rather 'on resolute anti-inflation measures.' Although 'the impact of these measures on their current account positions was dramatic' and had the consequence of putting 'strong downward pressure on the current account positions of other oil importing countries,' Witteveen's view was that the shifts were 'not in themselves an object of policy.' The between-the-lines message was that the US, Germany, and Japan had pursued sound and appropriate anti-inflation policies and that deficit countries should now also initiate appropriate stabilization policies. 'Payments difficulties do not arise from extraneous causes only,' Witteveen (1976b: 20) chided. 'They are frequently due, wholly or in part, to inappropriate policies in the deficit country. Even when they are not, adjustment cannot be postponed indefinitely. . . . There is now a need for all countries in external disequilibrium to intensify their adjustment effort, and to give the correction of disequilibrium a higher priority than it presently enjoys.'

Irrespective of whether the British and Italian current account deficits were attributable to excessive deflationary policies in other developed economies (see Healey 1989: 393, 1980: 39), to internal political divisions over the appropriate distribution of domestic income (see Simon 1976b), to the oil price shock (which both Healey and Simon acknowledge was important), or to some combination of these and other factors, the deficits still had to be financed. Witteveen's address at the 1976 meeting was indicative of a change in the broader international financial environment for countries in need of deficit financing. In 1974 and 1975, the Managing Director had sought to reassure deficit countries that the supply of balance of payments financing resources would be adequate; in 1976, however, he did just the opposite. 'To encourage adoption of adjustment policies,' Witteveen (1976b: 18) argued, 'it may be desirable for unconditional balance of payments financing to be somewhat less readily available than it has been for some countries in the recent past.' *Vis-à-vis* private commercial bank financing, Witteveen noted 'the risk that too ready availability of commercial bank lending may in cases retard the needed adjustment. I therefore welcome the increasing tendency for commercial banks to gear their lending to Fund stand-by arrangements.'

Creditor OECD countries at the 1976 IMF meeting endorsed the Managing Director's new emphasis on tightened conditionality and adjustment. German Finance Ministry representative Karl Otto Pöhl (1976: 92) stated that 'like Mr. Witteveen, I would consider it a healthy development if balance of payments credits extended by commercial banks and even by monetary authorities could be geared to IMF drawings and to their conditionality' (see also Simon 1976a: 94). As US Treasury Secretary Simon (1976a: 96–7) noted, 'recycling of funds from surplus countries to deficit countries can continue only to the degree that countries borrowing to finance external deficits can obtain credit. This in turn can only persist so long as lenders remain confident that borrowing countries can repay specific obligations and service their overall debt.' Simon clearly intended to raise concern and doubt among both borrowers and lenders with the warning that 'as debt grows to finance the continuing deficits, an increasing number of countries which have delayed adjustment will approach limits beyond which they cannot afford to borrow and beyond which prudent creditors will not lend to them. This is a serious matter, and it cannot be ignored by lenders or borrowers.' The only solution, Simon (1976a: 98) argued, was adjustment undertaken by the domestic political authorities or if necessary as part of a wider IMF stabilization program.

CONCLUSION

Secretary Simon (1976a: 102) concluded his 1976 IMF annual meeting address by stressing the inevitability of adjustment. 'For a time an increased inflow of real resources from abroad may enable a country to postpone the hard choices among competing domestic claims. . . . But sooner or later, the bills come due – the adjustment . . . has to be made. There simply is no substitute for the hard decisions and careful husbanding of resources that finance ministries traditionally espouse.' But with the financing-over-adjustment emphases that emerged for a time in the mid-1970s as well as the expanding role of commercial bank lending for balance of payments purposes, Simon's logic did not hold. External imbalances can be sustained as long as unconditional financing can be secured. It is only when such financing is cut off and/ or extended only on a conditional basis that deficit countries are forced into rapid adjustment.

This chapter has outlined how the United States and the IMF were seeking in 1976 to force more rapid deficit country adjustment by curtailing the access of deficit countries to unconditional sources of financing. Managing Director Witteveen (1987: 31) has recounted how the US Federal Reserve Chairman Arthur Burns 'considered Fund conditionality a kind of international rule of law. And I think that was quite right.' But the 'rule of law' assertion of Fund conditionality in 1976 was not an inevitability, but rather was a reflection of the policy preferences of the United States. It occurred at the expense of alternative cooperative policy arrangements and emphases that were articulated in 1974 and 1975 but were not sustained.

8 Currency Crisis and Restricted Policy Options, March–August 1976:
Opening 'Pandora's Box'[1]

With the passage of the Government's plans in March 1976 to freeze the level of public expenditure through 1979–80 (UK Parliament 1976), Chancellor of the Exchequer Denis Healey was of the view that enough had been done to assuage external confidence and to 'free up' domestic resources to allow an export-led economic recovery (UK Healey 1976a: 272). It became clear over the following months, however, that the policies adopted in early 1976 were deemed inadequate by actors who were in a position to have their policy preferences realized. The Government's expenditure plans would have to be revised downward twice again in 1976.

This chapter reviews the intensifying structural and bilateral pressures on the British Government for policy change, starting with the March 1976 run on sterling and continuing to the summer announcement of further retrenchment. The loss of confidence in the pound resulted in a sharp reduction in the room for manoeuvre for the Government. The means by which pressure was brought to bear was through sustained and increasingly alarming selling pressure on sterling, and after June 1976, through terms attached to a short-term multilateral loan that was offered to the British for currency defense.

STERLING WEAKNESS AND EXTENDING THE INCOMES POLICY, MARCH–MAY 1976

Denis Healey (1980: 21) has suggested that he was 'misled' by sterling's strength during his first two years as Chancellor, but that this changed in March 1976 when sterling came under sustained pressure. According to Healey, 'the initial fall in sterling was prompted in part by the market belief that the Government had decided on depreciation as a strategy for faster growth. From that moment on, the markets took the

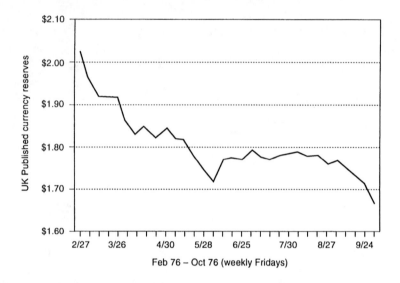

Figure 8.1   Sterling–dollar exchange rate 1976

Source: *Bank of England Quarterly Bulletin*, December 1976, Statistical Annex, table 29

most pessimistic possible view of any economic event in Britain' (see also Healey 1989: 426–7). There had been discussion among the British authorities in late 1975 and early 1976 about the desirability of a sterling depreciation, and this discussion had spread outside the confines of the Treasury and the Bank of England (see Chapter 6). Although it is likely that no formal decision was taken[2] (Bernstein 1983: 328; Holmes 1985: 82–3; Britton 1989: 42), the National Institute for Economic and Social Research (NIESR) was publicly advocating a 5 per cent depreciation while officials in the Treasury and the Downing Street Policy Unit were suggesting 10 per cent (*National Institute Economic Review*, February 1976, p. 5; Bernstein 1983: 324–5; Holmes 1985: 81; Donoughue 1985: 62, 1987: 86; Fay 1987: 73–4; Davies 1989: 43).

On 4 March 1976, sterling fell beneath \$2 for the first time (see Figure 8.1) in a foreign exchange market that currency dealers characterized as very confused (*The Times*, 5 March 1976, 'Sterling's sudden drop,' p. 19). When the Minimum Lending Rate (MLR) was cut the following day from 9¼ per cent to 9 per cent, markets interpreted the move as confirmation that depreciation was indeed official policy (Holmes 1985: 82–3; Brittan 1977: 88; *Financial Times*, 6 March 1976, 'Ster-

ling goes below,' pp. 1, 24; Fay 1987: 74). Selling pressure intensified; as Healey subsequently acknowledged, there was little incentive
to hold sterling if the impression was that the Government wanted the
currency to fall (Whitehead 1985: 184).

The Financial Times reported that it was the assumption of both the
Government and the market that sterling would continue to decline as
long as UK inflation outpaced inflation abroad (6 March 1976, 'Sterling
goes below,' pp. 1, 24); according to the Prime Minister's political advisers,
it was widely accepted within the Government that, given inflation differentials, further sterling depreciation would be necessary to maintain
external competitiveness (Donoughue 1985: 62; Haines 1977: 67). In
the German Bundesbank's view (1976: 51), the 'public debate' in early
1976 on the necessity of allowing sterling to decline further to offset
Britain's higher inflation rate reinforced sterling's decline once it had
begun. US Treasury officials thought that the initial sterling depreciation
had been deliberately engineered by British for unfair export advantage
and that it was 'dirty pool' (Fay and Young 1978, 1: 34). US Treasury
Secretary William Simon (1976b) wrote in an internal memo that the
US 'issued a clear warning to the British – with the French within hearing – that we will not tolerate deliberate competitive depreciations.'

Within days, sterling had fallen to approximately $1.90, depreciat-
ing in a little over a week by the same 5 per cent that the NIESR had
suggested occur gradually over a year (*Financial Times*, 11 March 1976,
'Pound loses 3 cents,' pp. 1, 36). The Bank of England sought to dis-
pel the now widely held view that it had deliberately pushed sterling
down, both by being very visible supporting sterling in the exchanges
(see *The Times*, 10 March 1976, 'Intervention by Bank,' p. 17; *Financial Times*, 11 March 1976, 'Pound loses 3 cents,' p. 1, 36) and by
taking the unusual step of explaining in detail its exchange market
position on the day sterling had fallen beneath $2. The pound's drop
was the result of a market 'misinterpretation,' the Bank argued; the
authorities had been resistant to any increase in sterling above $2.02
'which might prove unsustainable. Thus . . ., when a substantial but
short-lived demand for sterling appeared in the late morning and early
afternoon, it was met by them. By mid-afternoon . . . however, the dollar
was strengthening sharply; and against that abrupt turnaround, the authorities' sales of sterling earlier in the day were misinterpreted by the
market. The pound fell below $2' (*Bank of England Quarterly Bulletin*,
June 1976, p. 171; see also Browning 1986: 72; Brittan 1989: 42).

In Downing Street, the slide created 'the most terrible flutter'
(Donoughue 1989: 42). The Prime Minister sent for the Chancellor

Table 8.1   Labour Party leadership elections, March–April 1976

1st ballot: 25 March 76		2nd ballot: 30 March 76		3rd ballot: 5 April 76	
M. Foot	90	J. Callaghan	141	J. Callaghan	176
J. Callaghan	84	M. Foot	133	M. Foot	137
R. Jenkins	56	D. Healey	38		
T. Benn	37				
D. Healey	30				
T. Crosland	17				

Source: Wilson (1979: 236).

and asked him 'somewhat heatedly' for an explanation. Healey was 'most reassuring': the drop in sterling 'was not an action based on policy. It would be held at two dollars' (Wilson 1979: 227; see also Haines 1977: 67–8). When sterling was discussed in Cabinet the following week, the Chancellor continued to be reassuring: 'The Bank [of England] had *not* intervened to bring the rate down and it wasn't true that Nigeria was selling sterling;[3] so, though the pound had depreciated by 4 per cent since [4 March], the Treasury had allowed for a fall of this size and there was nothing to worry about. "The market has misunderstood the situation"' (Castle 1980: 683–4, original emphasis). In a Parliamentary statement, the Prime Minister was also reassuring, arguing that sterling's fall was an inevitable consequence of the inflation differential between Britain and the rest of the world. 'Although we have made substantial headway in bringing inflation down in this country . . ., our inflation rate is still above that of other important countries and it was inevitable that the markets should at some stage exert some downward pressure on the exchange rate, which is what we have seen in the last few days' (UK Wilson 1976: 640).

Privately, the Prime Minister was concerned whether the drop in sterling would necessitate a delay of his secretly planned resignation (Wilson 1979: 229). Following Labour's return to power in 1974, Wilson had decided not to continue as Prime Minister for more than two years and had set his sixtieth birthday in March 1976 as when he would resign. According to Wilson (1979: 227–8, 231–2, 301–4), sterling's weakness did not in the end affect his plans, and on 16 March he announced his resignation to a surprised Cabinet. Six candidates entered the contest that ensued among Labour MPs to select a replacement, and three ballots were necessary to choose Foreign Secretary James Callaghan as the new Prime Minister (see Table 8.1).

The ballots are interesting for what they reveal of the divisions among Labour MPs. Left–right cleavages that were well-defined on the first ballot (between the supporters of Callaghan, Jenkins, Healey, and Crosland on one hand, and the supporters of Foot and Benn on the other) remained well-defined throughout the contest; as Callaghan comments in his memoirs (1987: 394) of the final ballot between him and Michael Foot, 'it seemed that Benn's votes had gone to Foot, and I had gained nearly all the votes initially given to Crosland, Jenkins and Healey' (see also Barnett 1982: 85–6; Jenkins 1991: 436). The balloting indicated that the right's numerical superiority over the left in Parliament was by no means overwhelming and that policy disagreements on the Government's backbenches were likely to continue.

Through the winter and spring of 1976, the Government's left-wing supporters and critics continued to advocate an alternative economic strategy of reflation behind import restrictions.[4] Although the TUC seemingly acknowledged the external constraints posed by Britain's payments position and the need to borrow abroad 'at least £2 billion a year extra for at least the next three years,' it nonetheless called upon the Government to set a goal of reducing unemployment to 600 000 by 1978, arguing that 'on unchanged policies the prospects for reducing unemployment are limited as the likely growth of output over the next two years is incompatible with the reduction of unemployment' (TUC 1976b: 18, 20, 23–4, 1976a: 304–5). The TUC urged 'selective but nevertheless wide-ranging import controls' upon the Government; 'as the economy is reflated to achieve a level of 600 000 unemployed by 1978, there is a danger that imports will be sucked in, cancelling out, or more than cancelling out, the improvement in exports. The [TUC] General Council agree with the Government that . . . policies to prevent an in-rush of imports should form part of the strategy' (TUC 1976b: 24, 49). Although import controls became a central topic of discussion at TUC–Labour Party Liaison Committee meetings (Taylor 1987: 67–9; Castle 1980: 630–1, 657–60, 696–8), there was little movement in the Chancellor's opposition. Healey told the TUC that 'none of us in Government are against import controls in principle where no retaliation is likely and where a world trade war would not be triggered off,' but trade retaliation against British exports was a danger, he explained, and moreover cheap imports help the poorest people (private political diaries of Tony Benn, 22 March 1976; Castle 1980: 697–8).

Through the winter of 1976 as British unemployment rose above 5 per cent, the TUC pressed the Chancellor for reflationary measures in the upcoming budget that would reverse the trend (Taylor 1987: 67;

Castle 1980: 630–1, 657–60, 696–8; TUC 1976a: 301–2; TUC 1976b: 83; *The Guardian*, 1 March 1976, 'TUC to ask,' p. 1). At a January Liaison Committee meeting, the Chancellor informed the TUC that 'we haven't yet decided on budget reflation because . . . we are waiting to know what the trade unions will offer on wages. . . . The wage increase level is part of the budget strategy and will affect what I can do' (private political diaries of Tony Benn, 26 January 1976; see also Benn 1989: 507–8; Castle 1980: 630–1). The £6 pay policy was due to expire in August 1976. According to Treasury Minister Edmund Dell (1991: 216), the £6 policy had not 'achiev[ed] the reduction in inflation that had been hoped,' and thus the pay norm for the following year needed to be set 'as low as possible' at 3 per cent. 'If this did not prove feasible, higher unemployment could become the only alternative incomes policy.'

When the Chancellor presented the 1976–77 budget in April, he proposed to trade off personal income tax relief in exchange for agreement with the TUC on a second year of incomes policy. Healey emphasized that he was seeking a 'voluntary' agreement with the TUC – 'a policy which the General Council of the TUC and the Congress agree willingly to recommend to their members as something good for themselves and good for the country' – and that he was 'not seeking to dictate or impose a particular figure' for pay settlements. However, the proposed tax relief was based on the assumption that a pay limit 'in the area of 3 per cent' could be achieved. 'I do not believe that . . . a higher limit could be relied on to bring down our rate of inflation to that of our principle competitors' (UK Healey 1976b: 272–4).

The TUC was taken by surprise, both by the *quid pro quo* linkage of tax relief to pay policy agreement as well as by the small size of Healey's proposed 3 per cent limit (inflation was approximately 13 per cent). Although head of the Transport and General Workers' Union Jack Jones in his memoirs (1986: 305) characterizes the proposal as an 'ingenious approach,' negotiations between the TUC and the Government according to Healey (1989: 397) were 'extremely difficult. . . . At our first meeting the TUC representatives actually refused to say a word for several minutes – which seemed an eternity to me' (see also Jones 1986: 306). Early in the negotiations, Jack Jones stated publicly that 3 per cent was 'frankly not enough.' In his memoirs, he recounts that exchanges with the Government 'were often abrasive' (*The Times*, 12 April 1976, 'Mr Jack Jones,' p. 1; Jones 1986: 306). Healey (1989: 397) describes the many meetings between the Government and the TUC over the following month as 'long and exhausting . . . I had con-

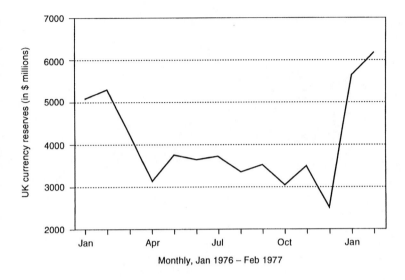

Figure 8.2   UK currency reserves, 1976–77

Source: *Bank of England Quarterly Bulletin*, September 1977, Statistical Annex, table 23

tinually to threaten the withdrawal of my promised tax cuts.'

Notwithstanding Healey's reassurance to Wilson in early March that sterling would be held at two dollars (Wilson 1979: 227), the pound experienced heavy downward pressure during both the balloting for Prime Minister and the incomes policy negotiations. Despite the authorization of the Bank of England to spend up to $500 million per day in currency defense (Donoughue 1987: 85), sterling fell beneath $1.90 in early April. Although external borrowing through the Bank of England's exchange cover scheme was adding $300–$400 million to the reserves monthly, the March and April losses as recorded in the published currency reserve figures were especially sharp (see Figure 8.2;[5] *Bank of England Quarterly Bulletin*, March 1977, Statistical Annex, Table 24; March 1978, Statistical Annex, Table 24/1). The press reported that approximately $1.25 billion and $1.5 billion had been spent on sterling support in March and April respectively, more than absorbing Britain's low-conditionality IMF drawings that had been arranged in 1975 (*The Times*, 5 May 1976, 'Defence of pound,' p. 1); internal US Federal Reserve figures show that the press reports were largely correct (see Figure 8.3[6]). Callaghan in his memoirs (1987: 414)

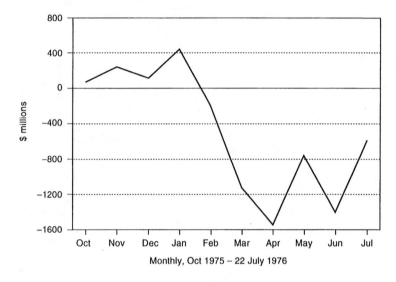

Figure 8.3   Bank of England exchange market intervention 1975–76

Source: McCormick (1976)

recounts that he was 'shocked' when he learned during his first meeting with Denis Healey how much had been spent in sterling support. Healey told him that the Government might have to approach the IMF during the summer to replace the reserves, 'but I did not fully take on board how significant that comment was to become.'

With sterling sinking beneath $1.84 on 9 April, the Treasury sought to make clear that it thought the slide had gone far enough by issuing a public statement: 'As the Chancellor has stated, the fact that our inflation rate was higher than that of our competitors was bound to be reflected in the sterling exchange rate. But there is no economic justification for the pressure which has pushed sterling down in recent days' (*The Times*, 10 April 1976, 'Pressure on sterling,' p. 1). Nevertheless the pound continued to sink through mid-April, with the slide now attributed largely to the less-than-enthusiastic public comments of trade union leaders regarding the Government's incomes policy proposals.[7] As *The Financial Times* commented ominously, 'there must be something drastically wrong with Government policy if a speech by some trade unionist or other or a strike by a few transport workers can send sterling into a virtually uncontrollable slide' (26 April 1976, 'Foreigners can read,' p. 14). As during the summer of 1975, the TUC again found itself negotiating on pay policy in the midst of an ongoing currency crisis with the TUC leadership having to offer public reassurances. When Scottish TUC delegates debated a resolution that called the proposed 3 per cent pay limit 'inadequate and unacceptable,' TUC General Secretary Len Murray publicly disavowed the Scottish TUC: 'I want to make it absolutely clear that trade union policy in this country is made by the Trades Union Congress covering the whole of Britain, including Wales and Scotland. . . . I have not the slightest doubt that there will soon be an agreement on wages for another year, and that the level set will be such as to enable the rate of inflation to be cut substantially still further in the next 12 months' (*The Times*, 22 April 1976, 'Mr McGahey,' p. 1; *The Times*, 24 April 1976, 'Agreement near,' p. 1). When sterling sank to yet another new low a few days later, Murray again spoke out to reassure 'anybody abroad' that the TUC and the Government were indeed going to reach agreement; he advised foreigners to 'buy pounds – because the pound is going to appreciate in value. I wish I could afford to buy some myself' (*Financial Times*, 27 April 1976, 'Chancellor to meet,' pp. 1, 40).

The TUC sought a flexible 5 per cent 'pegging' formula in the negotiations, but 5 per cent was publicly rejected by Healey as too much money 'sloshing around the country' (*The Times*, 14 April 1976, 'TUC chiefs,' pp. 1, 2; *The Times*, 26 April 1976, 'Tories demand statement,' pp. 1, 2). Jack Jones recounts in his memoirs (1986: 307) that 'we failed to make any real progress' during meetings with ministers and officials. TUC negotiators tried to broaden the talks to include not just wages, but also a strengthening of the price code and increases in pensions and industrial investment; 'we were rebuffed on every point. Denis Healey seemed to us intransigent. I sweated at the thought of what it might mean if we had to walk out with no agreement.' Pressure on the TUC was further intensified when the Prime Minister 'gave them a solemn warning that failure to reach an agreement on another round of pay restraints would mean the immediate end of the Government's life' (Callaghan 1987: 416). In the end, it was only with the involvement of the Prime Minister at a late-night meeting at Downing Street that a compromise settlement was achieved that limited average pay increases to 4.5 per cent, accompanied by the income tax relief offered in the budget (Healey 1989: 397; Callaghan 1987: 416; *The Times*, 6 May 1976, 'TUC chiefs,' p. 1). According to Jones (1986: 307), 'it was after 2:30 a.m. and everyone was very tired when we agreed to recommend the agreement. I felt terribly dissatisfied because I knew the figures were inadequate. . . . But in the end I felt we should not take the risk of a catastrophic run on the pound and a General Election. That is what a breakdown would almost certainly have meant, and the others in the trade union team took the same view.'

Despite agreement on another year of incomes policy, sterling continued to be weak. The pound traded in the mid- and low-$1.80s during the first half of May, falling beneath $1.80 for the first time on 21 May. According to the Bank of England, it 'intervened heavily in order to calm the markets' during this period, but 'the markets were largely one-way; intervention by the authorities as buyers of sterling to test the market . . . brought out each time a considerable weight of selling' (*Bank of England Quarterly Bulletin*, June 1976, p. 172). The continued pressure on sterling surprised the trade unions: as the TUC commented dispiritedly in an internal report, 'any doubts about the new [incomes] policy produce an immediate fall in the value of the pound, but confirmation of trade union support for the policy has little effect or at best produces only a steadying of the rate before a further fall' (*The Times*, 10 June 1976, 'TUC hold,' p. 1). The Bank of England's view was that 'the pound was initially unsettled by criticism from some trade unions of wage restraint, and later . . . by disappointment in some sections of the market that the pay policy . . . exceeded the limit of 3 per cent suggested in the Budget' (*Bank of England Quarterly Bulletin*, September 1976, p. 302). Callaghan (1987: 418) recounts that sterling 'seemed to have a self-perpetuating downwards momentum, and there were fears among the experts that the fall would not stop at any level.'

Interest rates had been held steady at 9 per cent for the month-and-a-half after the cut in March that had precipitated sterling's slide. But in the face of sustained currency weakness, the MLR was raised by $1\frac{1}{2}$ per cent in late April and by 1 per cent in May (see Figure 8.4). However, rate hikes appeared to have little effect on the pound's continued slide; according to *The Financial Times*, the $1\frac{1}{2}$ per cent April increase 'was not quite big enough to carry full conviction to the exchange market' (24 April 1976, 'Pound slips,' p. 1). After the second hike, a White House economic adviser who was watching the situation develop noted that 'there presently is nearly a 5 per cent differential on 3-month interest rates between the United States and the United Kingdom' (Malkiel 1976a), yet sterling continued to sink. By early June with the pound trading in the low $1.70s (see Figure 8.1 above), the situation had become alarming (*Financial Times*, 3 June 1976, 'Sterling falls,' p. 1, 34; *Financial Times*, 4 June 1976, 'Pound loses,' p. 1, 40; *Bank of England Quarterly Bulletin*, September 1976, p. 302).

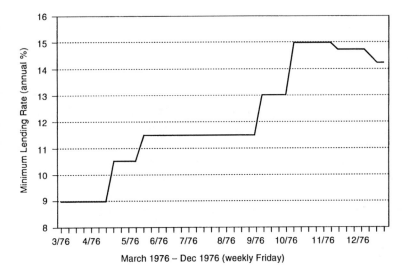

Figure 8.4 UK Minimum Lending Rate 1976

Source: Bank of England Quarterly Bulletin, September 1976, Statistical Annex, table 27; March 1977, Statistical Annex, table 27

THE JUNE 1976 CENTRAL BANK STAND-BY AND AMERICAN INVOLVEMENT

Officials in the United States were increasingly interested in and concerned about the British economic situation; according to US Under-Secretary for Monetary Affairs Edwin Yeo, by early 1976 'to our great dismay we realised we were going to have a major UK experience ahead' (Fay and Young 1978, 1: 34). *Vis-à-vis* sterling's slide, Yeo's view was that exchange rate stability was the product of 'attention to responsible management of underlying economic and financial policies in individual member countries' (US Congress, Senate, Committee on Foreign Relations 1976: 5), and US senior officials were increasingly of the view that sterling's weakness indicated that the British needed to undertake further fiscal and monetary policy retrenchment (Bernstein 1983: 338–9). With respect to the major policy development in Britain during the spring of 1976 – the extension of incomes policy for another year – the US Government was disapproving: 'In our view incomes policies . . . are likely to create distortions of a structural nature over time, and for that reason they cannot be used to solve basic economic policy problems. In particular, it is our view that when incomes policies are used *instead* of appropriate monetary and fiscal policies they tend to be counter-productive' (US State Department 1976a, original emphasis). Yeo recounts that 'the trouble in Britain was that people had a higher standard of living than the country was earning. . . . Our role . . . was to persuade the British that the game was over. They had run out of string' (Fay and Young 1978, 1: 34). His concerns extended beyond Britain itself: 'we feared that if a country like Britain blew up, defaulted on its loans, introduced foreign exchange controls and froze convertibility, we could have a real world depression' (Fay and Young 1978, 1: 34). Thus, it was with an ostensible concern about the preservation of global economic stability that US officials began to involve themselves in bringing about policy change in the UK (see also Bernstein 1983: 129, 339).

Initially, US officials kept their concerns largely to themselves. When Chairman of the Council of Economic Advisers Alan Greenspan sought to comment on British economic policy in his public statements, White House National Security adviser Brent Scowcroft (1976a) advised him to couch his comments in a 'positive framework' and suggested that he 'avoid criticism of the British Government's past or present economic policies. . . . Any such criticisms would most certainly be misunderstood and would have an adverse impact on US–British relations.' Yeo also took care initially to express his views quietly and tactfully, although he was less concerned with diplomacy and more concerned with confidence: 'If it had seeped out that we were so worried, that alone could have produced a severe financial recession' (Fay and Young 1978, 1: 34). Accordingly, the early expressions of American concerns occurred via official channels through a steering group of four international financial officials who met frequently and quietly to discuss international monetary affairs (Fay and Young 1978, 1: 34; Bernstein 1983: 340; Burk and Cairncross 1992: 38–9). The group was comprised of Yeo for the US, Derek Mitchell for the UK, Karl Otto Pöhl for West Germany, and Jacques de Larosière for France. At a meeting in late March, Yeo 'outlined for the first time the fears evolving in Washington. Mitchell heard them largely without comment and returned to Whitehall to tell his political masters' (Fay and Young 1978, 1: 34).

With the pound sinking from $2 into the low $1.70s between March and May, British Treasury ministers and officials were unsure how to halt the slide and restore confidence. TUC agreement on an additional year of restrictive incomes policy had been secured and interest rates had been raised by $2\frac{1}{2}$ per cent, but with no lasting effect on sterling.

Treasury official Leo Pliatzky (1982: 148) recounts the 'heated' argument inside the Treasury: 'Opinion went first in one direction and then in another. . . . One opinion which was urged upon the Chancellor with characteristic persuasiveness was that the most sensible and also the most painless course was to borrow our way through the situation; we should raise loans enabling us to put funds in the shop window on a scale large enough to demonstrate that there was plenty of backing for the pound and that speculators against it would burn their fingers' (see also Bernstein 1983: 358). The Chancellor of the Duchy of Lancaster Harold Lever was a strong proponent of a large external loan (Fay and Young 1978, 1: 34; Holmes 1985: 87; Dell 1991: 218–19). Treasury officials, however, countered with the argument that no one would lend to Britain without conditions and that there was no use asking for a loan unless the Government was willing to change its policies[8] (Fay and Young 1978, 1: 33, 34; Bernstein 1983: 358–9; Burk and Cairncross 1992: 39–40). UK Treasury official Derek Mitchell further argued that seeking a loan would be counter-productive: 'the mere request would raise suspicion that the Government was determined to evade the discipline of the IMF, and that would actually sharpen the threat to sterling' (Fay and Young 1978, 1: 34; see also Lever 1989; Burk and Cairncross 1992: 39–40).

But as sterling sank into the low $1.70s in early June, the situation was becoming desperate. Fearing that Britain risked running out of reserves, the authorities were increasingly reluctant to draw upon them for currency defense (Bernstein 1983: 359; interview material). Given the circumstances, the British authorities decided to seek an international loan. Over 3–6 June, Governor of the Bank of England Gordon Richardson, head of the Bank for International Settlements Dr Jelle Zijlstra, Chairman of the US Federal Reserve Arthur Burns, and other financial officials worked to put together a $5.3 billion multilateral stand-by loan for Britain, which was announced by Healey in Parliament on 7 June (Fay and Young 1978, 1: 33–4; Bernstein 1983: 359–60; Dell 1991: 219; Burk and Cairncross 1992: 40; UK Healey 1976c; *Sunday Times*, 3 October 1976, 'The crisis,' pp. 17, 19). Accounts vary on how the loan was raised and who organized it. Yeo has characterized the loan as 'bait,' thereby suggesting a planned and deliberate US strategy 'to hook the UK economy into IMF control when [the loan] had to be repaid' (Fay and Young 1978, 1: 35); Chancellor of the Duchy of Lancaster Harold Lever (1989) however recounts that the loan was arranged by concerned Europeans and was offered to the British over the opposition of certain UK and US officials (see also

Fay and Young 1978, 1: 33; Bernstein 1983: 359–60; Burk and Cairncross 1992: 39–40).

Britain's creditors in the arrangement were the central banks of the United States ($1 billion), Germany ($800 million), Japan ($600 million), Switzerland ($600 million), Canada ($300 million), France ($300 million), Belgium ($200 million), the Netherlands ($200 million), and Sweden ($150 million); the Bank for International Settlements also participated ($150 million) as did the US Treasury ($1 billion) (Simon 1976d; De Vries 1985, 1: 467). Two days after the loan was announced, the press reported that the US Treasury participated alongside the Federal Reserve in the stand-by because the Federal Reserve had declined to make available the full $2 billion that had initially been requested (*The Guardian*, 9 June 1976, 'US Bank,' p. 1; 'Healey's not-so-famous victory,' p. 15). Archival evidence suggests that UK officials were concerned about the appearance of American reticence to participate in the loan facility: among US Federal Reserve Chairman Arthur Burns' papers is a British proposal of text to be included in the Chancellor's statement to Parliament announcing the loan that would have addressed British concerns: 'It is wrong to suggest that there is any reluctance on the part of the United States authorities to provide $2 billion as part of an international operation. On the contrary, [the] US was very helpful in putting the package together. . . . In this connection it is relevant to recall that in a number of previous support operations the US contribution has been divided' (Burns 1976b). Significantly, however, this language was not included in Healey's statement in Parliament (see UK Healey 1976c: 912–27).

According to *The Times*' economics editor Malcolm Crawford (1983: 429), the US Treasury's participation in the arrangement 'inject[ed] an element of government-to-government conditionality.' Handwritten notes that US Federal Reserve Chairman Arthur Burns (1976a: 9, 11) took while the loan was being arranged make reference to 'steps to mop up excess liquidity' and record the terms of a new and attractive £800 million UK Treasury offering of long-dated paper that was announced by the Chancellor simultaneously with the announcement of the loan (UK Healey 1976c: 914). In a 6 June memo from US Under-Secretary Edwin Yeo (1976a) to US Treasury Secretary William Simon, Yeo characterized the British as 'now committed' to take 'prompt and vigorous policy actions' as a result of the stand-by. In a 7 June memo from Simon (1976d) to President Gerald Ford, Simon outlined to Ford that 'as a condition to our agreeing to provide financial support, the British Government has communicated to me their intention to take immediate steps to reduce the availability of domestic credit, followed by a series of steps over the next six months to tighten fiscal and monetary policy.' The 'immediate steps' in Simon's memo clearly referred to the new £800 million UK Treasury offering. However, when Denis Healey announced the offering in Parliament, he presented it as the Government's own decision. Replying to questions, the Chancellor stated unambiguously 'there are no strings to this money at all' (UK Healey 1976c: 914, 926; UK Healey 1976b: 236–7). Yet soon thereafter, Healey told his Cabinet colleagues that 'we've got to get public expenditure cuts for next year identified and published by July,' with the Prime Minister warning that 'we might have to take even more extreme measures' (Benn 1989: 577).

Although Yeo's and Simon's memos (quoted above) constitute strong evidence that monetary and fiscal policy stipulations were attached by the United States to the multilateral loan, it cannot be argued with certainty that the Chancellor and the Prime Minister were opposed to the stipulations.[9] The problem is well illustrated by an Economic Strategy Cabinet Committee discussion that occurred in mid-June regarding the possibility of a future UK drawing from the IMF. The Prime Minister commented to his colleagues, 'I don't understand why there is so much anxiety about the IMF. After all, they ask reasonable things, and I don't think we should make them into bogeymen. That's what the IMF are for' (Benn 1989: 580). Home Secretary Roy Jenkins concurred, recalling the UK's IMF stand-bys during his Chancellorship in the late 1960s: 'I gave them a letter of intent, but I had done it all before I went to the IMF because I thought what they said was sensible' (private political diaries of Tony Benn, 15 June 1976). Ministerial discussion moved into a consideration of public expenditure, with the Chancellor telling the Committee, 'we will have to have further cuts in public expenditure, and my plan is to make them before I go to the IMF.' In response to criticism from Minister of Energy Tony Benn, Healey elaborated: 'I didn't say I was going to do what the IMF wanted, but I thought [that] what the IMF would be likely to want would be right for Britain anyway, and I would want to do it anyway' (Benn 1989: 580; private political diaries of Tony Benn, 15 June 1976). According to Benn, 'Roy [Jenkins] then repeated that he had never done what the IMF wanted but always what he had wanted to do, and that was by coincidence what the IMF wanted. It was all very revealing' (private political diaries of Tony Benn, 15 June 1976).

Loan conditionality is more tolerable when the policy changes can be presented by the economic authorities as their own decision. In

June 1976, explicit bilateral conditionality – i.e., overt American involvement and intervention into British domestic economic policy decisions – would have been unacceptable. Policy conditions attached to American financial support could not be publicly acknowledged, and indeed given the sensitive nature of the situation, US officials were cautious in their on-the-record statements about the British economic situation. At a press conference in late June, Treasury Secretary Simon declined to discuss sterling or the extent of UK borrowing for sterling's defense (*Department of State Bulletin*, 26 July 1976, p. 121), while Under-Secretary Yeo was only somewhat more forthcoming when testifying before the Senate Foreign Relations Committee on his views about British (and Italian) economic problems: 'It is our view that it is time to adjust; that is what we need to do from the standpoint of the United States, realizing that these are sovereign countries' (US Congress, Senate, Committee on Foreign Relations 1976: 37).

Loan conditionality exacted through the IMF was a means by which 'sovereign countries' could be made to adjust. Accordingly, US officials insisted that the $5.3 billion stand-by loan be available for three months only, renewable once for a further three months, and that the British give written assurances and commit themselves publicly to going to the IMF if drawings from the stand-by could not be repaid when the six-month time limit expired. Yeo went to London to insist upon these stipulations: he recounts, 'Callaghan tried everything to prevent the six-month time limit. . . . First they didn't want any limit at all. When I wouldn't have that, they wanted a longer limit. And when I wouldn't have that, they wanted a longer take-down, which means that the six-month period would not begin until they started drawing the money' (Fay and Young 1978, 1: 33). There were no concessions. The six-month time limit and the commitment to go to the IMF should Britain be unable to repay were confirmed in a 6 June letter from Healey (1976a) that Treasury Secretary Simon regarded as binding[10] (Simon 1976d; Fay and Young 1978, 1: 33), and when announcing the loan in Parliament, the Chancellor duly stated that 'if any drawing . . . could not . . . be paid on the due date, Her Majesty's Government would be prepared to seek further drawing from the International Monetary Fund' (UK Healey 1976c: 915).

In his confidential summary of the arrangement to President Ford, Simon (1976d) explained that by agreeing to go to the Fund, 'the British Government has accepted the strict conditionality which the IMF would require.' Yeo made essentially the same point in public testimony before the Senate Committee on Foreign Relations:

It is important to note that the British have agreed that they will repay in six months any of the funds drawn, and that they will borrow from the IMF if necessary to meet that deadline. We feel this is an important commitment. It means that the United Kingdom is prepared, if necessary, to adopt the kind of fiscal and monetary policies which the IMF would require of a borrower in the higher credit tranches.

(US Congress, Senate, Committee on Foreign Relations 1976)

But the key point for the American officials was that it would be seen as the market and/or the IMF rather than the US that was pushing the British towards further retrenchment; as a 'very senior' US official pointed out to the press, 'policies must be able to stand the test of the market-place. If the market rejects them and goes on rejecting them, it is no use saying that the market is wrong. It is the policies which have to be changed' (*Financial Times*, 18 June 1976, 'A time for words,' p. 22; see also *Sunday Telegraph*, 13 June 1976, 'What it cost,' p. 18).

In Parliament, the $5.3 billion stand-by loan was presented as a 'massive international endorsement of sterling' (UK Healey 1976c: 916). Exchange markets had pushed sterling to a level 'which cannot be justified,' the Chancellor explained, and he quoted a statement issued through the Bank of England:

Financial authorities from the Group of Ten countries and Switzerland together with the Bank for International Settlements, noting that the recent fall in the value of sterling under exchange market pressure has led to disorderly market conditions which carried sterling to an unjustified level, today agreed in the common interest of the stability and efficient functioning of the international monetary system to make available to the Bank of England a stand-by credit in excess of $5 billion.

(UK Healey 1976c: 914–5)

In a television interview in early June, Healey asserted that 'I think *all* the finance ministers I've talked to and the central bankers too – the Americans, the Germans, the Dutch – believe that our performance is immeasurably better than it has been and that there is no economic justification for what's happening' (London Press Service, 3 June 1976, 'Healey on Falling Pound,' my emphasis); in his memoirs, Healey (1989: 427) writes that he got the stand-by 'without difficulty because *all* the contributors shared my view that the pound was then undervalued' (my emphasis).

It soon became clear, however, that US officials did not share the view that there was no justification for sterling's slide and that sterling was undervalued. The American announcement of its participation in the stand-by loan was word-for-word identical to the statement issued through the Bank of England (quoted above), except that the phrase 'which carried sterling to an unjustified level' was omitted (*Financial Times*, 18 June 1976, 'A time for words,' p. 22). US officials had discussed the phrasing of the US announcement, and Yeo (1976a) outlined the issues in a memo to Simon:

> The Bank of England is to issue a statement at 10:30 A.M. tomorrow. . . . The statement is mediocre at best from our standpoint, particularly in regard to our Congressional and other critics. It mentions that the rate of sterling has been unjustifiably low; this is true only if the British take prompt and vigorous policy actions – something that they are now committed to do. Up until yesterday the rate was probably too high re[garding] the policies that had been pursued.
>
> Arthur [Burns] and I have agreed that our statement will be short and will not mention whether the rate is too low or too high. We agreed that our statement will cite disorderly market conditions, and if the policy action Dennis [sic] has promised is signed, sealed, and delivered tonight we can accurately point to and comment favorably on the actions of the British authorities.

The omission of the 'unjustified levels' phrase from the US announcement was noted by the press, and as *The Times* correctly surmised, its absence was 'obviously intentional. The identical wording of the rest of the statement shows that it was agreed between the two sides before it was issued. The explanation for the discrepancy is equally obvious. The Americans do not believe that sterling is seriously undervalued' (19 June 1976, 'Fed silent,' p. 17; *Financial Times*, 18 June 1976, 'A time for words,' p. 22).

US officials expressed their concerns about Britain more directly in a public statement that Secretary Simon delivered at an OECD Ministerial meeting in late June. Simon called for deficit country adjustment, arguing that 'lenders will become increasingly reluctant to finance expanding current account deficits unless borrowing nations make fundamental changes in their domestic economic policies. . . . If the open trade and payments system is to survive, countries in a weak position must recognize the need to adjust and put the necessary economic and financial policies in place quickly' (US Information Service 1976). While Simon refrained from naming names, there was no doubt at the meeting that he was referring to Britain: Assistant Secretary of the Treasury Gerald Parsky was cited in press reports claiming that British policies needed to change in order to restore confidence and that the most urgent matter was a reduction of the British public sector borrowing requirement (*Financial Times*, 23 June 1976, 'Change domestic economic politics,' pp. 1, 32). Healey, who was also attending the OECD meeting, testily replied through the press that 'strictures from foreign sources are never helpful,' but he also hinted that additional public expenditure cuts would indeed be forthcoming (*The Times*, 23 June 1976, 'US Treasury,' p. 1).

PUBLIC EXPENDITURE CUTS AND 'UNBELIEVING'/ 'PRACTICAL' MONETARISM

Following the announcement of the $5.3 billion stand-by loan, sterling appreciated sharply to reach $1.80 on 8 June; it then fluctuated around $1.77 for the rest of the month with the aid of 'appreciable official support' (*Bank of England Quarterly Bulletin*, September 1976, p. 302). On 23 June, the Bank of England drew $1.03 billion from the stand-by to replenish reserves (Malkiel 1976b). The rate continued to be vulnerable to official sterling balance holders moving out of sterling; according to press reports, sterling balances declined by nearly £1 billion during the second quarter of 1976 (*Financial Times*, 8 September 1976, 'Record Fall,' pp. 1, 48). *The Times* argued that the approximately £4 billion remaining in sterling balances could put further downward pressure on sterling 'for years to come' and that something clearly needed to be done; 'the only solution to this particular dilemma would be to reactivate proposals that the official sterling balances should be "funded" through some mechanism like the IMF. . . . The essential mechanism would be that foreign official holders of sterling could exchange it for reserves from the IMF. The United Kingdom, in turn, would pay off the IMF in manageable amounts over say 50 years' (23 April 1976, 'Special protection,' p. 16). Prime Minister Callaghan also thought that the sterling balances presented a continuing problem. He recounts in his memoirs (1987: 419) that 'my idea was to fund the existing short-term liabilities and to spread repayment of them over a longer period into the 1980s. . . . I discussed the matter with the Chancellor and suggested that we should use the forthcoming visit to Puerto Rico [for the June 1976 G-7 summit] to explore the prospects with President Ford; Denis agreed with the general objective but preferred that he should first discuss the matter with . . . the United States Secretary to the Treasury.'

American officials were not at all receptive to helping the British on sterling balances. US policy objectives for the G-7 Puerto Rico summit were summarized in a confidential case-book as follows: 'We want to stress both privately and publicly the importance of relying on domestic fiscal and monetary policies as the means of strengthening countries' international financial positions, rather than on attempts to obtain international support for any particular exchange rate' (US Council of Economic Advisers 1976a). Secretary Simon briefed President Ford on the plane to Puerto Rico that he should tell Callaghan that 'a fundamental shift in British economic policy was necessary' (Fay and Young 1978, 1: 35). Callaghan too was preparing for the meeting with Ford on the journey to the summit: 'it was agreed that the most useful thing he could do was to persuade the President that economics was not a mechanistic activity divorced from politics. The Labour government, he would say, understood that changes were necessary; indeed, some were already in progress, but they would take time' (Fay and Young 1978, 1: 35).

Callaghan (1987: 420) recounts that on the day following the British delegation's arrival, 'the Chancellor reported to me that he had engaged [Simon] in talks about replacing the $5 billion loan with new long-term arrangements but had been rather discouraged.' The Prime Minister and President had a bilateral session alone and then had Healey and Simon join them. According to Simon, the meeting was 'a very quiet off-the-record session and we talked very freely about sterling and the market. I told the British I felt they had a couple of months, but that these should not be wasted by inaction' (Fay and Young 1978, 1: 35). Simon recounts that he and Ford 'were assured that the [six-month] stand-by was going to take care of the problem and, if they could weather the storm, it would all be over. I disagreed. . . . I just said that, in the absence of attacking the fundamental cause of the problem, monetary policy and the public sector spending, there was no way in which they could continue to support the pound at silly levels. The market would win out' (Whitehead 1985: 185–6). At a press conference following the summit, Simon made it clear that long-term arrangements to fund the sterling balances had not been on the agenda; summit participants had discussed only 'the possibility of those in temporary – and I underline temporary – need of financing for a transitory nature while they put their economic houses in order' (White House Press Secretary 1976). According to Callaghan (1987: 420), the summit 'was not a memorable meeting and we left without making any progress on the long-term stabilisation plan.'

There had been hints prior to the G-7 summit that the Government was contemplating further reductions in public expenditure. The Prime Minister in a televised interview had indicated that while there was 'no rational case' for cutting public expenditure in the current fiscal year, 'next year I'm not so sure about,' and at an acrimonious TUC–Labour Party Liaison Committee meeting, Callaghan reportedly told the Committee that, 'as leader of the party . . . I can give you no guarantees that there will not be further public expenditure cuts in 1977–78' (London Press Service, 15 June 1976, 'Prime Minister interviewed'; *The Times*, 22 June 1976, 'Mr Callaghan,' pp. 1, 2). Several articles about 'impending cuts' appeared in the press; although 'the sources of the stories . . . differed, the figure of £1 bn became firmly entrenched' (Browning 1986: 78–9). By the end of June, sterling had strengthened 'on expectations that cuts in public expenditure were being prepared' (*Bank of England Quarterly Bulletin*, September 1976, p. 302).

According to Bernard Donoughue (1987: 89), 'Callaghan personally authorised the Chancellor to lay down his proposals for further public expenditure cuts, telling Denis Healey that he "must bring them to Cabinet and win the support of Ministers."' In late June, a meeting was held of selected senior Ministers and officials to discuss proposals that would subsequently be presented to Cabinet (Crosland 1982: 343; Donoughue 1987: 89; Dell 1991: 225–6). The Chancellor employed two kinds of logic in advocating cuts, one focusing on 'resource-switching,' the other on confidence. The essence of the resource-switching argument was that expenditure cuts were necessary to 'make room' for the rapid growth that was to follow (Fay and Young 1978, 1: 35; see also UK Healey 1976d: 2012, 1976e: 1237–8). This argument did not go unchallenged, however; according to Donoughue (1987: 84–5), '[Foreign Secretary] Tony Crosland, supported by others close to the Prime Minister, pointed out [that] there was not the least danger in this new recessionary world of the mid-1970s of any economic overheating, so there was no need to create a hole. Indeed, a bigger hole of under-utilised resources was growing naturally in the British economy every month' (see also Crosland 1982: 343).

Inside the Treasury, the rationale for the cuts focused not on resource-switching but on external confidence (Pliatzky 1982: 149–51; interview material). 'There were those in the Treasury who put the Chancellor's dilemma to him with some brutality: either he changed policy in order to avoid the IMF, or he would be forced to go to the

Fund, where he would find policy changes among the conditions' (Whitehead 1985: 186; interview material; see also Fay and Young 1978, 1: 35). The size of the cuts package was also a matter of internal Treasury debate. Derek Mitchell, the Treasury official in charge of Overseas Finance and therefore most in tune with international opinion, argued that a large cut of say £3 billion was necessary to restore market confidence, while Permanent Secretary Douglas Wass and the Treasury official overseeing public expenditure Leo Pliatzky were more sensitive to the Government's political difficulties (Fay and Young 1978, 1: 35; Bernstein 1983: 371; Holmes 1985: 88; Whitehead 1985: 186). As Pliatzky (1982: 149) has recalled, the conflict was 'between what was required from the point of view of restoring financial confidence and what was considered feasible and negotiable in Cabinet.' A £1 billion package – 'the minimum which might have any hope of making the required impression' – was the starting point for discussion. 'Though £1 billion might be a minimum from one point of view, it looked like the maximum from the point of view of acceptability to the Cabinet.'

Accordingly, Healey proposed £1 billion in expenditure cuts to the Economic Strategy Cabinet Committee and then to the full Cabinet, employing both the resource-switching and the confidence arguments (Benn 1989: 588, 591; Fay and Young 1978, 1: 35). Foreign Secretary Tony Crosland, Minister for Energy Tony Benn, and others continued to dispute the resource-switching analysis, arguing that with the UK at the bottom of an economic slump and experiencing unprecedented levels of unemployment, resources clearly were not overstretched (private political diaries of Tony Benn, 2 July 1976). But the logic of the resource-switching argument was not simply macroeconomic; arguments for public expenditure cuts that anticipated strong economic growth were a 'politically less sensitive way' of presenting the cuts 'than if their sole justification had been foreign confidence in sterling' (Holmes 1985: 88). When the Chancellor explained the cuts to the TUC Economic Committee and to Parliament, the resource-switching argument and predictions of 5 per cent growth in 1976 were central (TUC 1976a: 309; UK Healey 1976d: 2010).

Vis-à-vis confidence, Foreign Secretary Tony Crosland and Minister for Energy Tony Benn both advocated an early approach to the IMF (Benn 1989: 588, 592; private political diaries of Tony Benn, 2 July 1976; Fay and Young 1978, 1: 35). The Prime Minister was not receptive to this idea, arguing with Benn that 'I think [the IMF] would demand things that we wouldn't be prepared to yield to them' (Benn 1989: 588). But moreover, the point of proposing expenditure cuts from the Treasury's perspective had been to avoid an upper tranche borrowing from the Fund by restoring external confidence; as Healey (1989: 427–8) recounts this period, 'I was determined not to go to the IMF for a conditional loan if I could possibly avoid it.'

According to Chief Secretary to the Treasury Joel Barnett (1982: 89–90), 'once the Prime Minister had agreed the need for the [expenditure] cut, there was never any real doubt we would achieve our objective. . . . The Prime Minister gently reminded Ministers that those who did not like the eventual package had only one option.' But Cabinet acquiescence on £1 billion in cuts was different from agreement on the composition of the cuts across departments, and Cabinet had to meet seven separate times before agreement on a final package was reached[11] (Donoughue 1987: 89). Healey (1989: 428) recounts these Cabinet sessions as 'appallingly difficult,' although in the Chief Secretary's view, the difficulty was due in part to the Prime Minister's decision to '"play it long", so as to avoid serious trouble' (Barnett 1982: 93).

It was during these Cabinet sessions that Minister for Energy Tony Benn and Minister for the Environment Peter Shore, supported by other left-wing ministers, presented to the full Cabinet what they called the 'alternative economic strategy' that was based upon the preservation of the Government's expenditure commitments through import controls and higher taxes (Benn 1989: 591–2, 594–5; see also *The Observer*, 18 July 1976, 'Pressure to raise VAT,' p. 1; *The Guardian*, 19 July 1976, 'Challenge to Healey,' pp. 1, 20). The 'real argument' for the expenditure cuts, Benn argued, centered on foreign confidence, and this argument was 'extremely dangerous because it is open ended. The IMF is in a position to press anything on us once we accept the confidence argument and there will be no end to it' (Benn 1989: 595; Barnett 1982: 93; Burk and Cairncross 1992: 49). Although Callaghan at one point cut Benn off in Cabinet, Barnett (1982: 94) recounts that the Prime Minister 'did not feel he could stop [Leader of the House of Commons] Michael Foot making a "Benn-style" contribution, pleading yet again for a substantial cut in the "cuts." Michael was extremely worried about the effect of the package on the TUC.'

Broader consultations about the package began in mid-July. Healey (sometimes with Callaghan alongside) presented both the resource-switching and the confidence arguments to the TUC Economic Committee, Labour MPs, and other groups of Labour supporters (TUC 1976a: 309; *The Times*, 15 July 1976, 'Cuts must be agreed,' pp. 1, 2). The presentations were not well received. At a meeting of the Tribune Group (a parliamentary grouping of left-wing Labour MPs), the Chancellor was repeatedly challenged on the 'confidence issue' (*The Times*, 13 July 1976, 'Left-wing warning,' p. 1). The TUC told the Chancellor and the Prime Minister that, although it wished to consider the proposals, 'it was not clear that the situation needed to be brought to an early point of decision' and reminded them that 'maintaining the confidence of the trade union Movement was vital' (TUC 1976a: 309). When the TUC and the Chancellor met again, the TUC rejected both the 'resource-switching' and the confidence arguments. The TUC's view was that the Government's current expenditure plans 'already provided for a massive switch away from the public sector.... Cutting public expenditure would increase unemployment for no reason. The Chancellor should consider import controls as an alternative.' *Vis-à-vis* confidence, the TUC argued 'there was no guarantee that a further round of cuts in public expenditure would secure foreign confidence in sterling. Furthermore cuts in public expenditure would also affect the confidence of working people in the Government' (TUC 1976a: 309–10). The TUC Economic Committee submitted a written statement to the Chancellor that condemned the forecast loss of 70 000 jobs as a result of the package, but that also acknowledged that the TUC's opposition was constrained by the desire not to see the Government fall (TUC 1976a: 310–12). In Cabinet, Healey characterized the TUC as wanting to preserve the Government but unwilling to go along with the cuts, and he took their position as a 'kind of endorsement' (private political diaries of Tony Benn, 19 July 1976).

After the £1 billion in expenditure cuts were finally agreed in Cabinet, the Chancellor, concerned that the cuts would not be sufficient to restore confidence, presented an additional proposal to raise an estimated £1 billion in new revenue by increasing employers' National Insurance contributions by 2 per cent (Whitehead 1985: 186; Fay and Young 1978, 1: 35). According to Chief Secretary to the Treasury Joel Barnett (1982: 93), the proposal had been withheld by Healey from an earlier Cabinet, with the Prime Minister's approval. 'This proposal was tacked on as a *caveat* to the public expenditure cuts in Cabinet and ideologically, as a tax on employers rather than workers, it evaded more general Labour Party opposition. The Cabinet, when it finally realised that Healey had railroaded the increase without proper consultation, was furious' (Holmes 1985: 89). Nevertheless, the tax increase was approved.[12]

Efforts to restore confidence were not limited to fiscal retrenchment, but also included the public announcement of a forecast for the growth rate of the money supply. Prior to July 1976, the Chancellor's comments about money supply growth had been confined largely to affirmations that the Government would not permit it to add to inflationary pressures (see UK Healey 1976b: 236–7; UK Healey 1976c: 914). In a televised interview in June, Healey was asked whether it would be helpful toward restoring confidence 'to fix, as many people advocate, a fixed level of the money supply that won't be exceeded?' Healey replied, 'I don't think that would help – I've looked into this very carefully in countries which have one. . . . Monetarism is a very trendy drug at the moment, and some people have gone overboard for it, but it's not got very much more sense you know than many other drugs. . . . To fix a target, and to make that govern the rest of your policy, I don't think that makes sense' (Ham 1981: 127; see also Healey 1980: 13; 1989: 376). But a week later, Bank of England Governor Gordon Richardson in a public speech weighed the advantages and disadvantages of announcing a quantitative monetary growth target (Bank of England 1984: 46). The major benefits, Richardson (1976a: 325) argued, were the positive confidence effects: 'it may make clearer what the aims of monetary policy are, and may give the public a greater sense that the authorities are committed to the achievement of their stated aim. . . . It may therefore have a useful effect on expectations, and may validate the belief of the public that inflation is being kept under proper control.' The disadvantages, Richardson noted, were the consequent instability in interest rates that would have to accompany a 'close adherence to a target.' The Governor ultimately reserved his position – 'all these factors need to be carefully weighed' – but at the US Federal Reserve, it was noted that Richardson's speech had been 'interpreted as a trial balloon,' and Federal Reserve Chairman Arthur Burns asked his staff to obtain a copy of the speech and to summarize it for him (Wallich 1976a).

A month later in a statement to Parliament, the Chancellor affixed a quantitative forecast to money supply growth in Britain. 'In the current year 1976–77 money supply has so far been growing at an annual rate of about 10 per cent. . . . For the financial year as a whole money supply growth should amount to about 12 per cent. . . . If inflation and output move as now forecast, I would expect the growth in money supply to be lower next year than this' (UK Healey 1976d: 2018–19; see also UK Healey 1976e: 1238). Healey concedes in his memoirs (1989: 491) that the decision to announce a monetary growth forecast was 'largely to placate the financial markets.' But the Chancellor's announcement was a forecast rather than a target, and the distinction was conscious and deliberate[13] (see Healey 1989: 434). In the view of

Financial Times columnist Samuel Brittan (1977: 89), the Treasury 'muffed' the announcement by expressing its policy commitment in this way. 'The July statement was originally supposed to contain a commitment to a 12 per cent limit on monetary growth in 1976–7; but this was vetoed at a late stage at a high official level, and the 12 per cent figure became something between an aspiration and a forecast. The potentially favourable effects on confidence and on inflationary expectations were thus thrown away.' US Federal Reserve officials held a similar view, commenting internally that 'by backing into a publicly-announced money target, [the British] have committed themselves to a perhaps overly restrictive or at least overly inflexible target without gaining the full favorable confidence/expectations effects that a firm, early commitment might have had' (Howard 1976c: 2–3).

At the official level within the British Treasury, the drift toward publicly announced monetary targets was viewed with a sense of defeat (Fay 1987: 80). Permanent Secretary of the Treasury Douglas Wass reportedly characterized himself as an 'unbelieving monetarist,' but rationalized the public announcement of monetary forecasts/targets by noting that since the financial community took monetary targets seriously, they might in fact stabilize the markets (Fay 1987: 80; Holmes 1985: 179; Brittan 1977: 89). Treasury official Leo Pliatzky (1989b: 122) has characterized the Chancellor as an 'unbelieving monetarist' as well; although Healey did not believe in monetary targets, he adopted them 'with a view to inspiring confidence in the financial world, which *did* believe in them' (original emphasis). Reportedly, Bank of England Governor Gordon Richardson was more of a 'practical' rather than an 'unbelieving' monetarist; in monetarism he saw 'a device which would shift the Government's focus away from employment to inflation' (Fay 1987: 80). As Bank of England economist John Fforde (1982: 72) has explained, a determined counter-inflation strategy outside of the 'political economy' of a monetary target would have been difficult in Britain: 'it would have been possible to initiate such a strategy with a familiar "Keynesian" exposition about managing demand downwards. . . . But this would have meant disclosing objectives for, *inter alia*, output and employment. This would have been a very hazardous exercise, and the objectives would either have been unacceptable to public opinion or else inadequate to secure a substantial reduction in the rate of inflation or both' (see also Pliatzky 1982: 176–9; Fay 1987: 80; Smith 1989: xiv–xv). The crux of 'practical monetarism' was the elevation of price stability as the pre-eminent goal of economic policy and the quiet relegation of other macroeconomic goals to a secondary level.

CONCLUSION

The Chancellor concluded his July statement to Parliament on public expenditure cuts by emphasizing the Government's 'full confidence that the remaining obstacles to our success are now removed' (UK Healey 1976d: 2020). He clearly did not anticipate having to come back to Parliament for additional expenditure cuts; the July measures, he believed, 'were sufficient to get our economy into balance. . . . I thought enough had been done' (Whitehead 1985: 187; see also Healey 1980: 21). Nor was he alone in this view; among Treasury officials, there was a 'feeling of subdued optimism . . . that economic Ministers had come to terms with Britain's underlying economic problems, and that insofar as government could ensure it, the conditions in which business operated had improved' (Middlemas 1991: 107). According to Treasury official Leo Pliatzky (1982: 147), 'we could feel by the summer [of 1976] that we had turned the corner.' Even US Treasury Secretary Simon (1976e) outlined the British economic situation with modest optimism in a July memo to President Ford: 'It appears that [the G–7 summit in] Puerto Rico gave added impetus to the Government's efforts to deal with their economic and financial problems. The Chancellor of the Exchequer is expected to announce substantial budget cuts soon. If these reductions are viewed as genuine and if they are complemented by a firm monetary policy, the UK might be able to avoid a large drawing from the IMF.'

Despite the efforts of the British authorities *vis-à-vis* incomes policy, public expenditure, and monetary policy, confidence was not restored. In the autumn, sterling's weakness re-emerged and the Government was driven to a crisis announcement of its intention to apply for an IMF loan. The view of Gavyn Davies of the Prime Minister's Policy Unit is that 'the markets wanted blood, and [the July measures] didn't look like blood. We didn't understand that in No. 10 at the time, we didn't know that what they wanted was a humiliation. . . . Trying to avoid the humiliation was a waste of time' (Whitehead 1985: 187, 1987: 256).

9 Driven to the IMF, September–November 1976:
'The Market's Verdicts are Merciless and Effective'[1]

During the winter and spring of 1976, the value of the pound against the US dollar fell by approximately 12 per cent, from above $2 to around $1.77. Commenting on the selling pressures on sterling, the Bank of England acknowledged that 'it is unlikely that events would have run the course they did had there not emerged a widespread view that sterling was overvalued' (*Bank of England Quarterly Bulletin*, September 1976, p. 308). But despite a 12 per cent depreciation, sterling's weakness persisted into the autumn. In late October, the pound fell into the mid-$1.50s, and it was apparent that the roots of the Government's confidence problem ran deep.

Pressures upon the Government for policy change during this period were multifaceted, occurring at the structural level from the financial markets, at the bilateral level from the United States and the Federal Republic of Germany, and at the multilateral level from the IMF. The various levels and forms of pressure were highly interconnected. This chapter outlines how the British authorities were driven to announce an application for an upper tranche drawing from the IMF by pressures stemming most immediately from the exchange markets as well as the various discussions and negotiations that occurred in response to the crisis.

THE COLLAPSE OF CONFIDENCE AND THE IMF LOAN APPLICATION, SEPTEMBER 1976

Several explanations were offered at the time for why sterling's weakness re-emerged in the autumn: the Bank of England's published currency reserves fell by $341 million in August 1976 (see Figure 8.2 above) raising the likelihood that the authorities would be both less willing and less able to defend sterling; it was announced that the overseas holdings of sterling balances had dropped by £905 million during the second quarter of 1976 and that the trade balance was worsening; the National Union of Seamen was threatening strike action in support of a pay claim that fell outside the pay policy limits.[2] Sterling's weakness was also related to what the Bank of England called a 'slackness of demand' for gilt-edged securities in August and September 1976 (*Bank of England Annual Report, 1977*, p. 8; Burk and Cairncross 1992: 52–3; Fay and Young 1978, 1: 35). During the summer, 'the expectation that the government might have to raise interest rates in order to persuade foreigners to hold sterling . . . made people reluctant to buy bonds. Unable to finance its deficit in this way, the Government then had to turn to bank borrowing, and the resulting increase in the money supply caused alarm among potential holders of sterling. And so the process could continue to feed upon itself' (Gardner 1986: 61; see also Donoughue 1987: 143; TUC 1977b: 14). But a buyers' 'gilt-strike' in anticipation of higher interest rates is largely a self-fulfilling prophecy, as the Government is compelled to raise rates in order to sell its debt. Accordingly, in September and October, the Minimum Lending Rate (MLR) was increased sharply from 11.5 per cent to 13 per cent to 15 per cent; according to Denis Healey (1980: 21–2; 1989: 428), the rate increases were 'fully justified' in order 'to get gilt sales moving' (see also UK Healey 1976f: 43–4; Fay and Young 1978, 1: 35; Burk and Cairncross 1992: 52–3; Browning 1986: 83).

During the first week of September, the Bank of England drew a further $515 million from the $5.3 billion stand-by (approximately $4 billion remained) and reportedly spent $400 million to support sterling at $1.77 (Browning 1986: 81; Fay and Young 1978, 1: 35; *Financial Times*, 5 October 1976, 'UK draws $500m,' pp. 1, 44). As Treasury official Leo Pliatzky (1982: 151) recounts, however, Bank of England support 'had at best only a temporary effect and merely depleted further our scanty reserves without restoring confidence. The Prime Minister and the Chancellor put the Bank on an increasingly short rein as to the extent to which they could use the reserves for intervention.' On 9 September, the Bank ceased intervention altogether, as 'the pressure on sterling was such that it was no longer possible to maintain the rate around $1.77' (*Bank of England Quarterly Bulletin*, December 1976, p. 430; see also *The Observer*, 3 October 1976, 'The Sterling Crisis,' p. 10). The decision to withdraw support had been approved at the most senior levels of Government. Some ministers argued for continued intervention, if need be, through further drawings on the stand-by loan, which was after all the reason why it had been provided (interview material; see also Browning 1986: 81). Callaghan in his memoirs

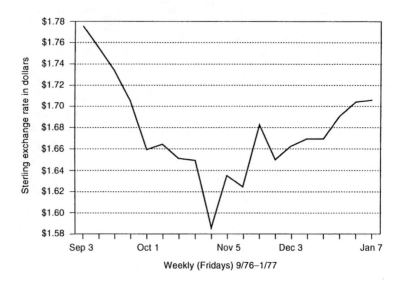

Figure 9.1   Sterling–dollar exchange rate 1967–77

Source: *Bank of England Quarterly Bulletin*, March 1977, Statistical Annex, table 29

(1987: 422) recounts that both the Chancellor and the Governor of the Bank of England were worried that 'the rate would fall heavily' with the withdrawal of support; however, in Callaghan's view, 'the reality was that as soon as the Bank repaid the $5 billion [stand-by], it simply would not have the resources to sustain sterling at $1.77. This seemed to both the Chancellor and me to be conclusive.' Without support, sterling fell by 3.5 cents within 30 minutes on 9 September; over the following two weeks, the pound sank into the low $1.70s (see Figure 9.1; *The Times*, 10 September 1976, 'Pound falls,' p. 1).

In early August, Financial Secretary to the Treasury Robert Sheldon stated officially for the Government that no decision had been made to apply to the IMF for an additional loan, and that beyond the Chancellor's scheduled attendance at the IMF's annual meeting in early October, no meetings were planned between the UK and the IMF at either official or ministerial levels (*Financial Times*, 4 August 1976, 'UK did not draw', p. 26). According to the IMF historian, however, 'frequent informal contact' had been maintained between the Fund staff and British economic authorities following the arrangement of low conditionality drawings for the UK in late 1975 (De Vries 1985, 1: 466). When the

annual UK–IMF consultations were held in May 1976, it was reported
in the press that no inquiries had been made about the possibility of a
further UK drawing from the IMF (*Financial Times*, 24 May 1976,
'Chancellor still reluctant,' p. 1). By August, however, 'UK officials
and the Fund management and staff were engaged in secret exploratory discussions about a stand-by arrangement,' including issues of
timing, the size of any UK stand-by, and whether the accompanying
policy package would prove acceptable to the IMF's Executive Board.[3]
(De Vries 1985, 1: 467).

During the first several months of 1976, the Fund appears to have
held a somewhat positive view of British economic prospects (see De
Vries 1985, 1: 467–8; *The Times*, 10 August 1976, 'Changes likely,'
p. 13). Following the IMF approval of Britain's first credit tranche and
oil facility stand-bys in late 1975, *The Financial Times* commented
that the loans constituted 'virtually an unsolicited IMF testimonial to
present official policies' and provided 'a strong motive for the Government to stick to the policies it has declared, but not to prepare fiercer
ones' (2 January 1976, 'IMF approves,' p. 20). Nonetheless, fiercer
policies were enacted in July. As late as August, *The Times* reported
that it was 'probable that the Government and the IMF share a wide
measure of agreement about the conduct of domestic financial policy
at present. An application for the second credit tranche . . . would not
involve a drastic change in direction with more spending cuts and higher
interest rates' (2 August 1976, 'Government rebuts,' p. 15). The view
that the IMF would not require additional policy changes should the
UK seek higher credit tranche drawings was held at the most senior
levels of the Government. At an Economic Strategy Cabinet Committee meeting in early August, the Chancellor was asked what conditions
would be imposed if the UK went to the IMF; Healey replied that
Britain could borrow from the Fund on existing policy (private political diaries of Tony Benn, 2 August 1976). Callaghan (1987: 423) recounts that he 'expected the Chancellor to have little difficulty' in
negotiating and arranging such a loan.

Inside the UK Treasury, there was active discussions of an IMF
application, but 'it was understood that the Government wanted to hang
on at least until after what was likely to be a tough annual [Labour
Party] Conference was out of the way,' which was scheduled for the
last week of September (Whitehead 1985: 188). At a meeting of the
Cabinet Economic Strategy Committee on 23 September, the Chancellor proposed to approach the IMF for an additional loan, telling his
colleagues that he expected to start loan negotiations at the upcoming

IMF annual meeting and that he expected no basic changes in the Government's economic policies. Ministers agreed that the Government would apply to the IMF, 'but no announcement was made as Healey did not wish it to be known before he attended the annual IMF Conference' (Dell 1991: 235–6; private political diaries of Tony Benn, 23 September 1976; Fay and Young 1978, 1: 35).

It is unclear how seriously Healey's stated expectation of no policy change was taken by his colleagues. While the position may have been Healey's genuinely held view, it was also a pragmatic stance for the Chancellor to take *vis-à-vis* Cabinet colleagues whose approval he needed (see private political diaries of Tony Benn, 23 September 1976; Bernstein 1983: 504, fn 88; Burk and Cairncross 1992: 57). Callaghan (1987: 422–3) suggests that the decision to apply to the IMF occurred simultaneously with his own decision to seek additional reductions in the Government's public expenditure plans; this account is suspect, however, in that it permits Callaghan to hold the position that his Government did not cave in to IMF pressure, but rather that he had already decided upon the need for expenditure cuts when the IMF application was made. Moreover, the Prime Minister's account is uncorroborated. The Treasury official responsible for public expenditure Leo Pliatzky (1982: 152) has recounted that 'there was *no* disposition in the Government to make concessions on their policies in order to get an IMF loan' (my emphasis), and according to Denis Healey (1989: 430–1), Callaghan never expressed to him any support for expenditure cuts until the high-point of the ensuing crisis in early December (see also Witteveen 1987: 31; Dell 1991: 252–3).

The annual Labour Party Conference was expected to be difficult for the Government, given the widening distance between party pledges (see Labour Party 1976a) and the direction of economic policy. In the weeks leading up to the Conference, attention focused on a party resolution calling upon the Government to nationalize private banks and insurance companies (Labour Party 1976b: 308). According to Minister for Energy Tony Benn (1989: 611), Callaghan 'was really worried about the bank and insurance nationalisation demands. . . . He and Denis agreed that if it were passed at the Conference the pound would fall. . . . Jim was absolutely convinced that if it was passed it would be disastrous.' The Government was also receiving pressure from the trade unions for import controls and reflationary measures. At a TUC–Labour Party Liaison Committee meeting prior to the Conference, TUC General Secretary Len Murray presented the argument for import controls 'very strongly,' arguing that unemployment was a problem, the TUC wanted economic expansion to create more jobs, and import controls were the key. 'The TUC was not interested in theoretical debate about import controls and retaliation. The TUC approached the issue in a more practical way by pointing to the constraint posed by the balance of trade to faster expansion' (private political diaries of Tony Benn, 20 September 1976; TUC–Labour Party Liaison Committee Minutes, 20 September 1976; *The Guardian*, 21 September 1976, 'A plain view,' pp. 1, 22; see also Taylor 1987: 73; Dell 1991: 242–5).

Three days before the Conference began, the Prime Minister sought to pre-empt the bank and insurance nationalization resolution by making public his position that the Government would not introduce such legislation during the life of the current Parliament, nor would it accept its inclusion in Labour's next election manifesto (*The Times*, 25 September 1976, 'Bank nationalisation,' p. 1). The Chancellor also sought to pre-empt on the subject of import controls; in a televised interview, Healey firmly rejected both import controls and import deposits, stating 'I see absolutely no employment advantage from either so long as I can run the economy as fast as it can run. . . . I don't believe that import controls can help.' In the interview, Healey also indicated that he had not yet made up his mind to apply to the IMF for an additional stand-by, but if he did decide to go to the Fund, it would be on the assumption that Britain could obtain the necessary assistance without changes in fiscal policy. The Government's current policies of monetary growth at 12 per cent and cutting public sector borrowing, Healey argued, would be likely to satisfy the Fund (*Financial Times*, 27 September 1976, 'Healey rejects,' p. 1).

But as the Party Conference approached, sterling began to sink rapidly. On 23 September the pound closed at a record low of $1.7115 with no evident support from the Bank of England (*Financial Times*, 24 September 1976, 'New low,' p. 1; 'Whitehall considers defences,' pp. 1, 40). On the day the Conference began, 27 September, sterling fell through the 'psychological barrier' of $1.70 to close at another record low of $1.6810. On the morning of 28 September, the Chancellor and the Governor of the Bank of England went to Heathrow airport outside central London for their scheduled departure to attend a Commonwealth Finance Ministers conference in Hong Kong and the IMF annual meeting in Manila. Healey (1987: 68) has recounted that as he prepared to leave,

> the pound went into a free-fall. . . . About every quarter of an hour, the pound dropped another cent . . . It seemed like the end of the

world. . . . In those days, there was no way of communicating when you were in the air. So I was going to be out of contact with my advisers for seventeen hours. I decided in the airport lounge that I couldn't afford that.

(See also Healey 1989: 428–9)

Prior to returning to central London, the Chancellor telephoned the Prime Minister. According to Callaghan (1987: 427–8), Healey told him that the Bank of England was forecasting a daily drop in sterling of about one cent to as low as $1.50 and that Bank was considering drawing on the reserves for sterling support. 'I said I was not in favour of spending a substantial sum from the reserves to bolster a falling rate. . . . I asked him whether a public announcement [of the UK's IMF application] would help to steady sterling. If not, I would prefer to sweat it out.'

The Chancellor's abrupt decision at Heathrow to stay in Britain was a clear indication that the Government was not in control of the situation. As Callaghan (1987: 428) recounts, 'hysterical panic set in for forty-eight hours. The markets behaved with all the restraint of a screaming crowd of schoolgirls at a rock concert.' Sterling fell by a total of 4.3 cents – its largest single-day fall ever outside of a formal devaluation – to close at yet another record low of $1.63775 (*Financial Times*, 29 September 1976, 'Pound loses 4c,' pp. 1, 36). That evening, Healey assembled his Treasury advisers for an emergency meeting. He recounts 'the only thing to do was to announce that we were going to the IMF, because that was the only thing that would hold the markets' The Prime Minister concurred (Whitehead 1985: 188; Healey 1989: 429; Callaghan 1987: 428). The following day, the Government announced that it would be seeking an IMF stand-by for the full amount of its remaining tranches. According to Healey (1989: 429), 'it was the lowest point of my period at the Treasury. For the first and last time in my life, for about twelve hours, I was close to demoralisation.'

At the Labour Party Conference in Blackpool, Callaghan sought to reassure the panicked financial markets; his Conference speech contained one paragraph that, as he seemingly boasts in his memoirs (1987: 425), 'made the fur fly' in which he not only chided the Party, but also seemed to repudiate the past thirty years of British economic management (Holmes 1985: 92–3).

For too long, perhaps since the war, we postponed facing up to fundamental choices and fundamental changes in our society and in our economy. . . . For too long this country – all of us, yes, this Conference too – has been ready to settle for borrowing money abroad to maintain our standards of life, instead of grappling with the fundamental problem of British industry. . . . We used to think that you could spend your way out of a recession and increase employment by cutting taxes and boosting Government spending. I tell you in all candour that that option no longer exists, and that insofar as it ever did exist, it only worked on each occasion since the war by injecting a bigger dose of inflation into the economy, followed by a higher level of unemployment.

(Callaghan 1987: 425–6; Labour Party 1976b: 185–94)

Callaghan (1987: 427) has noted that the speech was quoted 'extensively and approvingly throughout Europe and America.'[4] According to White House economic adviser Robert Hormats, the speech 'demonstrated to us that the UK had changed course. . . . With it, we could point to a genuine turn-around in thinking in Whitehall which merited our support' (Keegan and Pennant-Rea 1979: 166).

The Prime Minister telephoned West German Chancellor Helmut Schmidt and US President Gerald Ford to tell them 'how I saw the situation' (Callaghan 1987: 429; Daily Diary of the President, 29 September 1976). From Schmidt, Callaghan obtained a commitment that he would come to the UK in October 'to talk things over' (Callaghan 1987: 429). With Ford, Callaghan explained that 'we needed two things. First, an early intimation that a stand-by loan would be forthcoming. . . . Second, . . . sterling needed long-term protection against the volatility arising from . . . overseas holdings of sterling. In other words, we needed a safety net.' Although the President expressed concerns about the possibility of British import restrictions, according to Callaghan (1987: 429–30), 'Ford readily undertook to do everything in his power to be helpful on both matters.'

The Chancellor gave televised interviews about the IMF application, stating publicly his expectation that 'the condition [from the Fund] will be that we stick to the policy we've already got. I believe that in the fiscal field what we've already done will meet the requirements of those who lend to us. I think they may want rather more precision about monetary targets, though not a change in the monetary targets which I've indicated as guidelines earlier this year' (London Press Service, 29 September 1976, 'Chancellor's TV interviews;' *IMF Survey*, 4 October 1976, p. 301). The Prime Minister also in a televised interview echoed the message that the IMF would not require significant policy change 'because the policies the Government is following command a great deal of acceptance abroad. There is no doubt that those responsible for lending us money are impressed by the way the British people are facing this situation' (*The Guardian*, 1 October 1976, 'No strings,' p. 22).

With the Prime Minister's permission, the Chancellor flew to Blackpool to appear at the Party Conference to speak in debate on an emergency statement that asked the Conference 'to give its wholehearted support to the Government in resisting the present attack on the pound' (Labour Party 1976b: 317). Healey (1989: 429) recounts that the debate was already underway when he arrived and that 'the mood was ugly.' The Chancellor told the Conference 'I do not come with a Treasury view, I come from the battlefront,' and he urged caution. 'An unwise resolution, an ill-judged statement, can knock £200 million off the reserves in a minute, or if the rate goes down, it can add 20p to the price of the goods in your shopping bag in a minute – and that has happened before now' (Labour Party 1976b: 318–19). He attacked the 'siege economy' alternative of import controls, describing it as 'a recipe for a world trade war and a return to the conditions of the thirties. . . . General import controls – and do not kid yourselves that selective import controls is an alternative – means an immediate increase in the cost of living, an immediate fall in the standard of living, an immediate increase in unemployment, and immediate problems throughout our economy [*shouts from the floor*]. . . . How long do you think this Government would run under the sort of circumstances I have described?' (Labour Party 1976b: 319). To avert the collapse of the Government, Healey argued, 'we have got to stick to the policy we have got,' and he repeated what he had said in previous interviews:

> I am going to negotiate with the IMF on the basis of our existing policies, not changes in policies, and I need your support to do it [*applause*]. But when I say 'existing policies,' I mean things we do not like as well as things we do like. It means sticking to the very painful cuts in public expenditure [*shouts from the floor*] on which the Government has already decided. It means sticking to a pay policy which enables us . . . to continue the attack on inflation [*shouts of 'resign'*]. It means seeing that the increase in our output which has now begun goes not into public or private spending, but into exports or investment. That is what it means and that is what I am asking for. That is what I am going to negotiate for and I ask Conference to support me in my task [*applause*].
>
> (Labour Party 1976b: 319)

With Healey's absence from the IMF meeting in Manila, it was left

to Permanent Secretary to the Treasury Douglas Wass to represent the
UK, and Wass duly echoed the Government's public confidence that
any loan conditionality would not go beyond the kind of economic
policies that the British were already pursuing (*The Times*, 1 October
1976, 'Britain's IMF delegate,' p. 17; *Daily Telegraph*, 1 October 1976,
'£ erratic,' pp. 1, 36; Wass 1976, 1984: 48–9). But the timing of the
announcement of Britain's intention and expectation to borrow 'on
existing policies' was not opportune. IMF Managing Director Witteveen
in his public address at the meeting (1976c: 16–17) asserted that the
post-1974 period of easy financing for deficit countries was now over
(see Chapter 7). UK Executive Director to the IMF William Ryrie recounts 'squirming through a meeting in which Arthur Burns . . . just
gave us a hell of a time. . . . The gist of what we were saying was, we
need some more money, we need some more time, we need an extension of the stand-by credit, and Burns was saying 'no way''' (Burk
and Cairncross 1992: 57).

In the view of the IMF historian, because Denis Healey did not
attend the IMF meeting, the opportunity for 'frank, face-to-face talks'
was lost, and this missed opportunity may have contributed to subsequent problems (De Vries 1985, 1: 468). According to Managing Director Witteveen (1987: 31), the subsequent negotiations were 'difficult'
because of the UK's opening position: 'they came to the Fund saying,
"Our policies are all right, so now we want to draw the full four tranches
from the Fund." And it was a very considerable amount of money for
that time. Of course, we didn't agree that their policies were right.' At
a press conference in early October, Witteveen made it clear that normal channels would be followed *vis-à-vis* the British application: 'The
mission of the Fund will have to visit the United Kingdom to discuss
with the authorities the economic situation, their policies, the needs
for adjustment. In light of that, they will negotiate conditions of the
drawing and the amount of the drawing that can be made' (*IMF Survey*, 18 October 1976, p. 318). He categorically rejected suggestions
that IMF funds should be made available more easily, 'on the contrary, in the aftermath of recent world economic problems, the Fund's
conditionality tests are essential and should be kept intact' (*Sunday
Times*, 3 October 1976, 'Amount of IMF loan,' p. 1).

The British delegation at the IMF meeting sent 'insistent' cables to
London recommending that interest rates go up: 'it was not just the
Treasury and the Bank officials who thought that: everyone in Manila
did' (Fay and Young 1978, 1: 35). In light of sterling's weakness, the
renewed drying up of demand for gilts, and the expansionary effects

these two factors were having on money supply growth, the Chancellor in early October concurred (Browning 1986: 83; Healey 1989: 430; *Bank of England Quarterly Bulletin*, December 1976, pp. 409, 418; *Financial Times*, 7 October 1976, 'Sterling again,' p. 1). Healey (1987: 68) recounts that Bank of England Governor Gordon Richardson 'persuaded me that we needed to raise interest rates to 15 per cent, which was unheard of in those days, in order to sell enough gilts to get money under control. But I was also persuaded by him that we could then get them down within a year to 12 or 10 per cent, which was roughly the level of inflation.' According to Healey (1980: 21), this decision was 'politically, the most difficult of all the decisions I had to take.' When he brought the proposed increase to the Prime Minister, Callaghan refused to permit it; when Healey insisted upon taking the matter to Cabinet, Callaghan replied, 'all right, but I will not support you.' Healey (1989: 430–1) recounts, 'I knew I had no chance of persuading my colleagues without Jim's support. We both knew that I would have to resign if I was defeated.' He returned to his office to discuss the matter with Minister of Trade Edmund Dell – 'the only member of Cabinet on whom I could count' – when the Prime Minister's Private Secretary arrived to deliver a message from Callaghan that the Prime Minister 'was only testing the strength of your conviction. Of course he will support you' (Healey 1989: 431; Dell 1991: 238; see also Fay and Young 1978, 1: 35, 2: 33; Whitehead 1985: 190–1; Burk and Cairncross 1992: 61). Thus, with Callaghan's reluctant support, the Cabinet was informed on the following day of the rate increase. But as Minister of Trade Edmund Dell (1991: 238) notes, 'this incident must have created considerable doubt in Healey's mind as to how far he could rely on the Prime Minister's support.'

Monetary policy was also being tightened in other ways. The rate increase was accompanied by a call for special deposits from the banking system, which reduced domestic liquidity.[5] Two weeks later, publicly announced monetary growth targets were formally and unambiguously adopted when the Chancellor referred to the 12 per cent monetary growth 'forecast' as a 'severe target' and the Governor of the Bank of England announced that 'it is right to have a publicly-announced monetary target' and that the current M3 target was 12 per cent (Healey 1976c; Richardson 1976b: 454; Cobham 1991: 42; see also Richardson 1977a: 48). The IMF historian has pointed to Richardson's comments as evidence of the Governor's efforts (in light of the 'well known' emphases the IMF placed on credit and monetary restraint) 'to line up public support for whatever conditions might be necessary' from the Fund (De Vries 1985, 1: 470).

With loan negotiations lying ahead, Callaghan in early October made a plea for Cabinet unity. 'We have got to stick together now. I know it is very difficult for people who disagree, but if any impression gets about that there is disagreement within the Cabinet, then it does weaken our intent, people don't know where they are' (Benn 1989: 620). On the Cabinet right, Healey and Minister of Trade Edmund Dell must have found the Prime Minister's appeal for unity bitterly ironic, given the recent near-resignation of the Chancellor. On the Cabinet left, Minister of the Environment Peter Shore summed up the unhappiness, stating 'I don't mind sticking with the policy if it is working, but this one has failed.' He and Minister of Energy Tony Benn again advocated import controls (Benn 1989: 620–1). Callaghan 'by no means ruled these suggestions out,' confessing to Cabinet that 'the longer I am Prime Minister, the less sure I am that I know what is right and what is wrong' (Dell 1991: 238; Benn 1989: 622).

STERLING BALANCES, OCTOBER 1976

During the weeks before the loan negotiations began, the Prime Minister actively sought help from the Germans and the Americans on sterling balances, having raised the issue with Chancellor Schmidt and President Ford when the British loan application was announced. Schmidt visited Britain on the weekend of 9–10 October for talks; Callaghan told Minister for Energy Tony Benn that his plan with Schmidt was to have 'a long, comprehensive financial talk. . . . Schmidt has got $32 billion in reserves. They could fund the entire sterling balances' (Benn 1989: 624). According to Callaghan (1987: 431), Schmidt had been to the United States and found both President Ford and US Secretary of State Henry Kissinger 'sympathetic' to Britain's problems, but Secretary of the Treasury William Simon and Governor of the Federal Reserve System Arthur Burns were 'unhelpful.' When Callaghan asked Schmidt about German assistance in stabilizing the sterling balances, Schmidt in reply 'unfolded the picture of the German currency reserves. They were largely held in dollars and financed the American deficit. . . . If Germany were to recall part of her dollar reserves, this, together with similar assistance from the United States and one or two other countries, would make it possible to devise a plan that would offset the instability of the sterling overseas balances and bring much-needed relief. He promised to follow up this idea with the Americans' (see also Fay and Young 1978, 2: 33; Bernstein 1983: 450–1).

It was apparent, however, that there was disagreement among the

German authorities about whether Germany would or should assist the British with sterling balances. Simultaneous to the Callaghan–Schmidt talks, an unnamed German monetary official commented in the press upon the need for 'internal discipline' rather than 'large borrowings' (*Sunday Times*, 10 October 1976, 'Thumbs down,' p. 53). As an anonymous official in the British Cabinet Office recounts, what Schmidt 'had said expansively over dinner, his officials resisted right from the start. But Callaghan kept trying. [German Finance Ministry official] Pöhl was against it. Under the German constitution, it's not Schmidt's money, it belongs to the Bundesbank, and that was Pöhl's line' (Bernstein 1983: 451, 438, fn 65; see also Burk and Cairncross 1992: 66). American officials were adamantly opposed to any international funding arrangement for sterling balances in advance of the completion of the IMF negotiations (Bernstein 1983: 442–3, 449). When Under-Secretary for Monetary Affairs Edwin Yeo visited London in late September, 'Yeo threatened that Britain would not get the IMF loan at all if Callaghan continued to try to have a safety net for sterling. "It's very dangerous ground," said Yeo. "If you sign up with the IMF and take appropriate action, the balances will look after themselves"' (Fay and Young 1978, 2: 33; see also Lever 1989).

Callaghan in his memoirs (1987: 432) expresses exasperation with international financial officials who 'used the excuse that they wished the completion of the IMF negotiations to take place first. These officials were so short-sighted that they were unable to understand that the announcement of [a sterling balances] scheme would have made these negotiations more acceptable and enabled us to conclude them with less political difficulty.' The strength of the Prime Minister's determination *vis-à-vis* sterling balances was made clear in a televised interview in late October. Asked why the pound continued to be so vulnerable, the Prime Minister replied, 'basically it's because we are a reserve currency and I must say I rue it. . . . I would very much like to see us get into a position where these liabilities in ourselves which we have as a reserve currency were taken over in some form or another . . . I think Germany and the United States and perhaps Japan have got some responsibility here. They have got vast reserves' (Browning 1986: 86). In the interview, Callaghan linked the sterling balances to Britain's responsibilities and burdens as a NATO ally; according to *The Times*, 'the Prime Minister said Britain's contribution to the British Army on the Rhine was heavy and he did not want to have to choose between the country's short-term economic crisis and her contribution to NATO. "If we are to be equal partners in trying to keep the political stability of central Europe, then there is something which can be done"' (26 October 1976, 'Callaghan plea,' p. 1). The Germans and Americans faced important choices in how to respond to Britain's economic difficulties, Callaghan argued. 'If we are pushed into a position where we would have to make a choice between whether we carry on with these responsibilities or we have to say, "Sorry, our economic situation demands that we put our own position first," this would be a very serious matter for Europe' (Bernstein 1983: 453). The IMF also had a responsibility, Callaghan asserted, and would have to be 'very careful. . . . They will have to say, is it right to try to force Britain into courses which, unless the sterling balances are met in some other way, could be very harmful to the whole politics and the whole nature not only of Britain but of the West' (Browning 1986: 86). In Parliament the following day, Callaghan repeated his view that Britain's allies faced a choice: 'If they wish – as they do – to preserve the influence that Britain has politically, and which they value very much, and if they value the contribution Britain has to make, they should have regard to our problems in relation to our overhang of sterling balances' (*Financial Times*, 27 October 1976, 'Callaghan stands firm,' p. 12).

American officials responded to Callaghan's interview by reiterating to the press that the sterling balances problem should be settled after the IMF loan was completed and one unnamed US source noted dismissively that Callaghan's remarks needed to be seen in a domestic political context (*Financial Times*, 27 October 1976, 'Problem,' p. 32; *The Times*, 30 October 1976, 'Speculation,' pp. 1, 17). Some US Treasury officials did not think that Callaghan's attempt to link sterling balances with the UK's NATO burdens was credible, while economic advisers in the White House interpreted Callaghan's emphasis on sterling balances as 'a statement to the effect that no further stabilization measures were needed' (Bernstein 1983: 453–4; US Council of Economic Advisers 1976b; interview material). The German response was also varied. On one hand, Bundesbank officials made clear their view that any help with sterling balances should not proceed until the British had successfully negotiated the IMF loan; on the other hand, German government officials reportedly were trying to ensure that the conditions accompanying the IMF loan would be, as an unnamed Bonn official put it, 'a compromise between what is desirable and what is politically possible' (*The Guardian*, 27 October 1976, 'Bundesbank delays,' p. 17; *Financial Times*, 27 October 1976, 'Bonn seeks,' p. 32; *The Times*, 27 October 1976, 'Germany and Japan,' p. 21; *The Times*, 28 October 1976, 'Bonn reaffirms,' p. 21).

US Under-Secretary for Monetary Affairs Edwin Yeo became concerned by suggestions of equivocation in the German position on sterling balances and flew to Germany in late October to meet with Schmidt. 'He found, to his relief, that he was preaching to the converted. Schmidt's own advisers had been insisting that Germany must not undermine the IMF, no matter how keen the Chancellor was to help Callaghan.' After Yeo's visit, 'Schmidt remained worried and sympathetic, but he was not willing to act unilaterally to help the British' (Fay and Young 1978, 2: 34; Bernstein 1983: 451–2). Callaghan (1987: 432), however, contradicts this account. On 5 November he had a 'long telephone conversation' with Schmidt.

> From this emerged an unexpected offer that was to be of tremendous reassurance during the difficult weeks that followed. . . . Without any request or prompting from me, Helmut Schmidt said he felt Germany must be ready to act when required, in order to make the British Government feel a little more secure. Therefore, on a personal basis, he undertook that if ever an acute danger of necessity should arise, Britain could draw upon Germany within twenty-four hours, and the German Government would make whatever improvised arrangements were necessary. . . . Since he had asked me to regard this assurance as a personal one, I told only the Chancellor and then arranged for the Secretary of the Cabinet, Sir John Hunt, to pay a private visit to Bonn in order that both sides should be clear about what would be done if we ever needed his proffered assistance.

Callaghan's account is not corroborated by Healey (1989: 430), however, who recounts that the Prime Minister 'tried hard to persuade Helmut Schmidt and President Ford to offer unconditional assistance. Neither was willing. . . . Though I think Schmidt tried hard to convince his German colleagues, in the end both [the German and US] governments said they would not be prepared to make such arrangements [for sterling balances] before we had reached agreement with the IMF.'

STERLING'S PERSISTENT WEAKNESS AND THE START OF NEGOTIATIONS, LATE OCTOBER–EARLY NOVEMBER 1976

Exchange market pressure intensified still further in late October when sterling plunged to a new record low in response to a press account that outlined reported terms upon which Britain would be offered the

IMF stand-by and upon which the US and the IMF had reportedly agreed. According to *The Sunday Times* (24 October 1976, 'The Price Britain faces,' p. 1), 'the Fund thinks that sterling should be let down to about $1.50 ... (against today's $1.64) so that Britain's exports become more attractively priced. After the $1.50 figure is reached, sterling should be "managed" with a view to eliminating our balance of payments deficit in 1978'[6] (24 October 1976, 'The Price Britain faces,' p. 1). The story had a devastating impact on sterling. When exchange markets opened on Monday, 25 October, sterling slid by eight cents within the first two hours, recovering somewhat later in the day to close at $1.5950, but nevertheless setting a new record one-day drop of five cents (*The Times*, 26 October 1976, 'Bank support fails,' p. 1). 'Since the markets now believed that it was official policy to go down to $1.50, why should anyone hold sterling at $1.70?' (Donoughue 1987: 92). The pound continued to weaken over the remainder of the week, hitting $1.5550 for a time and recovering only somewhat at the week's end on a rumor that the Government was seeking to negotiate a £7–£10 billion loan that would fund the sterling balances (*The Times*, 29 October 1976, 'Simonet caution', p. 19; *The Times*, 30 October 1976, 'Speculation on huge loan,' pp. 1, 17; *Financial Times*, 30 October 1976, '£ closes,' pp. 1, 22; *Bank of England Quarterly Bulletin*, December 1976, p. 430).

Denials of the *Sunday Times* story were swift and unequivocal. US Treasury Secretary Simon called the article 'irresponsible and patently untrue ... Negotiations of any British drawing from the IMF is and shall remain a matter to be resolved solely by those two parties.' Deputy IMF Managing Director William Dale denied the report as well, stating that it had 'absolutely no basis in fact. The Fund does not and cannot determine its views on detailed measures until after careful examination of the economic indicators on the spot' (*The Times*, 25 October 1976, 'Negotiations,' p. 17). The truth of the report continues to be disputed. On one hand, the report's author Malcolm Crawford (1989: 173) argues that Denis Healey confirms the story in his memoirs (Healey 1989: 430) when he acknowledges that 'some IMF officials wanted a much lower exchange rate for sterling than the governments for whom they were supposed to speak.' On the other hand, the head of the soon-to-arrive IMF mission Alan Whittome has 'stated emphatically that "no one was talking about $1.50"' (Burk and Cairncross 1992: 68, 74). Significantly, the IMF's official historian avoids direct comment on the report's veracity, stating only that 'the Fund had to issue denials' in light of the market reaction (De Vries 1985, 1: 470).

According to Healey (1989: 434), the central claim of the article was 'patent nonsense as reported, since both the US Treasury and the IMF Board thought the pound was undervalued at that time. . . . But I suspect it reflected the views of some IMF official who still believed depreciation would engender an "automatic adjustment process".'

It is possible that all of the conflicting accounts[7] have some element of truth to them. The Fund as a rule does not hold a single view on technical matters when approaching stand-by negotiations, and Fund positions can and do evolve (Stiles 1991: 26–7, 34; interview material; Whitehead 1985: 191). However, 'perhaps the most remarkable aspect of the incident is the way in which an inherently implausible story, firmly denied on all sides, was so readily accepted by the markets' (Browning 1986: 85). In the UK Treasury, the market's reaction had underscored that the confidence issue simply had to be addressed and that there appeared to be 'no floor whatsoever' that was too low for sterling (interview material). As the US Council of Economic Advisers (1976b) matter-of-factly described the situation for the President, 'it is clear that the sterling rate will continue to be unstable and in fact, on balance, to erode further until a satisfactory economic program is announced.'

A six-person IMF negotiating team arrived on 1 November. The team was led by the head of the IMF's European Department and former Bank of England official Alan Whittome; also included was Deputy Director of the IMF's Exchange and Trade Relations Department C. David Finch, who was a member of past IMF negotiating teams sent to London in the 1960s[8] (De Vries 1985, 2: 1026; Finch 1989). Both the British and the IMF negotiators 'feared the repercussions if the Bank of England ran out of reserves' (Bernstein 1983: 488). On 2 November, the Bank published figures showing that reserves had fallen by $455 million in October to stand at $4.7 billion, the lowest level in five years (*Financial Times*, 3 November 1976, 'UK reserves fall,' p. 36). The $1.6 billion that the British had drawn from the June central bank stand-by was due for repayment on 9 December. As an anonymous member of the IMF negotiating team recounts, 'you come and they've got a problem, they're running out of money. They couldn't hide behind controls, so they must reestablish confidence and must figure out how. The real thing was to stop speculation against the pound' (Bernstein 1983: 488).

The British tended to drag their feet at the early negotiating sessions with the IMF. Dwindling reserves notwithstanding, the IMF team was told that the economic forecasts upon which the Fund would base its analysis of the British economy were not yet ready (Fay and Young 1978, 2: 33–4). However, this was at best only a partial explanation for the initial lack of progress.[9] Another almost certainly more important reason for British foot-dragging was political. As Denis Healey recounts (1987: 68), 'the Prime Minister was very nervous about the political consequences of bringing in the IMF, so he kept the IMF team . . . hanging around their hotel for a week or two before he would allow any Treasury officials to talk to them' (see also Healey 1989: 430; Bernstein 1983: 492; Burk and Cairncross 1992: 70).

The awaited National Income Forecasts were presented to the Cabinet Economic Strategy Committee on 3 November and were discussed indirectly in Cabinet the following day (Barnett 1982: 101–2; Benn 1989: 635–8; Dell 1991: 252–3; private political diaries of Tony Benn, 4 November 1976). The Treasury's 1977–78 PSBR forecast had risen from the £9 billion estimate during the summer to £11 billion,[10] with unemployment rising to 1.75 million (Benn 1989: 636; Dell 1991: 252; Barnett 1982: 102). The increases were largely due to lowered growth expectations and pressures on public expenditure associated with rising unemployment (private political diaries of Tony Benn, 3 November 1976; *Financial Times*, 6 November 1976, 'On unchanged policies,' p. 1; see also Brittan 1977: 91).

Ministerial reaction to the deteriorating economic outlook can be divided into three factions – left, center, and right – that would dominate Cabinet discussion during the following weeks. On the left, Leader of the House of Commons Michael Foot argued that 'the unemployment level is unacceptable and we will have to have import controls put on the agenda again' (Benn 1989: 636). Minister of the Environment Peter Shore concurred, declaring that 'all our targets have collapsed at the same time. We do have a PSBR problem but though important, it's secondary' (Benn 1989: 637). Foot, Shore, Minister of Energy Tony Benn, and Minister of Employment Albert Booth all advocated import controls over additional deflation (Benn 1989: 637; private political diaries of Tony Benn, 3 November 1976). In the center, Minister for Education Shirley Williams 'rejected dealing with the situation by public expenditure cuts, rejected import controls, and favoured a huge loan' (Benn 1989: 637). The case against import controls, she argued, 'is that the IMF would have to agree, which they wouldn't' (private political diaries of Tony Benn, 3 November 1976). Chancellor of the Duchy of Lancaster Harold Lever also rejected protectionism – 'in 1978, the balance of payments problem will be solved anyway' – and argued that the UK could get the loan on current policies; 'we should say to the IMF "don't push us too far" and indeed, we should have said it ages ago. The Social Contract is our greatest asset' (private political diaries of Tony Benn, 3 November 1976). Foreign Secretary Tony Crosland would later become the nominal leader of this center faction.

On the right and in relative isolation, Minister of Trade Edmund Dell bluntly warned his colleagues that 'there was no escape except for major cuts which would be a main condition of the loan' (Benn 1989: 637; Dell 1991: 253). The Chancellor of the Exchequer more euphemistically called for 'reshaping' the PSBR to fortify confidence, but it was clear additional expenditure cuts would be involved. Regarding import controls, Healey noted that other countries had even higher unemployment than Britain, that retaliation was 'certain,' and that the US, Germany, and the IMF would neither allow nor accept them (Benn 1989: 637; private political diaries of Tony Benn, 3 November 1976). According to Dell (1991: 253), 'there was no conclusion to the discussion because what Healey was proposing was unacceptable to a majority of the [Economic Strategy] Committee, and yet there was no agreement about alternatives.'

Healey (1989: 381) has argued that the £11 billion 1977–78 PSBR forecast was twice what it should have been and was one of the primary causes of the subsequent crisis: 'if I had been given accurate forecasts in 1976, I would never have needed to go to the IMF at all' (see also Healey 1980: 21–2). Some suspected that the £11 billion figure was 'massaged upwards' by Treasury hard-liners who wanted the IMF to be tough with the Government on public expenditure (Crawford 1983: 432); as an anonymous Policy Unit official recounts, 'I thought [the Treasury] were manipulating it, but you can't prove it' (Bernstein 1983: 494). Doubts about the integrity and loyalty of Treasury officials began to appear in the press; reportedly, there was a 'growing suspicion that some senior officials, though not actually sabotaging the negotiations with the IMF, are trying to use the loan application as a lever to impose their own political values on the elected government of the country' (*The Times*, 8 November 1976, 'Government seeking,' p. 1; see also *The Guardian*, 28 October 1976, 'Divide or Rule?' p. 12). Chief Secretary to the Treasury Joel Barnett (1982: 104) recounts that these suspicions were shared by at least one Cabinet minister who 'claimed to have a reliable report that a senior Treasury official had told Washington to be firm and we would cut public expenditure by the required amount.'[11]

According to Treasury official Leo Pliatzky (1982: 138–47), one of the primary reasons for the PSBR overestimation was the failure to take account of the extent of under-spending that was occurring as a result of the introduction of 'cash limits,' a system of expenditure control that had been extended to cover three-quarters of Government spending by early 1976 (Middlemas 1991: 103; Burk and Cairncross 1992: 15, 184–6). Cash limits 'convinced departments that if they overspent they would run out of money and there would be no more. . . . And so at each level in departments, those responsible for controlling budgets were holding something back and not committing it' (Pliatzky 1989a: 44). The consequence was substantial, though unplanned, under-spending. Although in real terms public expenditure had been planned to rise by 2.5 per cent, in the event it fell by 2 per cent (Browning 1986: 94; Jackson 1991: 84). But because the under-spending was unplanned and hidden from view, it had no impact on confidence where 'what mainly mattered was not reality, but the market's perception of what appeared to be going on' (Fay and Young 1978, 1: 35; Bernstein 1983: 383–4).

STERLING BALANCES, NOVEMBER 1976

The Prime Minister continued to press for action on sterling balances. In early November, he sent a letter to President Ford 'in which he stressed the intense political difficulties which harsh IMF loan conditions would create and proposed again that the only way the pill could be made less bitter was by creating a safety net for sterling which would enable the British to follow a more expansionist policy' (Fay and Young 1978, 2: 34). Callaghan (1987: 432) recounts that the IMF view was that the British would use a sterling balance loan to evade IMF conditionality and not reduce the PSBR. 'I had met the leader of the IMF team at the Chancellor's request and informed him this was incorrect, but I am not certain he believed me. . . . In an attempt to remove this impression, I asked [Chancellor of the Duchy of Lancaster] Harold Lever to go to Washington to talk to the American Treasury, the IMF,[12] and the Federal Reserve Bank.' According to Callaghan (1987: 433), President Ford agreed 'at once' to receive Lever. The US Treasury and Federal Reserve, however, would have preferred no discussion of sterling balances occur and were not enthusiastic about Lever's visit[13] (Fay and Young 1978, 2: 34; Bernstein 1983: 456). Denis Healey also opposed Lever's trip (Burk and Cairncross 1992: 78).

Lever met first with Treasury Secretary Simon and Under-Secretary for Monetary Affairs Yeo, and then separately with Chairman of the

Federal Reserve Burns and Secretary of State Henry Kissinger (Bernstein 1983: 455; Burk and Cairncross 1992: 78). Lever recounts that he found Simon 'like a brick wall,' while the meeting with Burns was inconclusive (Burk and Cairncross 1992: 78; see also Lever 1989). It was only with Kissinger that Lever received a sympathetic hearing; if a sterling balances arrangement was that important to the Prime Minister, Kissinger suggested, Lever should have Callaghan make a direct telephone appeal to the President (Burk and Cairncross 1992: 78; Lever 1989; see also *The Times*, 16 November 1976, 'Kissinger assurance,' p. 23). The British took up the suggestion, and Callaghan and Ford had a 13-minute telephone conversation just prior to Lever's meeting with the President the following morning (Daily Diary of the President, 16 November 1976).

The American objectives at the Ford–Lever meeting were outlined in a briefing paper prepared for the President by White House adviser Brent Scowcroft (1976b). The meeting was

> an opportunity to indicate our belief that every effort should be made to reach early agreement between Britain and the IMF. ... It will also enable [the President] to underline our position that we cannot outside of the context of such an agreement lend support to any proposals designed to finance sterling balances, as we do not believe that such a step would address the basic problems faced by the UK or constitute an appropriate way of providing any needed additional financing.

Of the meeting itself, Lever has recounted that he argued that a sterling balances arrangement was 'quite separate' from the IMF loan and that the UK would be 'settling with the IMF if they could agree reasonable terms.' He asked Ford for a 'firm undertaking' that once a UK–IMF agreement was reached, 'you would do everything in your power to bring [a sterling balances arrangement] about at the earliest date.' According to Lever, Ford agreed[14] (Burk and Cairncross 1992: 80).

At a press conference following the meeting, Lever said that he had conveyed the message that the British wanted multilateral talks on sterling balances to start as soon as the UK–IMF negotiations were over and that he was confident that 'there would be a positive response within the time required;' resolving the sterling balances question in his opinion was 'neither difficult in principle nor in terms of the mechanics, so long as there is sufficient international goodwill' (*Financial Times*, 17 November 1976, 'UK seeks talks,' pp. 1, 46; *The Times*, 17 November 1976, 'Lever hopes,' p. 27). But it was soon apparent that 'sufficient international goodwill' was going to be a problem. When informed by the press of Lever's comment that the sterling balances problem 'must be dealt with straight away,' Secretary Simon replied that he thought it was 'premature' to talk about financing the sterling balances and that he would be discussing the IMF loan and British economic problems with the President in a few days (*International Herald Tribune*, 18 November 1976, 'UK Aide,' p. 9).

Callaghan was seeking 'simultaneity,' in which the IMF loan and the sterling balances arrangement would be announced at the same time (Fay and Young 1978, 2: 34). During Lever's final evening in Washington, he was informed that the President had not meant to agree to a simultaneous announcement at his meeting with Lever; 'there really was a good possibility that it would all work out, but the administration was making no final commitment [on sterling balances] until the IMF terms had been settled.' Lever reportedly 'blew up,' asking his American hosts 'did he now have to tell the Prime Minister that the President was going back on his word?' (Fay and Young 1978, 2: 34–5). The following morning, US officials tried to clarify what had been agreed at the Ford–Lever meeting. White House adviser Robert Hormats called the British Embassy to say that 'the administration would keep its commitment on the sterling balances – but there was still a question of the mechanics and the timing of the funding.' Secretary of State Kissinger also called: 'Lever should go back to London content, said Kissinger. He should just try and understand that Washington like London had inter-departmental difficulties. These included disagreements about what Ford had actually told Lever, but Kissinger would sort things out' (Fay and Young 1978, 2: 35).

Prior to his departure, Lever telephoned Callaghan and at the Prime Minister's request, the British Embassy sent to the White House a message (British Embassy 1976) that sought to clarify further the British position on simultaneity. 'The Prime Minister's view is that, while initially the whole substance of the IMF terms could be agreed before there is agreement on how best to deal with the problem of sterling balances, it is essential that the finalisation of the IMF loan and an agreement on the sterling balances should be announced simultaneously.' The ambiguity implicit in Kissinger's assurance to Lever that he would 'sort things out' as well as Callaghan's reiteration that simultaneity was 'essential' suggest that neither the Americans nor the British considered the US Government's view on sterling balances to have been settled by Lever's visit. But Callaghan must have been guardedly optimistic: on 17 November he repeated the need for a sterling balances safety net to the Cabinet Economic Strategy Committee and commented that there was sympathy for Britain in the US (Benn 1989: 646; private political diaries of Tony Benn, 17 November 1976).

Two days after Lever's return, American officials held a meeting at the White House to discuss the British economic situation (Daily Diary of the President, 19 November 1976). It is not known what specifically was discussed,[15] but it is reasonable to assume that it was here that the American view on sterling balances was hammered out. The following day, President Ford (1976a) sent a message to Callaghan that further refined the US position on Britain's IMF loan application and Callaghan's sterling balances appeal. Following the introductory pleasantries, the President wrote that the United States was

> encouraged that your government is now actively involved in discussions with representatives of the IMF. . . . In the expectation that your government will, as your message of November 17 suggests,[16] come to substantial agreement on conditions deemed necessary by the Fund to achieve stability, I can assure you that we will, once such agreement has been reached, work sympathetically with you on a responsible way of addressing various aspects of the sterling balances and related concerns. Should a resolution be reached, and we have confidence in prospects for success, it could be announced simultaneously with the announcement of your agreement with the Fund. As your efforts to achieve a major stabilization of Britain's internal and external positions proceed, we hope that you will be able to avoid injurious consequences in the defense and trade areas.
>
> I have obtained support from my colleagues for this approach with a deep sense of your commitment, and that of your government, to a strong and vital Britain, and of appreciation for our nations' deep and long-standing friendship. I hope the negotiations will go well and look forward to hearing soon that agreement with the Fund has been reached.

Given the conflicting signals that Lever had received while in Washington, the President's assurance that 'I have obtained support from my colleagues for this approach' might have been regarded positively in London, but there was little else in the letter that was encouraging. The US view continued to be that a sterling balances arrangement was contingent upon prior agreement with the IMF. Moreover, once agreement with the Fund was reached, the United States was committing itself only to 'work sympathetically' on sterling balances.[17]

In late November, the Federal Reserve staff at Chairman Burns' request produced a paper (Truman 1976) outlining the arguments for and against different approaches to dealing with sterling balances. In the end, the staff recommended against action in part because 'a full refinancing of these balances through official international credits would weaken British efforts to develop and implement an effective stabilization program.' In other words, a sterling balances arrangement would lessen the market pressures that had driven and were driving the British towards IMF conditionality.

NEGOTIATION DIFFICULTIES, NOVEMBER 1976

It was obvious by mid-November that IMF and UK negotiators were thinking in very different terms. 'IMF calculations suggested that the PSBR ought to come down radically: maybe by as much as £4 bn in two years. Also on their programme was stricter controls of the money supply and of Domestic Credit Expansion[18] (DCE)' (Fay and Young 1978, 2: 34). But discussions were still at a preliminary stage: As an IMF staff member recounts, 'there is a negotiating tactic in all this. Before formal discussions I offered fairly large figures – not by mistake. You know it will come down. Each side needs to look victorious' (Bernstein 1983: 504). But the British were 'solidly refusing to play the game according to the Fund's rules' (Fay and Young 1978, 2: 34); an anonymous IMF official recalls that 'in the first stage the British officials had instructions that they weren't allowed to discuss any changes in policies – it was a very tough and uncooperative attitude. This lasted until [IMF negotiating head] Whittome told Healey that if he kept it up he would go back to Washington' (Bernstein 1983: 493; Whitehead 1985: 193).

Confederation of British Industry (CBI) officials met with the Fund mission on 10 November. According to CBI Chief Economic Adviser Donald MacDougall (1989: 45), 'we said . . . we thought a savage deflationary policy would be quite counter-productive from the point of view of the TUC and moreover it would be bad for business confidence. We later sent [Whittome] some notes about the parlous state of company finances.'[19] TUC General Secretary Len Murray met with the IMF team later in the month and took the opportunity to warn Fund negotiators that the incomes policy was in danger: 'if your conditions are too onerous, it will not be a question of Phase Three of incomes policy, there won't be a Phase Two; it will collapse' (Jones 1986: 325; see also Fay and Young 1978, 2: 35; Bernstein 1983: 513; Burk and

Cairncross 1992: 83; *The Times*, 30 November 1976, 'Cuts could imperil,' p. 1). According to the IMF historian, one line of argument inside the Fund 'suggested that the social and political framework of the United Kingdom was under such heavy pressure that the Government's ability to take decisions was impaired.' The Fund management and staff however 'considered these views exaggerated' in light of the Government's successful limitations on public expenditure during the summer, its ability to raise interest rates, and the success of pay policy in reducing the level of wage settlements (De Vries 1985, 1: 468–9). The Fund position appears to have been that since the Government had been able to undertake tough deflationary measures earlier, it could go still further. Accordingly, although both the TUC and CBI had based their opposition to deflation by emphasizing the likely reaction of the unions, these arguments appear to have made little difference in the Fund's negotiating position; as an unnamed IMF staff member recounts, 'that's not the kind of thing that changes opinions' (Bernstein 1983: 513; interview material).

The Chancellor's position was increasingly difficult, not just *vis-à-vis* the IMF negotiating team in London, but also *vis-à-vis* the Prime Minister and Cabinet (Healey 1989: 429–30; 1991: 251; Burk and Cairncross 1992: 83). Despite the fact that the IMF team had been in London since 1 November, a 'mandate to talk to the IMF' was obtained by Healey from the Cabinet Economic Strategy Committee only on 17 November (Benn 1989: 646). Minister of Trade Edmund Dell (1991: 254) recounts that 'Callaghan at first appeared to believe that the Government could dictate to the IMF the terms on which they were to lend to us. Although he had come to accept that the PSBR was the key, it was Healey who had to insist that there had to be a reduced target for the PSBR.'

On 19 November, IMF negotiators presented their PSBR proposals to the British: a £3 billion reduction for 1977–78, rising to £4 billion in 1978–79[20] (Pliatzky 1982: 153). Treasury official Leo Pliatzky (1982: 153, 1989a: 44) recounts that although the IMF 'conceded that it was for the British Government to choose between different ways of reducing the PSBR,' the Fund team was 'talking in terms of achieving [the PSBR reduction] entirely by a reduction in public expenditure.' Pliatzky's view (1982: 153) is that 'it was never on the cards that Treasury ministers would put such proposals to Cabinet, let alone succeed in getting approval for them.' Pliatzky (1989a: 44) has recounted that, in light of the proposals, he asked the Fund team, 'do you want to bring this government down?' IMF negotiating head Alan Whittome replied, 'we are not in the business of bringing governments down.' Pliatzky responded, 'in my judgement, if you pressed for those reductions and succeeded in getting them, you would bring this government down, and you would do great harm to democracy in this country' (see also Pliatzky 1982: 155; Dell 1991: 250).

There was, however, maneuvering room in the Fund's proposals. According to Fund staff, their opening bid was '10 per cent more' than they felt was necessary so that they could later appear flexible (Stiles 1991: 134, 138). When told that their figures were unrealistic, the IMF team 'indicated that these were not their final terms, that they were looking for information, and that they would carefully consider whatever was disclosed' (Dell 1991: 249). On the British side, there was flexibility as well. The Treasury's initial negative response 'did not mean that . . . nothing could be done,' Pliatzky (1982: 153–4) recounts. 'But the negotiating gap was immense. . . . Terms had somehow to be worked out which on the one hand would produce agreement with the IMF and on the other hand would not destroy the Government.'

It was clear that the Cabinet discussions were going to be difficult. Minister of Trade Edmund Dell (1991: 256–7) recounts that the Prime Minister called together 'a small private meeting' of selected ministers 'to discover whether there was any meeting of minds. . . . Denis Healey explained why it was vital that the negotiations with the IMF should be successful. That could only mean further cuts in public expenditure.' Dell and Foreign Secretary Tony Crosland squared off at the meeting. Crosland's argument, which would subsequently be put before Cabinet, was that with 1.25 million unemployed, there was already sufficient spare capacity in the economy for an export-led recovery. Expenditure cuts would only increase unemployment and could thus perversely worsen the PSBR through additional social expenditure and reduced tax revenues. Moreover, expenditure cuts would result in the collapse of Social Contract wage restraint, especially in the public sector (Dell 1991: 257; Benn 1989: 653–4; Crosland 1982: 377–8). 'The only serious argument for cuts was one in terms of international confidence,' Crosland argued. 'But what would happen to confidence if the Government bowed down and accepted the package, and as a result the Social Contract broke, and the smouldering resentment of the [Parliamentary Labour Party] meant that the Government could not deliver the cuts in the House of Commons?' (Crosland 1982: 377). Dell countered by focusing upon the confidence argument: even if Crosland were correct that everything was in place for a British economic recovery, 'the disbelief of the market could undermine it and, indeed, bring down the Government before we reaped the benefit of having at last got everything in place. There was just too strong a basis for the market's lack of confidence for the Government to behave as [Crosland] was proposing. . . . Our application to the IMF had been forced on us by the incredulity of the market and therefore we had to make the choice, to negotiate successfully with the IMF, or to be swept from office' (Dell 1991: 257–8). Callaghan 'made no commitment to either side of the argument. The whole question would have to go to Cabinet. He had wanted to listen' (Dell 1991: 258).

Callaghan (1987: 433–4) has explained that his strategy during this period had three aims: (1) to keep the Government intact by preventing ministerial resignations; (2) to keep the Party together by emphasizing that a failure to support the Cabinet's conclusions would mean a general election; and (3) to avoid a break with the TUC. He recounts that he had indicated to the IMF his own idea of an 'appropriate settlement;' although in agreement that the most recent 1977–78 PSBR forecast of £11 billion could not be sustained, 'I was not willing to go below the £9 billion [PSBR] that the Cabinet had agreed as recently as July. . . . I was ready to go with the IMF as far as was necessary to restore validity to our July estimates, but no further. The IMF took this badly, and the Chancellor and I had to decide what to say to Cabinet.' Callaghan recalls (1987: 434) that 'it would have been best if we could have reached a quick decision, but I knew this would not be possible if we were to remain together, so by instinct more than by rational judgement, I decided not to bring matters to a head. . . . Although I knew how far I was ready to go to secure agreement with the IMF, I saw no advantage in making my position clear at an early stage.'

He did, however, discuss the situation privately and frankly with Foreign Secretary Tony Crosland: 'I said I recognised his intellectual difficulty with our policy – indeed I shared some of his reservations, but supposing his tactics turned out to be wrong? He might think the Government would be in danger from our own supporters if we reduced the following year's expenditure, but did he believe the Government could survive without the loan? If so, how?' (Callaghan 1987: 436–7). Crosland later told his wife that for the first time he wondered whether the Government would survive, but then asked himself 'even if the Government survives, does it make such a difference if Labour measures can't be implemented?' (Crosland 1982: 376). Callaghan (1987: 437) comments of the Foreign Secretary's position that 'I began to get the impression that in the last resort he would regard the break-up of the Government as the lesser evil.'

Within the Cabinet, two factions formed out of ministers opposed to IMF deflation (Bernstein 1983: 550–60; Whitehead 1985: 194–5). On the Cabinet left, Michael Foot (Leader of the House of Commons), Peter Shore (Environment), Tony Benn (Energy), Stan Orme (Social Security), Albert Booth (Employment), and John Silkin (Agriculture) had met among themselves as early as 8 November to discuss their views; a central policy alternative for the group was some kind of employment-preserving restriction on imports (Benn 1989: 639; Burk and Cairncross 1992: 88–9). The 'social democratic' group of ministers met for the first time on 22 November and included Tony Crosland (Foreign Secretary), Shirley Williams (Education), Harold Lever (Chancellor of the Duchy of Lancaster), David Ennals (Social Services), Roy Hattersley (Prices and Consumer Protection), and William Rodgers (Transport). According to Hattersley, everyone who was present opposed public expenditure cuts, but 'their opposition was based on different arguments. Ennals and [Williams] wanted to protect their departments' budgets. Lever, like Hattersley – and [Crosland] – thought the whole exercise unnecessarily deflationary' (Crosland 1982: 377). Of the two groups, Callaghan (1987: 435) recounts that they 'were playing a dangerous game which I was determined to circumvent. It was apparent that if the two groups were to coalesce the Chancellor would not have a majority in support of his negotiating stance.'

There were two additional groups of ministers that, although not organized, were nonetheless important. On the right and in favor of public expenditure cuts were Denis Healey and Edmund Dell (Trade). According to Dell (1991: 259), he and Healey met 'from time to time' during this period, 'but when we met, we were alone.'[21] There was also a group that Bernard Donoughue (1985: 64; 1987: 90–1) has called a 'rump' or 'King's party,' consisting of ministers who 'gave their ultimate support to the Prime Minister, though hoping to minimise the particular cuts in their own departmental budgets.' This ill-defined group was the largest and included Elwyn Jones (Lord Chancellor), Merlyn Rees (Home Secretary), Eric Varley (Industry), Roy Mason (Northern Ireland), Bruce Millan (Scotland), John Morris (Wales), Fred Mulley (Defence), and Fred Peart (Leader of the House of Lords).

The full Cabinet discussed the IMF negotiations for the first time on 23 November. Callaghan opened the discussion by posing the question whether the Government 'could afford to pay the price that the IMF were asking of us. Either way we could go into the abyss' (Benn 1989: 653). The Chancellor outlined the state of the negotiations: the Government had been 'negotiating hard' and the IMF had accepted the

Government's forecast that the PSBR for 1977–78 on unchanged policies was £10.5 billion (revised downward from £11 billion earlier in
the month). 'The IMF think a dramatic improvement is possible. . . .
The IMF would accept £9 billion next year [1977–78] and £6.5 billion
the year after [1978–79]' (Benn 1989: 653). A £9 billion PSBR limit
would require a £1.5 billion reduction from the £10.5 billion forecast,
but the Chancellor told the Cabinet that the IMF would accept a £500
million sale of state-owned shares in British Petroleum as part of the
£1.5 billion. Therefore, the Government would only have to find an
additional £1 billion to reach the proposed ceiling. As the IMF Executive Board would not like the £1 billion to be found through increased
taxation, Healey told the Cabinet, he was therefore proposing expenditure cuts and suggested finding nearly half of the £1 billion by delaying the uprating of social security benefits and pensions (private political
diaries of Tony Benn, 23 November 1976).

Foreign Secretary Tony Crosland spoke next. He pressed the Chancellor on the logic underlying expenditure cuts, pointing out that resources were under-utilized and that the cuts therefore could not be
sold on the grounds of industrial policy. Crosland also was suspicious
that the Treasury's £10.5 billion PSBR forecast (downwardly revised
from £11 billion) would still turn out to be an overestimate; he pointed
out that outside forecasters were predicting a lower figure.[22] Crosland
doubted whether the Social Contract would survive with expenditure
cuts, and the Government's support in the House of Commons would
be further eroded (Fay and Young 1978, 2: 35; private political diaries
of Tony Benn, 23 November 1976). According to Dell (1991: 260–2),
Crosland repeated earlier arguments that he had made, but with two
significant revisions: first, Crosland conceded that confidence was
important – 'the Government had made its negotiations too public to
do nothing now' – and that therefore he was now prepared to accept a
£1 billion PSBR cut, to be achieved by selling £500 million of British
Petroleum shares with 'the other half to be found in the least deflationary way possible.' Second, Crosland argued that by threatening
protectionism, the UK could get the IMF loan without unacceptable
conditions. 'Politically the IMF could not refuse the loan. If the Government kept its nerve, it could insist on its own terms – could limit the
cuts to "window-dressing"' (Crosland 1982: 377– 8; private political
diaries of Tony Benn, 23 November 1976; Fay and Young 1978, 2: 35;
Benn 1989: 653–4; Burk and Cairncross 1992: 86–7).

Other ministers began to weigh in (see the private political diaries
of Tony Benn, 23 November 1976), but the Prime Minister 'cut the

discussion short. Of the thirteen people who spoke, ten took the view that the loan could be obtained on the terms set out by the Foreign Secretary' (Crosland 1982: 379). Callaghan reminded the Cabinet that even if the IMF were to accept Crosland's strategy, other constituencies – the 'Party in the country, the overseas and Common Market constituencies' – would also have to agree because of interdependence, and 'if we didn't convince them, we wouldn't satisfy the markets.' Even with the alternative strategy, Callaghan argued, Britain must have a loan (private political diaries of Tony Benn, 23 November 1976). When Chancellor of the Duchy of Lancaster Harold Lever pointed out that the £500 million gap between Healey's and Crosland's PSBR proposals was not great, the Chancellor replied that the difference was much more 'because in effect the argument was whether it was in cuts or tax increases' (private political diaries of Tony Benn, 23 November 1976).

Callaghan (1987: 437) recounts that in his communications with President Ford and Chancellor Schmidt, he used Crosland's opposition 'to make sure that both knew the strength of feeling in the Cabinet,' and that he gave himself 'a little margin' by telling Ford and Schmidt that 'Cabinet would agree to nothing less than £9.5 billion' for the 1977–78 PSBR. Callaghan told them that Cabinet had objected strongly to deflation with higher unemployment 'which would utterly destroy our hard-won agreement with the TUC on pay,' and that he would not be able to obtain approval from Parliament. 'I asked them to talk to their representatives in the IMF.' According to German finance ministry official Karl Otto Pöhl, Callaghan asked Schmidt to send an envoy to London to 'cool things down' (Burk and Cairncross 1992: 87; Fay and Young 1978, 2: 35); according to Callaghan (1987: 437), 'Helmut Schmidt recognised our political difficulties and was fearful of the world moving down a protectionist path. He undertook to telephone President Ford.'[23]

Callaghan on 23 November sent Ford a message (Callaghan 1976a) that conveyed the sense of the Cabinet. Callaghan thanked Ford for his message of 20 November (quoted above), noting that 'what you say about the sterling balances is very encouraging.' But sterling balances were no longer the Prime Minister's central concern, and aside from this opening reference, were not mentioned again. Callaghan laid out to Ford the negotiations with the IMF and in Cabinet.

We have . . . now reached a most critical point in our negotiations with the IMF. The Cabinet discussed the matter at length this morning and find the proposals unacceptable. They wish me to put the position before you.

On present forecasts our public sector borrowing requirement in 1977–78 will be £10.5 billion. The IMF are saying that we should cut this to £8.5 billion with a further reduction in 1978–79 to £6.5 billion. Our immediate problem concerns 1977–78. Denis Healey thinks that he can negotiate the IMF up to a figure of £9 billion and put this to Cabinet this morning. The Cabinet were however not prepared to agree to either £8.5 or £9 billion. They feel that the lowest PSBR which is politically acceptable next year is £9.5 billion. In other words they are willing to contemplate, with great difficulty, making a reduction in the PSBR next year of £1 billion of which half would be found from further cuts in public expenditure. There is no need for me to tell you how uncertain all these figures are.

Callaghan then outlined the two arguments underlying Cabinet opposition to the IMF's terms.

First. Economic. Unemployment here is higher than at any time since the 1930s and is forecast to rise again next year even on the basis of existing policies. This situation, which provides no case for a further release of resources into exports, would be worsened if we took the action the IMF recommended. In short, the Cabinet's objection is to substantial deflation with even higher unemployment. The balance of payments is forecast to come into surplus next year. No independent economist here is advocating further substantial deflation on top of the £2 billion cut in the PSBR for next year which we made in July. The proposed deflation would reduce our expected rate of growth of GDP to no more than $1-1\frac{1}{2}$ per cent.

Second. Political. The Cabinet's view is that cutting the PSBR by more than £1 billion would utterly destroy the partnership with our trade unions upon which our successful policy of wage restraint depends. They do not believe that we would be able to carry the necessary legislation in the House of Commons. Even a reduction of £1 billion will involve very grave risks for us. In any case, with cuts of the order the IMF are suggesting on top of those we made only four months ago [in July], it would be impossible to spare our defence programme.

Callaghan then made a direct and unvarnished appeal for the President's intervention.

Forgive me for putting these points to you so tersely. But time is very short. Denis Healey is reporting the Cabinet's view to the leader of the IMF mission this afternoon and I shall be seeing him myself later today. I cannot of course forecast how [IMF head of negotiations] Whittome will react but I thought I should let you know the position at once since the Cabinet will have to take a final decision on Thursday[24] [25 November]. I hope that you will feel able to intervene with the Managing Director of the Fund and impress on him the need to moderate their terms to what can be made politically acceptable in this country.

Ford answered Callaghan's appeal the following day (Ford 1976b); his response was lukewarm at best. Ford noted that as Callaghan had said that he thought the Chancellor could narrow the differences with the IMF, this was encouraging; there was no change expressed in the message in the US Government's position on the sterling balances.[25] As Callaghan (1987: 437) comments in his memoirs, 'in Washington Secretary Simon's influence was paramount, and the President could not deliver beyond repeating his assurance that the United States would move sympathetically on creating a sterling safety net as soon as we had reached substantial agreement with the IMF on the conditions for the loan.'

Both the 'left-wing' and 'social democratic' factions of ministers met following the initial Cabinet discussions. According to Minister of Energy Tony Benn, the leftist group 'discussed the situation in detail' and was

> all very optimistic about Tony Crosland's position, saying we should rally round him. . . . Michael [Foot] was worried and thought that [Callaghan] was going to come down against [Healey], and [Healey] might resign. Of course if he does resign, the pound will go through the floor, even if we get the IMF loan. In order to keep [Healey], you have to have more deflation, but the trick is to keep [Healey] and have less deflation.

(Private political diaries of Tony Benn, 24 November 1976; Benn 1989: 656–7)

Minister of Education Shirley Williams recounts that the view among the social democratic faction was that 'the IMF could be faced down to some extent; one had to make concessions to it, but nothing like as much as was asked for' (Whitehead 1985: 196). When they met and counted Cabinet votes, 'they discovered that, between left and centre, there was actually a Cabinet majority against a deflationary package' (Fay and Young 1978, 2: 35). According to Tony Crosland's wife, Crosland and Minister of Prices and Consumer Protection Roy Hattersley wondered if an alliance between the two groups was possible; 'Hattersley thought it best to make the approach through political advisers. His own adviser, David Hill, approached Tony Benn's, Frances Morrell. . . . As both groups were fighting the Treasury's deflationary package, Hill said, could they not join forces in a united front? Morrell replied that the Bennites were not willing to play that game with the Crosland group' (Crosland 1982: 379). Minister for Energy Tony Benn, however, doubts the accuracy of this account (interview material). Minister of Trade Edmund Dell's view (1991: 259) is that 'the position of the Benn group was that they would not ally with Crosland but would support him, except perhaps to the degree that the Crosland proposals also involved attacks on the social services' (see also Benn 1989: 656). In the event, there appears to have been no formal cooperation between the two opposition factions.

When Cabinet met again on 25 November, the Prime Minister told ministers that he and the Chancellor had met personally with the IMF mission's leader Alan Whittome. 'Jim said that the IMF knew about our fear of deflation, and we faced a serious dilemma between retaining on the one hand the confidence of the TUC and, on the other, the confidence of the markets. . . . Whittome had asked us to look at three scenarios for 1977–78: one was a PSBR at £8.5 billion, another at £9 billion and a third at £9.5 billion.' The Prime Minister outlined a schedule into the following week for further discussion and a decision: 'he felt nothing further could be said today' (Benn 1989: 658). The Chancellor assured Cabinet that 'when he met the IMF, he had expressed the Cabinet's view powerfully, and his own motive was to ensure minimum damage to the British economy, but he said we had to satisfy three groups: the staff of the IMF; the United States and Germany; and the markets' (Benn 1989: 658). Healey continued to stress the confidence argument: 'arm-twisting by the UK to force the IMF to agree to something that in their hearts they didn't think was right, would be damaging. . . . It would look as if we were not doing what was necessary' (private political diaries of Tony Benn, 25 November 1976; see also *Financial Times*, 'An honest man,' 26 November 1976, p. 23).

There was little agreement in the discussion that followed. Foreign Secretary Tony Crosland spoke after Healey; he and Minister of Prices and Consumer Protection Roy Hattersley advocated an import deposit scheme 'which they thought that Healey could use at least to frighten the IMF' (Fay and Young 1978, 2: 35; Crosland 1982: 379; Dell 1991: 266). Minister of Trade Edmund Dell argued that 'we had to stop borrowing. Borrowing with menaces was no more acceptable.' Minister for the Environment Peter Shore pointed out that although the Government must restore confidence, it must also put its own view forward. Minister of Energy Tony Benn told the Cabinet that he hoped 'the real options would be before us, . . . not just a Yes or No to the IMF proposals. We had to have broad discussions about the political implications of various courses of action.' Leader of the House of Commons Michael Foot made the observation that 'the Cabinet was anti-deflation and that it was bound to be, given that unemployment was at 1.75 million in the forecasts' (private political diaries of Tony Benn, 25 November 1976; Benn 1989: 658).

The Chancellor summed up the discussion by emphasizing that the Government was spending more than it was earning and that

> one of the things we had to go for was the real value of protected [state-provided] benefits. . . . So long as we lived in an open and a mixed economy, we shall depend on the market judgment to determine our future. If we couldn't persuade our followers that these were the facts, we would fail in our leadership, and then another Party would have to take over. . . . We would have proved that our brand of social democracy doesn't work.
>
> (Benn 1989: 659)

Tony Crosland countered that 'social democracy doesn't depend on deflation. . . . Speaking for himself, Tony Crosland concluded that rationally he didn't believe that further cuts were sensible or necessary' (private political diaries of Tony Benn, 25 November 1976; Benn 1989: 659).

The Prime Minister reminded Cabinet that addressing the sterling balances problem depended upon obtaining the IMF loan and then closed the meeting (Benn 1989: 659). Once again, he had not supported Healey in Cabinet (Fay and Young 1978, 2: 35). Tony Crosland after the meeting 'was in a good mood: it was still possible that a united front would break the IMF's hold on Healey. Callaghan had still not supported his Chancellor in Cabinet, but he consistently told Tony that he expected to do so. Therefore it was imperative that Healey be shifted' (Crosland 1982: 379). With the benefit of hindsight, however, this appears to have been largely wishful thinking. Healey viewed Crosland's argument dismissively: 'Tony Crosland was saying . . . we don't understand economics at all – you can run a much bigger deficit than this without damage. The trouble with theoretical economists is that they don't understand that when you have a deficit, you can only finance it by borrowing, and you've got to persuade people that it's worth lending to you, and that they'll get their money back' (Whitehead 1985: 196–7; see also Healey 1989: 431). The Chancellor remained strongly opposed to the alternatives of his Cabinet opponents.

CONCLUSION

When the IMF negotiating team arrived in London in early November, the prerequisites for a major crisis were in place. The exchange market had forced the Government into announcing its intention to apply to the IMF for a conditional loan; when the Government then took the position that no policy changes were necessary, conflict was inevitable. As an unnamed IMF staff member recounts, 'if the UK wanted a large drawing, the Fund would have to examine British policies, just like any other country. I couldn't accept without examination the British argument that their policies were adequate' (Bernstein 1983: 589). Less than a month after the application on existing policies announcement, the exchange market again demonstrated its ability to push for policy change when the pound was driven into the $1.50s.

Earlier in 1976, when the Government had turned to its OECD partners for assistance *vis-à-vis* the exchange market (e.g., the $5.3 billion central-bank stand-by loan), help was furnished only with strings attached. The Government had to commit to going to the IMF. When in October and November the Prime Minister appealed to Chancellor Schmidt and President Ford for assistance on the sterling balances, he found them insistent that Britain conclude a conditional loan with the IMF first. The Government was regarded by the international financial community with distrust and skepticism. As US Federal Reserve Chairman Arthur Burns has commented, 'I had my doubts whether the British could correct the faults in their economic management on their own. You must remember I am a neanderthal conservative, and naturally suspicious of a Labour Government. I thought it was a profligate government' (Fay and Young 1978, 1: 33). In the final months of 1976, Burns and others who regarded the Government with suspicion and doubt were able to have their preferences for economic retrenchment in the UK realized through the IMF.

This chapter has reviewed the intensification of the various levels of pressure for policy change (structural, bilateral, and multilateral), as well as how this pressure was initially resisted within the Cabinet. The process by which the resistance gave way and the Government capitulated is addressed in the following chapter.

10 Crisis Resolution, December 1976 – January 1977:
'It is Mad but we have No Alternative'[1]

The sustained crisis of confidence that had put downward pressure on sterling throughout 1976 was resolved only with the Government's capitulation to external pressures for change, in which its policy autonomy was explicitly bound for almost the entirety of its remaining term of office. Although the IMF's demands *vis-à-vis* public expenditure were reduced by £500 million at the eleventh hour and the Cabinet left-wing was able to defeat demands for a reduction in the level of social benefits, these were small victories at the margins of a larger and more significant defeat in which the Cabinet acceded to demands that were contrary to its initial assessment of what was appropriate. The Cabinet debates were intense and soul-searching; the Government was on the verge of collapse and the Prime Minister wondered repeatedly whether it would survive (Callaghan 1987: 437–8). Visitors from abroad including US Treasury Secretary William Simon and the IMF Managing Director Johannes Witteveen arrived in London for clandestine meetings with British authorities in which 'parameters' were set (Whitehead 1985: 197–8). In the end, the Government survived only with the sacrifice of its own policy judgment in favor of the judgment of its external critics who were lending it money – specifically, the IMF and the US Treasury. As Foreign Secretary Tony Crosland reportedly commented when he reluctantly shifted his position on the IMF package from opposition to support, 'it is mad but we have no alternative' (Whitehead 1985: 199; Benn 1989: 685).

AMERICAN AND GERMAN VISITS TO LONDON, LATE NOVEMBER 1976

US Treasury Secretary Simon, accompanied by Under-Secretary Yeo and other American financial officials, flew to London in late November (Seidman 1976; *The Guardian*, 27 November 1976, 'Treasury group,'

p. 20; Fay and Young 1978, 2: 35). Although Simon told the press that he was 'just here to see the sights,' it was obvious under the circumstances that the visit had a more important political purpose, indeed, according to an unnamed White House official, 'the United States Embassy in London had been instructed to assist the Simon party by establishing a special communications and security "command post" in the group's hotel' (Fay and Young 1978, 2: 35; *New York Times*, 26 November 1976, 'Simon Will Travel,' p. A21). Simon, while in London, met with the head of the IMF negotiating team Alan Whittome to encourage him not to give way to the British (Fay and Young 1978, 2: 35). Simon and senior US officials also met with Chancellor of the Exchequer Denis Healey and Chancellor of the Duchy of Lancaster Harold Lever where, according to contemporary press accounts, Lever put forward the view that 'in the present state of continued recession, any moves to reduce public sector demand for resources or raise indirect taxation will be counter-productive' (*Financial Times*, 29 November 1976, 'Healey and Lever,' p. 1). Although the British were hoping for talk about compromise, 'Simon's message was negative: he did not believe there was anything to discuss. There was no alternative' (Fay and Young 1978, 2: 35). Yeo has recounted of the meeting with Healey, 'he didn't whine, but he thought he was ruined, and so did we' (Fay and Young 1978, 2: 35).

Simon has recounted of the London visit that 'it was felt that I should . . . have informal and hopefully secret discussions with the members of the Bank [of England] and the [UK] Treasury. . . . Unfortunately the press was hounding me wherever I went, and as a result I had to devise something rather devious.' Simon along with Yeo went to a London tailor where, as he recounts, 'we met the Treasury people, and there was generally a small parade of folks coming in and out of this tailor, and I ended up buying three suits I didn't need; but nonetheless we pretty well set the parameters' (Whitehead 1985: 197; Fay and Young 1978, 2: 35). Although Simon suggests that subterfuge was necessary because 'the press were all over the place' (Fay and Young 1978, 2: 35), it seems likely that meetings occurred clandestinely because he was seeking inside information with officials from one or both sides of the negotiating table. Although a Fund official has recounted of the meetings with Simon and Yeo that 'we discussed where we were, but only in the broadest terms' (Bernstein 1983: 515), US officials upon their return to Washington were nonetheless able to summarize the remaining differences between Healey's and the IMF's positions in a one-page table for President Ford (see Table 10.1; Seidman

Table 10.1   Summary of Healey and Witteveen negotiating positions, December 1976 (in £ billion)

	1976	1977		1978	
		Healey	*Witteveen*	*Healey*	*Witteveen*
Cuts in expenditure	—	1.0	1.5	1.5	2.0
Expenditure cuts or increases in indirect taxes	—	—	—	[0.5]	—
Sale of [British Petroleum] oil shares	—	0.6	—	—	—
PSBR	11.3	8.7	8.2	8.5	8.0
PSBR as a GDP%	11.3%	7.5%	7.1%	6.6%	6.2%
Current account balance of payments	−3.2	−1.0	—	+2.8	—
Increase in money supply M3	16.1%[3]	11.8%	10%	14%	12%
Changes in public expenditure programs at 1976 prices (New Definition)	—	−2.4%	—	−0.4%	—
Domestic credit expansion	—	7.7	—	6.2	—
Tax cuts (if IMF estimates of PSBR on present policies are accepted)	—	—	0.8	—	0.4

Source: Simon (1976f); brackets and endnote in original document.

1976). It is likely that the confidential bargaining positions summarized in the table were obtained during Simon's discussions in London[2] (see Simon 1976k).

German Finance Ministry official Karl Otto Pöhl was also in London in late November, having been sent there by Chancellor Schmidt (Fay and Young 1978, 2: 35; Burk and Cairncross 1992: 90). He met with Healey who, Pöhl recounts, was 'cool, if not rude' (Burk and Cairncross 1992: 90) and contacted Whittome to tell him that 'the German government was not going to ask the IMF to weaken their position' (Fay and Young 1978, 2: 35). Pöhl also met with the visiting US officials in London; they 'agreed that they should put pressure on the British to fulfil the conditions set out by the IMF and not make an exception' (Burk and Cairncross 1992: 91; Simon 1976k). When he returned to Germany, Pöhl 'told Schmidt that he could not put pressure on the IMF to lighten conditions on Britain, because he would destroy the IMF' (Burk and Cairncross 1992: 91).

CONTINUED CABINET DISCUSSIONS, LATE NOVEMBER 1976

Formal negotiations between the Fund team and the British had not been making progress. 'Whittome had drunk much whisky with the Chancellor and still the message was the same: that the IMF was asking far too big a piece of flesh, that the cuts would be unnecessarily deflationary, and that there was a political dimension to the crisis which Whittome had omitted from the Fund's models of sound economic behaviour' (Fay and Young 1978, 2: 35). Whittome has recounted how the Prime Minister 'would have me around at midnight to soft talk [me] into taking a softer line' (Burk and Cairncross 1992: 90). There was little movement in the IMF's position, however, and it was at Managing Director Witteveen's suggestion that the Fund team 'let the negotiations proceed slowly to give UK officials time to come to an agreed position among themselves' (De Vries 1985, 1: 471).

The Prime Minister had an opportunity to discuss the situation informally with Foreign Secretary Tony Crosland at a European Council meeting in the Netherlands at the end of November. Callaghan (1987: 438) recounts that at the meeting

> I made a special point when talking with Helmut Schmidt to involve Tony Crosland in our conversations. . . . I took the opportunity, while Tony Crosland was there, to enquire if [Schmidt] would be willing to intervene with the IMF to secure better terms. He made a temporising reply, but it was obvious to Tony that he believed we should reduce our borrowing requirement and was politely saying "No." I was not surprised.

On the return journey to London, 'I made use of the time to press the Foreign Secretary once more. . . . I told him that at our next [Cabinet] meeting, I would indicate that Ministers must now reach a conclusion on their general strategy. I knew where I stood; what would he do?' Crosland was non-committal: his response was 'to remind [Callaghan] of the growing general opinion against the IMF's terms' (Crosland 1982: 380; see also Fay and Young 1978, 3: 33). That evening, however, the 'social democratic' faction of ministers led by Crosland gathered for a 'disappointing' meeting: '[Minister for Transport] Bill Rodgers had gone over to the Prentice-Dell hard line. [Minister for Education] Shirley [Williams] and [Minister for Social Services] David Ennals were undecided what was best to do. . . . Tony [Crosland] and [Chancellor of the Duchy of Lancaster] Harold Lever and [Minister of Prices and Consumer Protection] Roy Hattersley alone were unchanged in their opposition to the IMF's terms' (Crosland 1982: 380).

In addition to Crosland, Callaghan also sought out Leader of the House of Commons Michael Foot for a private talk. Foot was 'deeply unhappy,' Callaghan (1987: 438) recounts. 'Michael's concerns were with the consequences for unemployment and the level of social benefits, but his overriding consideration was that there should be no whiff of 1931' when the minority Labour Government of Ramsay MacDonald collapsed in the midst of a financial crisis and splintered the Labour Party. Callaghan summed up Foot's view 'as being that it would be better to stay together than to stay in government. Fortunately he understood that I was as determined not to split the Party as he was.' The 'left' ministers group met on 30 November and discussed the Chancellor's Cabinet paper that rejected alternative strategies and insisted upon cuts in social benefits; according to Minister of Energy Tony Benn (private political diaries of Tony Benn, 30 November 1976):

> we agreed we should let Denis and Jim report back. Then Denis will make his statement saying that he has to have it this way. . . . I think there is a good chance that Denis will get absolutely drubbed [in Cabinet] tomorrow. It is simply not on. . . . If Healey is defeated a second time tomorrow in light of his further attempt, then I think the possibility is that he'll resign. If he threatens to resign, Jim either has to support him, or switch him with Crosland, or repudiate him and let him go. If Denis went, I think there would be an absolutely major crisis.

IMF MANAGING DIRECTOR WITTEVEEN'S VISIT TO LONDON, 1 DECEMBER 1976

The Cabinet meeting scheduled for 10 a.m. on 1 December to discuss the IMF package was unexpectedly delayed by 40 minutes. Minister of Energy Tony Benn commented to his diary (1989: 661) that 'this made us a bit suspicious. You don't normally delay a Cabinet of that importance unless there's some hiccup.' Unbeknownst to Benn, the delay

was due to the short-notice arrival in London of IMF Managing Director Johannes Witteveen. During the last days of November, Alan Whittome
had returned to IMF headquarters in Washington for further consultations. With the Cabinet's decision close at hand

> some US officials and the Fund staff team considered it essential for
> the Managing Director to meet with the Prime Minister before the
> Cabinet meeting to elicit his support for macroeconomic policies in
> preference to use of restrictions on imports. . . . US Treasury officials
> transmitted to Mr. Witteveen President Ford's belief that it would be
> desirable for Mr. Witteveen, in the interest of the international com-
> munity, to go to London to help persuade Mr. Callaghan to support
> a reduction in the public sector borrowing. Mr. Witteveen was asked
> to keep secret President Ford's request. He was fully aware that
> such a trip was risky and would have to be secret or the negotiations
> between the Fund and the United Kingdom could be in jeopardy.
>
> (De Vries 1985, 1: 471–2)

Witteveen (1987: 31) has recounted that upon arriving in London, 'I
talked first to Healey and his officials and then with Callaghan himself.' Healey (1989: 431) recounts that 'when [Witteveen] asked me
for another £2 billion spending cuts next year, I told him it was out of
the question. I took him to see the Prime Minister.' The meeting between Prime Minister and Managing Director reportedly was 'highly
unpleasant' (Fay and Young 1978, 3: 33). According to one account,
'Callaghan called the IMF Managing Director "Boy," and lost his tem-
per in a rather calculated way' (Whitehead 1985: 198). According to
the IMF historian, 'UK officials had on the table a copy of the charter
of GATT. Apparently they were seriously considering imposing import
restrictions' (De Vries 1985, 1: 472). Witteveen argued that:

> Britain could not expect special treatment and that the Fund had the
> full support of the US. Further bargaining would therefore not help
> Britain and could even be counterproductive. Witteveen tried to con-
> vince the Prime Minister that the stand-by would be less onerous
> than he feared, because it would lower interest rates and stabilize
> sterling. Callaghan argued that union, party and Cabinet opposition
> limited what the British could accept in the way of conditions. . . .
> Witteveen, however, did not see the political opposition as a major
> factor.
>
> (Bernstein 1983: 522; see also Dell 1991: 268; Burk and
> Cairncross 1992: 94)

According to Whittome, following the Managing Director's presentation, Callaghan told Witteveen '"You never mentioned the word unemployment," . . . Witteveen mumbled . . . that in the short-term it may be higher than it would otherwise have been, but ultimately, surely, it will be better, and Callaghan said, "Well, if that's all you can say, you'd better get back on the next plane to Washington." Then Healey and I came in with some remark which allowed it to get going again' (Burk and Cairncross 1992: 94).

Callaghan and Healey left for Cabinet. According to the IMF historian, a second session of talks with Witteveen and Whittome was held over lunch and it went better. 'Mr. Callaghan finally agreed to support a reduction of the public sector borrowing requirement. Although this reduction was not as large as that proposed by the [IMF] staff, it was, nonetheless, substantial' (De Vries 1985, 1: 472; see also Fay and Young 1978, 3: 33; Whitehead 1985: 198). Healey recounts (1989: 431) that it was only at the discussions between Callaghan and Witteveen that he obtained Callaghan's support for expenditure cuts of £1 billion. According to Witteveen (1987: 31), the meeting 'apparently . . . was the first time that Callaghan as Prime Minister had expressed a view [to Healey] on the whole issue. He had always remained kind of neutral, not supporting the Chancellor on this, and that made it very difficult for Healey to get any kind of decision out of the Cabinet that would be acceptable to the Fund.' According to the IMF historian, 'Mr. Healey was especially pleased with the successful outcome of Mr. Witteveen's trip and told him so'[4] (De Vries 1985, 1: 472).

CABINET DECISIONS, EARLY DECEMBER 1976

In Cabinet on 1 December, the Prime Minister reiterated the need to reach a majority agreement that would be accepted by all in order for the Government to survive (Benn 1989: 662). Before discussion of the various Cabinet papers began,[5] Callaghan and Healey were asked to report on their discussions since Cabinet's last meeting; Callaghan replied, 'there's not much I can say. The formal position is that the IMF is considering the matter, but the IMF is not the only leg, it's a three-legged stool, and [West German Chancellor Helmut] Schmidt is impressed with the gravity of the situation, though his fears are more global and are not really restricted to problems about us' (Benn 1989: 662). Minister of Energy Tony Benn, unaware that Callaghan and Healey had just come from a meeting with the IMF Managing Director, pointed out that Healey had had meetings with US Treasury Secretary Simon. The Chancellor replied, 'I talked to Simon and a German official [Pöhl] and trying to bully the Fund won't help us. The US are being very difficult, there is no bilateral borrowing available to us, even if the Fund helps us, but if a safety net [for sterling balances] is required, the US would be prepared to look at it' (Benn 1989: 662).

The Prime Minister called upon Minister for Energy Tony Benn to present his paper first. Benn argued his case that 'there are two alternative strategies, the Chancellor's and mine, and there is a very big choice to make. My paper warns against deflation of any kind, imposed or self-imposed. I have been driven to the conclusion, very reluctantly, and I hope the Cabinet will believe me, that expansion requires protection' (Benn 1989: 663). Benn linked his opposition to Healey's proposals with the problems the Government would have with its own supporters. 'Our political stance would be untenable if we deflate in a slump because it would undermine the industrial strategy, involve accepting international control and, if cutting benefits were thrown in, it would be impossible' (Benn 1989: 663–4). When asked how the Government could survive electorally with his alternative strategy as Government policy, Benn turned the question around and replied that 'nothing would be more fatal to Labour's electoral chances than the Party going to the country having laid off employees in manufacturing industries and in the public service sector on the grounds that the bankers wanted unemployment to restore confidence' (Benn 1989: 665).

Benn neither impressed nor persuaded his colleagues. Minister of Education Shirley Williams asked if his proposals were 'a threat or a real policy' (Benn 1989: 665). Minister of Trade Edmund Dell (1991: 266) recounts that 'Benn's paper was treated dismissively by the Cabinet as a whole.' According to Denis Healey, Benn 'didn't really have alternative proposals. I think that on many of the big issues of the time he was simply agin' it' (Whitehead 1985: 195). Even Benn's leftist colleague Minister for the Environment Peter Shore was dismissive, commenting during his own Cabinet presentation that 'it was all very well to tease and hound Tony Benn, but the alternative policy needed to be looked at properly' (Benn 1989: 666; see also Foot 1986: 114, 118–19; Whitehead 1985: 196).

Peter Shore was called next to present his proposals. As Benn recounts (1989: 665–6), 'he said . . . we could either go for deflation or import controls. Denis was for deflation which would encase us in a two-year tomb. The IMF tranches would come bit by bit; we would be drip fed to police us. . . . He believed we were not paying our way and the easiest way to deal with that was to control imports.' Shore argued that Britain had little alternative to import controls, and 'was empowered under the GATT rules to use temporary controls. He suggested a two-year period of controls until North Sea Oil revenues began to flow' (Bernstein 1983: 568–9; see also Fay and Young 1978, 3: 33; Whitehead 1985: 196). Shore argued that 'our real problems were the short-term ones – how to get additional finance in the interim period. Only the Treasury technicians would know the answer to this. We knew emergency plans existed, and the IMF would help because they could not humiliate and break a democratic government' (Benn 1989: 666).

Shore was pressed by his colleagues on Britain's short-term financing needs. Repayment of $1.6 billion in drawings on the June central bank stand-by was due on 9 December, and an expected external deficit of £2.5 billion would need to be financed in 1977. In response, Shore argued that, first, 'the current account would be closed in 1977 under his proposals. Second, we could push forward the impending dollars repayment [of Britain's drawings on the June stand-by] for three months. Third, we would get the IMF's backing, but if we didn't we might have to mobilise [Britain's external] assets and then release them in an orderly way'[6] (Benn 1989: 666–7).

Foreign Secretary Tony Crosland presented his argument next in which he developed the points he had put to Cabinet previously that there was no economic case for a policy shift. 'I want us to stick to our existing strategy. We have had deflation, we have had devaluation, we've got a wages policy, and it will work. There is no case for a change' (Benn 1989: 667). Crosland did acknowledge, however, that the Government was facing a confidence crisis.

> We live in the real world of expectation and there are two scenarios to consider. One is the £1 billion net cut [in public expenditure] which is unacceptable, and the IMF won't really press us for it. If they do, we should resist and threaten a siege economy, or talk about our role in Cyprus, or our troops in Germany, or our position in Rhodesia, membership of the EEC, etc. Schmidt and Ford would soon give way. The other alternative is tolerable: to get £1 billion off the PSBR by selling [£500 million in British Petroleum] oil shares, having import deposits which are a bit deflationary and have political advantages, and to do a presentational job to the IMF by announcing now the cuts we had decided on in July but which have not yet become known, and possibly some extra cuts.
>
> (Benn 1989: 667)

Minister for Trade Edmund Dell pressed Crosland, asking how under his proposal confidence would be restored; Crosland replied that 'these were all matters of political judgment . . . and he believed in our present policy, and that confidence would be restored' (Benn 1989: 668; see also Bernstein 1983: 565).

The Chancellor attacked all three of the alternatives presented (private political diaries of Tony Benn, 1 December 1976). Dealing with Crosland's 'soft option' first, Healey argued that 'Crosland was wrong because he underestimates the importance of money. We had to cut the PSBR to satisfy the IMF, to avoid printing money, to deal with interest rates, to finance the external deficit. Even any doubt about whether we were going to accept the IMF terms,' he argued, 'would lead to the plummeting of the pound. . . . If we accept, we'd get the loan, the safety net, and we might get import deposits.' The Chancellor attacked Benn's 'alternative strategy' proposal as 'tempting but only rhetoric. . . . Tony Benn really wanted a command economy which is incompatible with [a] mixed economy. The only basis of increasing employment was [a] real fall in the take home pay for everyone or to borrow abroad.' The Chancellor concluded with an attack on Shore's 'less radical' import control alternative on employment grounds: 'Peter's alternative would not cut unemployment. . . . We had [the equivalent of] a 25 per cent tariff from depreciation last year, and that hadn't been effective, and it threw doubt on the whole effectiveness of import controls.' The Chancellor told Cabinet that it 'had to choose between real alternatives and his was the best, involving sacrifices now' (private political diary of Tony Benn, 1 December 1976).

The Prime Minister ended the meeting without disclosing his own view. He summed up the discussion and told Cabinet that 'we were ready for a general decision tomorrow . . . but the majority were not agreed on the size of the package. Tomorrow we would discuss the quantum and the make-up of it generally. He said he supported the Chancellor in saying the IMF should know the [Government's] position tomorrow and then we'll allocate it [i.e., decide how the PSBR cut was to be achieved]' (private political diary of Tony Benn, 1 December 1976).

The Prime Minister sought to widen the discussion by inviting TUC General Secretary Len Murray and General Secretary of the Transport and General Workers' Union Jack Jones for a private talk. Callaghan (1987: 438–9) recounts that with each of them, 'I explained my views about a solution and told them how the negotiations stood.' With Murray, 'I limited my conversation to the financial and economic implications

of the alternative courses, and sought his advice on the reactions of
the TUC. As ever, he was extremely helpful, enabling me to gauge the
severity of the unions' response.' With Jones, however, Callaghan 'went
further' in stressing his determination to avoid the break-up of the
Government and the Party. 'Jones warned me strongly about the consequences to the Social Contract if there was a large increase in unemployment or reductions in social benefits, but he gave me every
encouragement to maintain a Labour Government, even if it meant taking
some decisions the TUC would not like and would oppose' (see also
Jones 1986: 309; TUC 1977a: 218–19).

Callaghan also had a 14-minute telephone conversation with President Ford about the loan terms[7] (Daily Diary of the President, 1 December 1976). As Callaghan recounted the conversation to Cabinet:

> '[Ford] said that if the Fund came through, he would try to help
> with the safety net. He said he felt sure it would be acceptable to
> the Congress. . . . What I said to Ford is this. I would like to pro-
> pose a three-legged stool: a cut of £1–1.5 billion in the PSBR; a
> [sterling balances] safety net; [and] import deposits on the same basis
> as Italy. I might be able to sell it.' Ford said their attitude was to be
> firm but fair.
>
> (Benn 1989: 672–3)

Callaghan told Cabinet that he had delivered the same message to German
Chancellor Schmidt as well (Benn 1989: 673).

The 'social democratic' faction of ministers met to discuss the situation. Foreign Secretary Crosland's support among his colleagues was
eroding. Chancellor of the Duchy of Lancaster Harold Lever was 'openly
hostile' *vis-à-vis* the import deposits in Crosland's proposal and 'had
been converted by the Chancellor' (Fay and Young 1978, 3: 33; see
also Crosland 1982: 381; Bernstein 1983: 552; Donoughue 1987: 97,
1985: 68). Minister of Education Shirley Williams was writing a compromise paper, 'trying to find a method of meeting the IMF's PSBR target with the least damage to public spending and jobs' (Fay and Young
1978, 3: 33; see also Crosland 1982: 381). Moreover, Crosland's own
resolve was beginning to waver. Although he continued to believe that
there was no economic case for public expenditure cuts, he began to
consider the political consequences if the Prime Minister were to be
defeated by Cabinet, reasoning that 'if the Prime Minister joins with
the Chancellor, they probably are unbeatable and indeed shouldn't be
beaten. If it became known . . . that Jim had been defeated by Cabinet,
it would be murder.' He told his wife, 'I may well switch my argument . . .

and say this: that we cannot afford not to support the Prime Minister. He is crucial' (Crosland 1982: 381).

Crosland met privately with Callaghan to tell him of his decision to abandon his opposition. As Callaghan recounts (1987: 439), Crosland 'remained unconvinced about the policy but . . . he recognised the Government could not survive on such an important issue unless it backed me.' The Prime Minister was 'both grateful and relieved.' With Crosland's support, 'I would be able to secure a majority in Cabinet for the Chancellor's approach. I could therefore declare my hand without the necessity of delivering an ultimatum to the Cabinet.' With a reasonable certainty of majority support among the Cabinet, Callaghan met with Labour Chief Whip Michael Cocks. 'I asked him for an assessment of the mood of the Party' (Callaghan 1987: 439). Cocks was not encouraging. 'There was pretty general despondency with a left-wing group almost certain to vote against any particular piece of legislation which involved a reduction in public expenditure. They might however sit on their hands in a vote on the package as a whole, if it was an issue of confidence in the Government; they did not want the Government to fall' (see also Benn 1989: 671–2; Fay and Young 1978, 3: 34).

Cabinet met again on 2 December for the 'moment of decision' (Callaghan 1987: 439; Benn 1989: 670). The Chancellor began by noting the general feeling in Cabinet that had led to a rejection of the alternative strategy and the siege economy, and reminded his colleagues of the currency reserve situation. After repaying the drawings on the central bank stand-by on 9 December, Britain would have only £2 billion in reserves. 'If we failed to agree with the Fund, it would be a disaster. Then much more drastic measures would have to be taken, and there would be higher unemployment. The question was: what adjustments should we make, and would they satisfy the Fund and meet criticism at home and abroad?' (Benn 1989: 670). The Chancellor insisted that the PSBR forecast for 1977–78 had to be cut; 'friends and creditors thought we were not creditworthy' (Benn 1989: 670; Callaghan 1987: 439). Healey told Cabinet, 'I now recommend that we go for a £500 million sale of [British Petroleum] shares; for a net reduction of £1 billion in the PSBR in 1977–78, mainly by cuts, with another £1.5 billion reduction in 1978–79. Therefore the PSBR would be £8.7 billion in 1977–78' (Benn 1989: 670). A substantial negotiating gap still remained between the Government and the IMF, the Chancellor told his colleagues, but anything less than his proposal would not restore confidence.

Crosland's package is quite unsaleable, and the markets would remain unconvinced. If we can [cut the PSBR by £1.5 billion and get the IMF to agree], we will get the borrowing, and the safety net [for sterling balances], and possibly import deposits. . . . The Crosland plan is unacceptable to the IMF, to other countries, and to the markets; it only offers a 20,000 gain in jobs; there is a risk of another demand for a package and it is better to overkill now.

(Benn 1989: 671; see also Callaghan 1987: 439–40)

Following the Chancellor's presentation, the Prime Minister spoke. Callaghan (1987: 440) recounts that 'I had no hesitation in accepting his proposal and said so at once to my colleagues.' The Prime Minister outlined three elements to the proposed settlement: 'First, we should go for a quantum with £1 billion of [expenditure] cuts; and to this extent I support Denis. . . . Secondly, we must reduce tax levels at the top and bottom, and for this we can expect wide public support. Thirdly, we must deal with social security benefits' (Benn 1989: 672). As presented by Callaghan, the question for Cabinet to decide was whether to obtain the needed expenditure savings from social security cut-backs or from expenditure reductions in the Government's capital building programs which would harm the construction industry (Benn 1989: 672). Callaghan argued:

There is no doubt which would be more harmful in terms of jobs. We are committed to raising benefits by statute . . . and pensioners have therefore got a 16 per cent increase this year, which is more than those at work have got under the pay policy. But that can't go on on that basis. There is a good case in logic for saying that if we have to choose between the construction industry or deferring the increase in benefits, we should defer benefits; but that would require supporting legislation, and [because parliamentary support for such legislation was not secure] it would put the life of the Government at risk.

(Benn 1989: 671–2; see also UK Healey 1976h: 494)

Callaghan stressed that there was no agreement with the Fund as yet, and he told Cabinet of his efforts to soften the loan terms with Managing Director Witteveen as well as with President Ford and Chancellor Schmidt (Benn 1989: 672–3). 'We do put our lives to the test and our life as a Government could come to an end. We must all understand that if we reject this, our overseas friends and critics will bring the life of this Government to an end and the tremors will shake us' (Benn 1989: 673; Callaghan 1987: 440).

Leader of the House of Commons Michael Foot, who for the most part had not participated in earlier discussions, spoke next. Foot told the Prime Minister that the package was 'not satisfactory' and that the consequences that would flow from the expenditure cuts were 'inconceivable. The whole position has been changed by unemployment rising to 1.75 million in the forecasts, and we would be accepting an increase in that.' The proposal to cut social security benefits was particularly objectionable, Foot argued, and threatened to divide the Party. 'If you tried to deal with benefits by statute, it would destroy TUC support. The legislation would not be passed, and we would be in a position where, if the Government was defeated, Labour candidates would be fighting an election in favour of cuts in social benefits.' He 'recoiled in horror' at the unemployment effects and the benefits cuts, and urged the negotiation of a different package with the IMF. If the Government followed the course proposed by Healey

> we would forfeit our agreement and our association with the unions and would be ground to death. We must connect what we do to our own beliefs. We may not get the loan, but we have better prospects than a course that would be a disaster for the movement. We need more time; we want to sustain the Government; or, if forced into Opposition, sustain ourselves in unity rather than be split into snarling groups.
>
> (Benn 1989: 673–4)

According to Minister of Trade Edmund Dell (1991: 269), 'for a moment it appeared that Callaghan's intervention [in support of Healey] had not had the desired effect.' But Foreign Secretary Tony Crosland then intervened in support of the Prime Minister and the Chancellor, and according to Benn (1989: 674), 'this was a completely new factor.' Crosland told his colleagues that he continued to believe the package was wrong – indeed, it was 'destructive of what he had believed in all his life.' Nevertheless, 'the new factor is your view, Prime Minister' (Benn 1989: 674). Like Michael Foot, Crosland was concerned about maintaining Party unity; however, his view was that 'the unity of the Party depends upon sustaining the Prime Minister, and the effect on sterling of rejecting the Prime Minister would be to destroy our capacity. Therefore I support the Prime Minister and the Chancellor' (Benn 1989: 674; see also Barnett 1982: 105; Crosland 1982: 381–2).

As other ministers made their views clear, concern focused upon the proposed benefit cut, the effect it would have on the Party, and whether the Government could survive (see Benn 1989: 674–5). The Prime

Minister intervened to simplify the choice for Ministers: 'The choice . . . is between hitting the construction industry with the high unemployment that would follow or reducing the upgrading of the benefits. It is a stark choice' (Benn 1989: 675). According to Callaghan (1987: 440), he 'went around the table one by one, inviting the opinion of every member of the Cabinet. . . . it was obvious that there was a substantial majority for the Chancellor's proposal, although a minority found it unacceptable.' The meeting was winding down and the Prime Minister attempted to draw the discussion to a close: 'I want now to sum up as best I can. . . . I now think we should authorise Denis to offer to the IMF £1 billion in [expenditure] cuts, £0.5 billion in sale of shares [of British Petroleum], and test out the import deposit argument' (Benn 1989: 678). Healey emphasized that IMF acceptance of the Government's offer was by no means assured (Benn 1989: 678; Healey 1989: 431–2). Regarding the composition of the PSBR cut, the Chancellor warned, a tax increase 'would be much less acceptable because they want cuts not tax increases' and expenditure cuts harmful to the construction industry would have the most negative impact on jobs while cutting social security benefits would have much less effect on unemployment (Benn 1989: 678). Leader of the House of Commons Michael Foot clarified with the Prime Minister the scope and nature of the decision the Cabinet had made, asking 'is it clear that the Cabinet can suspend its final judgment until the very end of this whole business when we know the quantum, we know the response, we know the allocation, we know whether we can get import deposits, we know the whole acceptability?' (Benn 1989: 679). The Prime Minister agreed (Callaghan 1987: 440; Benn 1989: 679).

FURTHER NEGOTIATING DIFFICULTIES, EARLY DECEMBER 1976

The Prime Minister and the Chancellor both emphasize that it was by no means clear to them that the Fund would accept the proposals that the Cabinet had agreed of a £1.5 billion PSBR cut for 1977–78, made up of £1 billion in public expenditure cuts and £500 million in the sale of state-owned British Petroleum shares (Callaghan 1987: 440; Healey 1989: 431–2). Callaghan (1976b) sent a message to President Ford to bring him up to date. He began by thanking the President for 'your continuing interest and our close contact during this difficult period,' telling Ford that the Cabinet meeting had been 'long and difficult . . . and I do not yet know whether I shall be able to carry all the Cabinet with me.' Callaghan then outlined the difference between the Government's PSBR proposals and those of the IMF.

> Denis Healey has been authorised by a majority decision [of the Cabinet] to put to the IMF an adjustment of £1½ billion which he and I had recommended. This would be achieved by the sale of assets worth £½ billion and by fiscal changes – mainly public expenditure cuts – worth £1 billion. This would have the effect of reducing the PSBR in 1977–78 to £8.7 billion, a very substantial reduction. The IMF were asking for public expenditure cuts of £1½–£2 billion but at the lower end of this range there is a gap of £½ billion between our position and theirs.

The Prime Minister did not mince words in describing to Ford the political difficulties the crisis was presenting him.

> I am not positive that I can keep all the Cabinet on board even yet, until they see how the details of the savings are to be made. We are getting down to this next Monday [6 December]. Denis Healey has been authorised to put the Cabinet's position to the Fund and I will of course keep you posted of developments should it not be possible to reach agreement. I must tell you that I am not sanguine, and I can only hope the IMF really understand the consequences.

West German Chancellor Helmut Schmidt at about this time sought to soften the American hard-line by sending German Finance Ministry official Karl Otto Pöhl to Washington 'to try and weaken the conditions' (Burk and Cairncross 1992: 91). An anonymous Bundesbank official (most probably Pöhl himself) has recounted that 'when I went to Washington, I saw [US Federal Reserve Chairman Arthur] Burns, and he was furious about Schmidt's intervention – said we shouldn't meddle with the Fund's business from a political point of view, that it was a bad precedent' (Bernstein 1983: 519; see also Burk and Cairncross 1992: 91). The appeals from Callaghan and Schmidt had little if any influence on the American position; according to IMF Managing Director Witteveen (1987: 31), 'the Americans didn't give in to this pressure.... They didn't press me to be easy. In fact, Arthur Burns ... was very supportive. He called me on the telephone one evening to tell me that he was behind the Fund's position.'

Callaghan's message (1976b) to President Ford took up again the question of a sterling balances safety net. The US position was that any potential sterling balances arrangement was contingent upon prior agreement on the terms of a conditional IMF loan (see Chapter 9).

Now that agreement with the Fund appeared imminent, Callaghan pressed Ford on the issue.

> Assuming . . . that agreement can be reached with the Fund in the next few days, I hope we can make rapid progress on the safety net. I will understand your position that agreement with the Fund is an essential prerequisite and also that there is a Congressional angle that must wait for January, but I think that you also understand that if I am to have the best chance of acceptance of the package firstly in Cabinet and secondly in the country, I shall need to be able to say when we announce it something fairly positive about the safety net. As you know, what we have in mind is a multilateral facility arranged between central banks on which we would be able to draw in event of any net fall in sterling balances which involved a cost to our official reserves. It would help me a great deal if in the announcement we plan to make on or around 15 December, if all goes well about an agreement with the IMF, we could include something on the following lines:
>
>> President Ford has indicated to me that he will be recommending Congress to approve United States participation in this facility and I now expect that negotiations on it can be brought to a speedy conclusion.[8]

The negotiations with the IMF almost collapsed when Healey met with Whittome to present the Government's PSBR proposals. Healey (1989: 432) recounts that he was able to convince Whittome to accept no more than £1 billion in public expenditure cuts, 'but Witteveen rang Whittome from Washington and asked for yet another billion. I told Whittome he should tell the Managing Director to "take a running jump." He smiled and said, "We seem to have reached an impasse." I told him to warn Witteveen that if he persisted, we would call a general election on the issue of the IMF versus the people' (see also Healey 1987: 68; private political diaries of Tony Benn, 6 December 1976). Callaghan (1987: 441) recounts that 'I had not given the Chancellor any authority to threaten a general election but I was quite happy that he should have done so.' Late into the evening, he and Healey 'talk[ed] over the various drastic policy changes that would be needed if a loan was not forthcoming. They would have meant a bumpy ride not just for the British people but also for the international community, with serious implications for our relations with the GATT, the European Community and NATO, as well as the United States. On that night anything seemed possible.'

The following morning, Callaghan recounts (1987: 441), he was 'handed a message I had not expected. . . . The IMF negotiators had . . . suggest[ed] a renewal of contacts between them and our Treasury officials. I was of course agreeable.' However, emergency preparations in the event agreement was not forthcoming commenced. Callaghan subsequently revealed to Cabinet that Downing Street and Treasury officials had been 'going over the crisis measures to brush them up,' and according to Healey, the emergency measures would have been introduced on 7 December had agreement with the IMF not been achieved (private political diaries of Tony Benn, 7 December 1976). But agreement with the Fund was forthcoming. Healey recounts (1989: 432) that 'Witteveen surrendered. I suspect he had put forward his demand only because he had been gotten at by Ed Yeo, who was trying to mastermind the whole negotiation from the US Treasury' (see also Healey 1987: 68; 1989: 430). According to Callaghan (1987: 441), the negotiations after the breakdown 'proceeded much more easily than before,' and the Chancellor was able to tell Cabinet that 'he had reached an agreement that he was ready to recommend to his colleagues. Put simply, he would limit borrowing by the Public Sector to £8.7 billion in 1977–78 (plus £500 millions from the sale of British Petroleum shares) and to £8.6 billion in 1978–79, although there was no conclusion on how the latter figure would be arrived at.'[9]

FINALIZING THE TERMS, DECEMBER 1976

When Cabinet met again on 6 December, the Chancellor brought his colleagues up to date on the negotiations, including the IMF's request for additional expenditure cuts and Healey's response that Witteveen 'could take a running jump' (private political diaries of Tony Benn, 6 December 1976). Regarding import deposits, Healey pointed out to Cabinet that 'we might have to choose between import deposits and the [sterling balances] safety net' (private political diaries of Tony Benn, 6 December 1976). As the session progressed, expenditure cuts were made in defense, overseas aid, food subsidies, and the capital expenditure of the publicly-owned water authorities. The discussions were extended into the following day and were 'very difficult' (Barnett 1982: 106–7). The Chancellor argued strongly in favor of benefits reductions – 'we would be swept out of office by the anger of the low paid if we didn't deal with the level of benefits' – but Ministers' views were mixed, and the Prime Minister 'proposed deferring the point. We had

£700 million [in cuts] already' (Benn 1989: 683). Other politically difficult proposals were discussed without much progress or agreement.[10] According to Chief Secretary to the Treasury Joel Barnett (1982: 106), the Prime Minister

> appeared to lose his patience. . . . He said, as we could not agree, he and Denis would go away, make up a package and present it to the House and the Parliamentary Party. If it was thrown out by the Party, that would be that; if it was approved, then those Cabinet Ministers who wanted to resign should do so then, but not before. There was an appalled silence before Michael Foot, Peter Shore and a number of others said there was no need for that, and that we were not far from agreement.
> (See also Benn 1989: 685; Fay and Young 1978, 3: 34)

When Cabinet convened again, the Chancellor presented a new paper that asked for nearly £1.2 billion in cuts rather than the £1 billion total that had already been agreed: 'Denis said that confidence had been undermined by the [press] leaks and therefore we'd have to make more cuts in public expenditure to prevent further loss of confidence' (Benn 1989: 685). When some of his colleagues (including the Prime Minister) suggested that the additional £200 million be achieved through excise tax increases that would permit the Government to direct additional resources to industry, the Chancellor argued that tax increases 'would destroy our credibility with the markets' and that 'I am afraid the package will fail if there is a tax element in it' (private political diaries of Tony Benn, 7 December 1976). A wide range of expenditure cuts in environmental services, nationalized industry prices, and housing were discussed and agreed (private political diaries of Tony Benn, 7 December 1976; Fay and Young 1978, 3: 34; Barnett 1982: 106). At the close of the meeting, the Prime Minister emphasized the need for secrecy – 'if it was known what the Treasury asked, and what it had got (which was much less), it would damage the package' – and summed up what had been concluded: 'we have . . . given authority to the Chancellor to offer the IMF £1 billion cuts in public expenditure in 1977–78, £2 billion in 1978–79, of which half a billion will be in tax. We have agreed to sell the [British Petroleum] shares [and] we would consult on the letter of intent to the IMF' (Benn 1989: 686). The Chancellor was defeated in his opposition to excise tax increases – the Prime Minister summed up that £200 million in taxes would be raised in 1977–78 for an 'add-back' to industry – as well as on the proposed cuts in social security benefits (Benn 1989: 686; see also Burk and Cairncross 1992: 105–6).

Although most of the conflict surrounding the loan centered on the PSBR limits, certain other details of the loan agreement were also problematic and were not fully agreed until the weekend of 11–12 December (De Vries 1985, 1: 472). One of the stickier problems was the phasing – the timed release of borrowed funds – that would accompany the loan. 'UK officials understandably wanted to be able to have as large a "front-loading" as possible, while the Fund management and staff considered about SDR 1 billion more appropriate as a first drawing' (De Vries 1985, 1: 471). Unable to reach agreement with the IMF, Healey sent a message (1976d) to US Treasury Secretary Simon on 5 December, reviewing the disagreement.

> We quite accept that our drawings must be phased over the two-year period of the stand-by: but we have urged that we need some front-loading – in particular that we must take a substantial immediate drawing to replenish our reserves after the 9 December repayments [of drawings from the June central bank stand-by] and give us some visible freedom of manoeuvre in markets during the next few months. So far, the IMF have conceded that we might draw up to about $1 billion initially, but no more.

The Chancellor laid out the case to Simon for a large early drawing.

> The world knows that we have some $1½ billion to repay this month: it is also well-known that when we have done this our reserves will be far below the safe $5 billion mark which has long been regarded as the safe minimum to have in the shop-window. I greatly fear that, apart from its constraining effect on our freedom of manoeuvre, the announcement that we are getting only $1 billion immediately, after all the arguments we have been through with the Fund, would come as a disappointment, even a shock, to domestic and market opinion. It would appear inconsistent with the conditions on which the June stand-by was offered. . . . I would ask you to press on the Fund the need for us to replenish our 9 December repayments [of $1½ billion] fully.

Healey anticipated the counter-argument that with front-loading, the Fund could be perceived to be treating the UK with partiality.

> I can well understand the fear of the Fund that they may be thought to be making a favourable exception of the UK from the general practice of conditionality. But there are two respects in which our case is exceptional:

(a) We are specifically applying, in line with the terms of the June agreement with the G-10 countries, for a drawing to reimburse a substantial short-term credit which is now due for repayment.

(b) We are being asked to accept phasing of drawings over two years instead of the customary one. We are not opposed to this, but consider that a concession to us on the initial drawing sufficient to enable us to repay the stand-by is a more reasonable quid pro quo from the IMF point of view as well as being implicit in the June arrangement with the G-10 countries.

The Fund had been unpersuaded by British front-loading arguments; as late as 14 December, UK Treasury official Derek Mitchell was asking German Finance Ministry official Karl Otto Pöhl 'to keep up the pressure to allow the UK a large initial drawing from the IMF' (Burk and Cairncross 1992: 118; see also *Financial Times*, 13 December 1976, 'IMF may release,' p. 1). In the end, the Fund appears to have given in slightly; when Healey introduced the package in Parliament on 15 December (UK Healey 1976g: 1535), he announced that $1.15 billion of the nearly $4 billion stand-by would be 'immediately' available, with 'over $1 billion more before the end of 1977.'

Healey told Simon that, as an alternative to front-loading

> the Fund themselves have suggested that we might look to some of our G-10 partners to provide new 'bridging finance' for six or nine months until our Fund drawings have accumulated to $1½ to $2 billion. This would be less attractive, but I accept it as an alternative if you thought it appropriate and if arrangements could be made for it very quickly. . . . You will recognise that this matter must be cleared up before I make my statement to Parliament in the week beginning 13 December.
>
> (Healey 1976d)

Notwithstanding the British expression of urgency, American officials were not quick to act. US Under-Secretary for Monetary Affairs Edwin Yeo telephoned his British counterpart Derek Mitchell on 9 December[11] to tell him if he wanted to come to Washington to discuss possible swap arrangements and sterling balances, he could do so any time the following week. Mitchell met with Yeo and Burns in Washington on 12–13 December (Burk and Cairncross 1992: 117–18; *The Times*, 13 December 1976, '"No American pledge",' p. 19). It was only on 14 December – one day before Healey was to announce the IMF package in Parliament – that Simon sent a short message to Healey regarding bilateral swaps with the US: 'I am pleased to be able to assure you, in response to the request in your letter of December 6 [quoted above], that we will be able to offer additional short-term financing to supplement your initial drawings from the IMF. Ed Yeo will discuss the details of what we can provide with your representatives here' (Simon 1976g).

When Healey announced the IMF loan in Parliament, he also announced that supplemental financing had been arranged with the US Treasury and Federal Reserve for $500 million and with the German Bundesbank for $350 million 'in anticipation of further drawings under the agreement with the IMF which will take place later in the year' (UK Healey 1976g: 1536). However, the last-minute nature of the US–UK swap was not kept secret from the press: *The Times* reported that the arrangements had been put together hurriedly 'just hours before Mr. Healey made his statement' (16 December 1976, 'Pound dips,' p. 19). Moreover, two other important features of the swap with the US were left unsaid by the Chancellor: first, the $500 million was not as yet available to be drawn; second, drawings on the arrangement were conditional upon UK compliance with the terms of the IMF standby (Burns 1977). One possible reason for Healey's lack of candor is the likely possibility that these details had yet to be worked out with US officials. 'Agreement in principle' for the swap with the US Federal Reserve was only confirmed through an exchange of cables in late December (Burns 1977), and it was not until early January 1977 that US Federal Reserve Chairman Arthur Burns sent a message to Bank of England Governor Gordon Richardson to inform him that 'the Bank of England may initiate drawings on our swap line' and that 'I would like you to note as a mutual understanding that drawings and renewals are to be conditioned on the fulfillment by your Government of the terms of the IMF stand-by'[12] (Burns 1977).

Another element of the policy package surrounding the IMF loan that appears to have been worked out at the eleventh hour was whether the Government would introduce import deposits. Callaghan had outlined to Cabinet in early December his '3-legged stool' strategy involving 'import deposits on the same basis as Italy' (Benn 1989: 673). However, he had also told President Ford at the same time that the Government had not yet taken a decision on import deposits (Callaghan 1976b). Minister of Trade Edmund Dell (1991: 268) argues that Callaghan's advocacy of import deposits was largely 'bluster' and that Callaghan 'did not appear to realize that [import deposits were] irrelevant, once he had supported Healey, because the IMF would not consent.' There is, however, contrary evidence suggesting that the IMF was at least somewhat open to the possibility of temporary import restrictions. Leader of the IMF negotiating team Alan Whittome has commented that 'the Fund would probably have accepted short-term import controls' (Burk and Cairncross 1992: 87, fn 114), and indeed, Italy in the mid-1970s was able to arrange upper credit tranche IMF stand-bys while having an import deposit scheme (see De Vries 1985, 1: 448–9, 452; Spaventa 1983: 452, 458–9).

But import deposits were not part of the final package. When Cabinet met to review the letter of intent, the Prime Minister informed his colleagues that import deposits had been ruled out (Benn 1989: 687). Earlier, he had warned the TUC–Labour Party Liaison Committee that direct action on imports 'could well prejudice the satisfactory resolution of the sterling balance issue' (TUC–Labour Party Liaison Committee, Minutes, 6 December 1976). The accuracy of this view was confirmed when German Finance Ministry official Karl Otto Pöhl told UK Treasury official Derek Mitchell of Chancellor Schmidt's relief that the British were not in fact taking any action on imports; such action, Pöhl told Mitchell, would have seriously affected Schmidt's ability to assist the British in other ways, including the arrangement of a sterling balance safety net (Burk and Cairncross 1992: 119).

Other policy measures accompanying the loan appear to have been more easily agreed. With respect to monetary policy, the Fund and the Treasury agreed early on 'that the £9 billion DCE [Domestic Credit Expansion] target for 1976–77 which was included in the 1975 letter of intent should be the starting point for the negotiations' (Bernstein 1983: 510; Healey 1975a). The Chancellor had already adopted a policy of publicly announced monetary growth targets before the IMF arrived in London. The UK and IMF negotiators agreed upon DCE ceilings of £9 billion in fiscal year 1976–77, £7.7 billion in fiscal year 1977–78, and about £6 billion in fiscal year 1978–79. In his 15 December announcement to Parliament (UK Healey 1976g: 1534), the Chancellor linked the £9 billion 1976–77 DCE target to an M3 target growth range of between 9 and 13 per cent.[13] 'While this range suggested virtually no change in the monetary stance, financial markets viewed the new commitments as more binding and sentiment shifted almost immediately' (OECD 1978: 29–30).

During the Cabinet discussion about the loan terms, 'little account was taken of the potential reactions of the unions and the Parliamentary Labour Party to the conditions.... It was only later, when the Cabinet was decided where and how to make cuts, after the total amount had been agreed, that the reactions of the unions and the party became important considerations' (Bernstein 1983: 556). The Chancellor discussed the economic situation at a 6 December meeting of the TUC–Labour Party Liaison Committee. The IMF loan was 'essentially a form of bridging finance,' he explained, and his main objectives were 'to stabilise the value of the pound and to reduce interest rates, which would in turn have a beneficial effect on demand in the economy' (TUC–Labour Party Liaison Committee, Minutes, 6 December 1976; see also Benn 1989: 680). Reportedly, the TUC leadership's response to the Chancellor's Liaison Committee presentation was 'measured.' TUC General Secretary Len Murray emphasized the broader and more constraining 'international context' of the loan, and the TUC side more generally 'stressed the importance of maintaining the Social Contract and the industrial strategy and of avoiding any division in the Labour Movement which would prejudice the Labour Party in Government.' Healey commented that he was grateful for the tone of the discussion (*The Times*, 7 December 1976, 'TUC wrings,' p. 1; TUC–Labour Party Liaison Committee, Minutes, 6 December 1976; Benn 1989: 680–1; private political diaries of Tony Benn, 6 December 1976).

The tone of the meeting changed, however, when the Chancellor referred to the proposals on social benefits cuts that were being discussed in Cabinet (see above). When he told the Committee that 'as for the level of benefits compared to the income of those at work, . . . the only way of dealing with that was by reducing the rate of increase of benefits or by taxing them,' Jack Jones shot back 'or by increasing wages' and Len Murray added 'or by getting more people back to work' (private political diaries of Tony Benn, 6 December 1976). Although the TUC leadership wanted to maintain the Government in power, they continued to be at odds with the Government's economic priorities (see Jones 1986: 324; *The Times*, 7 December 1976, 'TGWU move,' p. 4; *The Times*, 14 December 1976, 'Murray warning,' p. 19; *Financial Times*, 17 December 1976, 'After the economic package,' p. 32).

The Prime Minister was concerned about the acceptability of the package on Labour's back benches. The Tribune group of approximately 80 left-wing Labour MPs issued a statement in early December warning the Government that it could not count on the group's support if further cuts in public expenditure demanded by the IMF were agreed (*The Guardian*, 7 December 1976, 'Tribunites fire,' p. 1). At a meeting of the Government's whips, the Prime Minister asked whether Labour MPs would remain united. Callaghan (1987: 442–3) recounts they told me that it was demoralising for the Party to have agreed to a set of measures in July and then to learn that more was required in December, and a group of those they called 'kamikaze' members might vote against the Government on specific issues. Nevertheless, the Government would win if it came to an issue of confidence, but they advised me, if possible, to avoid reductions in expenditure that would require legislation, for they could not guarantee a majority.

The Fund negotiating team returned to Washington on 13 December, six weeks after they had first arrived (*The Times*, 15 December 1976, 'IMF likely,' p. 1; *Financial Times*, 14 December 1976, 'IMF team,' p. 42). Cabinet met on 14 December to review the letter of intent (Benn 1989: 687–8). On 15 December, the Chancellor in a statement to Parliament (UK Healey 1976g) made public the letter of intent and announced the policy package that would accompany the loan. The stand-by and policy conditions were to cover a two-year period. The PSBR was to be reduced to £8.7 billion in 1977–78 and to 'somewhat less in the following year – on present forecasts I expect a figure of some £8.6 billion' (UK Healey 1976g: 1525; Healey 1976e: paras 12, 14). The PSBR adjustment, the Chancellor told Parliament, 'will come mainly from savings in public expenditure' and he broadly outlined where the expenditure cuts would fall (see Table 10.2). He assured Parliament that 'once again we have avoided mechanical cuts across the board and have not reduced the main social security benefits, although we are concerned about the narrowing gap between them and the income of those in work' (UK Healey 1976g: 1525–7). As a part of the 1977–78 PSBR reduction, he also announced that £500 million of the Government's holdings in British Petroleum would be sold (UK Healey 1976g: 1532; Healey 1976e: para. 12).

With respect to monetary policy, Domestic Credit Expansion (DCE) ceilings were set. DCE would be limited to £9 billion in 1976–77, £7.7 billion in 1977–78, and about £6 billion in 1978–79 (UK Healey 1976g: 1534; Healey 1976e: paras. 18–22; see also Donoughue 1987: 100; Dell 1991: 272–3). Regarding import controls, the Government pledged that it 'remains firmly opposed to generalized restrictions on trade and does not intend to introduce restrictions for balance of payment purposes'[14] (Healey 1976e: para. 24). The letter of intent concluded with a densely worded statement about Fund monitoring of the agreement,[15] which was subsequently clarified by the Chancellor the following day. 'On the question of performance,' Healey explained, 'we are not on this occasion inviting the Fund to monitor our performance by visits every quarter.[16] We have told the Fund how we hope to achieve our targets in the early stages of the programme, and, therefore, we shall be subject only to the normal annual visits of the members of the Fund which all members agree to accept' (*The Times*, 17 December 1976, 'Only annual visits,' p. 12).

The Chancellor tried to put the best face possible on the package when he asserted that 'the Government have taken decisions because they believe them to be necessary. . . . They are Government decisions. They would have been more necessary if we had not been able to count on the endorsement of our policies by the IMF and on the assistance to our resources which we shall get from IMF borrowing' (UK Healey 1976g: 1543). Nevertheless, the wider reaction to the policy changes was mixed. On one hand, US Treasury Secretary William Simon said he believed the program as announced was 'excellent,' and Managing Director Johannes Witteveen indicated that he was prepared to recommend that the IMF Executive Board approve the UK's stand-by request (*The Times*, 16 December 1976, 'Pound dips,' p. 19). In Parliament, however, Shadow Chancellor of the Exchequer Geoffrey Howe characterized the measures as an 'IMF budget' and scornfully gibed that 'it seems that Labour Governments can be prevented from steering the economy towards disaster only when they are under the firm surveillance of the IMF' (*Hansard*, 15 December 1976, col. 1538). Callaghan (1987: 443) recounts that on the Government's back benches, 'there was a lot of criticism from left-wing members. I replied with the question, "Do you want us to go on?" Faced with that, there was no doubt about their answer' (see also Benn 1989: 689–90). However, the degree of unhappiness on Labour's back benches was revealed when, with the Conservatives abstaining, 27 Labour MPs defied a three-line whip to vote against the Government on the policy measures, and about 30 Labour MPs abstained. The vote was 219–51, with the Liberals and Scottish and Welsh nationalists voting alongside the Labour rebels against the Government[17] (*The Times*, 22 December 1976, 'Labour MP revolt,' p. 4).

The TUC General Council's response to the package was also mixed. Some members were hostile: General Secretary of the National Union of General and Municipal Workers David Basnett argued that the Government was taking the wrong path and urged the implementation of the TUC's alternative strategy; General Secretary of the National Union for Public Employees Alan Fisher warned that 'in meeting the conditions made by the IMF, the Government have accepted a cheque that may bounce at the next general election.' The public responses of General

Table 10.2   1977–78 and 1978–79 public expenditure savings, announced 15 December 1976 (£ million at 1976 survey prices)

	1977–78	1978–79
Defence budget	100	200
Overseas aid	50	50
Food subsidies	160	57
Regional employment premium	150	170
Refinancing of fixed rate credits	100	200
Capital spending at Colleges of Further Education	10	10
Nationalised industries	110	130
Road construction	75	50
Housing	-20	300
Regional water authorities etc. construction	75	130
Local environmental services: construction and other capital	50	50
Community ownership of development land	35	35
Courts – purchase of sites	2	—
Education – construction	22	11
Other education expenditure, including school meals	20	30
Health and personal social services – construction	10	20
Other National Health Services expenditure	5	5
Northern Ireland	5	10
Property Services Agency	27	45
Expenditure on the Civil Service	30	10
Total	1016	1513

Source: UK Healey (1976g: 1558–8)

Secretary of the Transport and General Workers' Union Jack Jones and TUC General Secretary Len Murray were more measured, however: Jones commented that although the Social Contract would be 'bruised' as a result of the measures, 'the essential unity of the Labour Party and the trade unions, despite our concern about a lot of these measures, will be maintained;' Murray told the press that the Government had 'clearly fought to minimize the cuts and their deflationary impact, and trade unionists will understand that if the United Kingdom did not get the IMF loan the alternative would be even worse' (*Financial Times*, 16 December 1976, 'Some Tory approval,' p. 1; *The Times*, 16 December 1976, 'Mr Jones sees,' p. 4, 'TUC Committee,' p. 1).

The TUC Economic Committee issued a statement that reflected the conflicting views of its members (TUC 1977a: 219; *Financial Times*, 17 December 1976, 'After the economic package,' p. 32). It began sympathetically, noting that the TUC 'understands' the Government's circumstances and 'recognises' the efforts to limit the deflationary impact of the IMF's conditions. 'It has to be accepted that there was no real alternative to seeking financial support from abroad if the pound was to be protected against continuing downward pressure, the consequence of which would have been even more difficulties on the balance of payments and even more unemployment' (TUC 1977a: 219). The statement quickly became more critical, however. The TUC renewed its call for selective import controls, and stated bluntly that the cuts 'will result in the continuation of quite unacceptable levels of unemployment [and] do not make a positive contribution to the growth path in the industrial strategy' (TUC 1977a: 219–20). The statement concluded with a warning to the Government on the need for 'an orderly return to collective bargaining' which 'must be set in the context of an effective strategy to tackle unemployment and inflation' (TUC 1977a: 220). In the Prime Minister's view, while the general tone of the TUC statement was 'supportive,' the emphasis on the return to collective bargaining was 'ominous' (Callaghan 1987: 443). Indeed, even before the letter of intent was announced, TUC General Secretary Len Murray was warning the Government that union loyalty 'depends on replenishment and cannot be taken for granted' and that the Government was going to have problems extending pay policy into a third year (*Financial Times*, 14 December 1976, 'Murray warning,' p. 19).

Currency markets were skeptical on the day of the letter of intent announcement; sterling fell by three-quarters of a cent. At a press conference, the Chancellor noted the pound's relative strength over the past two weeks (it was trading in the mid-$1.60s) and explained that the markets had already 'discounted the measures' (*The Times*, 16 December 1976, 'Pound dips,' p. 19). He was proven right. By the end of December, sterling had risen back above $1.70, and financial market commentators were soon speculating that sterling's strength might in fact pose problems (see *The Times*, 30 December 1976, 'Pound at three-month peak', p. 1; Samuel Brittan, *Financial Times*, 30 December 1976, 'Lombard,' p. 2; *National Institute Economic Review*, February 1977, p. 4). By early 1977, the return of confidence was so strong that when IMF Managing Director Witteveen visited London, 'UK officials were informally asking him how much to let sterling appreciate' (De Vries 1985, 1: 476) and the Minimum Lending Rate (MLR) began what was to become a quite substantial decline from 15 per cent in November 1976 to a low of 5 per cent in October 1977 (see *Bank of England Quarterly Bulletin*, December 1977, Statistical Annex, Table 9; Donoughue 1987: 140–1; Middlemas 1991: 144).

STERLING BALANCES, DECEMBER 1976–JANUARY 1977

The most important issue that remained outstanding with the mid-December announcement of the letter of intent was the question of sterling balances. Despite the pressing appeal from the Prime Minister for 'simultaneity' (see Chapter 9), an agreement on sterling balances was not announced until nearly a month after the announcement of the IMF loan. The British clearly would have preferred an earlier announcement, and they appear to have expected one. The Prime Minister expressed to President Ford in early December the hope that 'we can make rapid progress on the safety net' (Callaghan 1976b), and the Chancellor indicated publicly that he hoped to announce an agreement in principle on sterling balances when he announced the measures accompanying the IMF loan (*The Times*, 8 December 1976, 'Healey hint,' p. 1; *Financial Times*, 8 December 1976, 'Healey hint,' p. 1, 34; Fay and Young 1978, 3: 34).

Starting at different times and in varying degrees, the Federal Reserve, the Bundesbank, the Bank of England, and the Bank for International Settlements (BIS) had all done preliminary work on possible solutions to the sterling balances problem (see Burk and Cairncross 1992: 112–15). By early December in the Federal Reserve, two different proposals were under consideration – one written by President of the New York Federal Reserve Bank Paul Volcker and labeled the 'Volcker Plan,' the other labeled the 'Treasury Plan' and most probably written by Under-Secretary for Monetary Affairs Edwin Yeo (Volcker 1976; US Federal Reserve System 1976b). A third plan arrived on 9 December when General Manager of the BIS René Larre sent to G-10 central bank governors a paper intended to serve as a basis for possible informal discussions on sterling balances (Larre 1976). While the three plans differed in the type of sterling balances to be covered, in the size of the proposed safety net, in the location of the facility, and in the more technical aspects of resolving the sterling balances problem (see US Federal Reserve System 1976b), the Treasury Plan was distinct from the others in wanting to 'ensure IMF conditionality' as a specific objective of any sterling balance arrangement and in suggesting that the safety net could 'tighten conditionality by making access . . . conditional upon *quarterly* satisfaction of IMF conditions'[18] (US Federal Reserve System 1976b, original emphasis).

British Ambassador to the US Peter Ramsbotham was in frequent contact with White House officials about sterling balances, and he reported to London that 'all hope of an announcement at the same time as the IMF loan conditions were revealed should be abandoned.' Federal Reserve Chairman Arthur Burns in particular was 'intractable. He not only refused to discuss the agreement, he attacked Ford and Kissinger for meddling in a technical matter, and was furious at Callaghan's consistent pressure' (Fay and Young 1978, 3: 34). Although relatively optimistic reports about the likelihood of a sterling balance agreement were appearing in the British press,[19] a well-informed report appeared in *The New York Times* on 9 December ('British sterling,' pp. 71, 80) that focused on the choices facing US policy-makers and speculated that 'it is possible that nothing at all will be done. The United States Government is not yet committed to anything. . . . Top American officials retain considerable skepticism about how serious the problem is. A common view here is that if Britain's Government ran the economy properly, the sterling balances probably would not be much of a problem.' When on the following day a wire service reported that Congressman Henry Reuss, the Chairman of the House of Representatives Banking Committee, had indicated that the US, Germany, and Japan were 'very near agreement' on a $5 billion sterling balances safety net, Treasury Under-Secretary Yeo publicly denied the report, stating that 'there have been no substantive talks between US and British officials on sterling balances' (*Financial Times*, 11 December 1976, 'Commitment,' p. 1).

With the IMF loan announcement drawing near, the lack of progress on sterling balances must have worried the Prime Minister (see Callaghan 1987: 431–2, 437). Callaghan again appealed for assistance. US Secretary of State Henry Kissinger was in London on 11 December, and Callaghan 'asked Kissinger to intervene once more with the President to get the sterling balances agreement through. Kissinger obliged by sending a message . . . reporting the British anxiety at the bloody-mindedness of Yeo and Burns and told the PM that he would do what he personally could on his return' (Fay and Young 1978, 3: 34). The Prime Minister himself also sent a message to the President.[20]

According to press accounts, the discussions between US and UK officials about sterling balances in the days leading up to the IMF loan announcement did not go well. 'Authoritative sources' in Washington commented that the British had been overconfident about the support they could expect to obtain from the US on sterling balances. UK officials reportedly were 'surprised at the determination with which some US officials have expressed their views on the UK's plans to improve the economic situation.' Federal Reserve Chairman Burns was characterized as 'quite blunt' (*The Times*, 13 December 1976, '"No

American pledge"',' p. 19). 'Yeo was intensely suspicious' (Fay and Young 1978, 3: 34). He and Burns insisted that there was no real problem regarding sterling balances, and that in any event, little could be done by the US during a period of Presidential transition (Burk and Cairncross 1992: 117–18). According to Yeo:

> I was afraid of . . . sabotaging the IMF agreement by having a sterling balances deal which just provided a lot of unconditional money by the back door. We had sweated blood, and believed it was absolutely essential that the market perceived that the centrepiece was the IMF deal and not a sterling balances agreement that looked like a crock of gold in disguise. With that we would have been finessed at the last moment.
>
> (Fay and Young 1978, 3: 34; see also Bernstein 1983: 587)

Simultaneous to the discussions in Washington, central bankers (including Governor of the Bank of England Gordon Richardson and Bundesbank Deputy Governor Otmar Emminger) were meeting at the Bank for International Settlements (BIS) in Basle to discuss sterling balances (*Financial Times*, 13 December 1976, 'IMF may release,' p. 1; *The Times*, 13 December 1976, 'Pound backing,' p. 19). German officials Karl Otto Pöhl and Otmar Emminger had tried prior to the BIS meeting to persuade Arthur Burns to move forward on sterling balances, arguing that

> there was no reason why the agreement should not be put through. . . . Burns . . . told them that Chancellor Schmidt had no business interfering and that he would not accept the dictates of anybody, PM, Chancellor, even President. He refused point-blank to send his international expert Henry Wallich to Basle to discuss the details. He was afraid of being outflanked at the last moment by an irate British Government.
>
> (Fay and Young 1978, 3: 34)

Reportedly, the progress made at the Basle meeting was 'considerable.' A West German central banker told the press afterwards that on the basis of the discussions held thus far, the Chancellor of the Exchequer would be able to state in his announcement of the IMF package on 15 December that 'it will be possible to reach an agreement [on sterling balances] before long' (*Guardian*, 15 December 1976, 'Banks stable,' p. 1).

Federal Reserve Board Governor Henry Wallich had worked out the wording of the Chancellor's comments on sterling balances in Healey's public announcement of the IMF loan to Parliament, and Chairman Burns had scribbled 'for Dennis [*sic*]' across Wallich's draft (Wallich 1976b). Healey followed Wallich's wording almost verbatim, telling Parliament that

> as the House knows, the Government have been concerned to re-move the pressures exerted on the sterling exchange rate by the overhang of the sterling balances. Considerable work has already been done on this problem in the Bank for International Settlements in Basle, where Central Bank Governors have had constructive dis-cussions over the last weekend. At the same time, the matter is also under discussion with the Treasury and the Federal Reserve in Wash-ington. These talks have revealed a general desire on the part of those concerned to achieve a satisfactory arrangement for the ster-ling balances, and I believe it will be possible to reach an agree-ment before long.
>
> (UK Healey 1976g: 1535–6)

In the Cabinet session on 14 December to review the letter of intent, there was bitterness about how little had been obtained on sterling balances. Healey told his colleagues on 14 December that 'the US Fed and the US Treasury are being very unhelpful and [President] Ford insists on an IMF settlement first.' The Prime Minister said that he was 'disappointed. . . . Ford and Schmidt had let him down and that Burns of the Fed was most unhelpful, and it was the first time in his life that he felt anti-American' (private political diaries of Tony Benn, 14 December 1976).

Nonetheless, Callaghan maintained his contacts with President Ford: on 16 December he sent a one-page telegram to Ford regarding ster-ling balances.[21] The question now received attention at the highest levels of the US Government. On 18 December, a meeting was held at the White House among the relevant senior officials so that an American view could be worked out. In attendance were President Ford, Secre-tary of State Henry Kissinger, Federal Reserve Chairman Arthur Burns, and Under-Secretary for Monetary Affairs Ed Yeo[22] (Fay and Young 1978, 3:34). 'Burns delivered a vigorous attack on the way the White House had handled the affair: if the politicians had kept out of it, he and the technical people could have fixed it all up in a couple of weeks. But, Kissinger replied, it was a political problem, and the sterling bal-ances were a key decision: they would help end the sterling crisis.' It was decided at the meeting that there would be a sterling balance agree-ment, but the participants argued over what kind of agreement it would be: 'Kissinger wanted a broad, generous agreement which would be a political bonus to Callaghan, while [Burns and Yeo] wanted something more limited. Kissinger scored some points, because Yeo was told to stop being so bloody-minded, but the President gave [Yeo] the vital job of drafting the deal' (Fay and Young 1978, 3: 34).

Further discussions on sterling balances occurred when financial and monetary officials from the G-10 countries met in Paris to activate the IMF's General Arrangements to Borrow (GAB) to raise the necessary funds for on-lending to the UK (*The Times*, 17 December 1976, 'Paris move,' p. 21; *Financial Times*, 20 December 1976, 'Talks this week,' p. 1; *IMF Survey*, 10 January 1977, pp. 2–3). 'The agreement that was beginning to take shape had two main components: sufficient reserves to resist any renewed [downward] pressure on the pound – the safety net – and arrangements to phase out the balances' (Burk and Cairncross 1992: 121). Despite these areas of agreement, however, there is evidence to suggest that the Americans were continuing to raise difficulties.[23] After the meetings, Bundesbank official Otmar Emminger reported to the Bundesbank Central Bank Council that 'it was likely – although not certain – that in January central bank governors would have before them a paper setting out the basis for [a sterling balances safety net]' (Burk and Cairncross 1992: 121) and Bank of England Governor Gordon Richardson sent a telex to Arthur Burns proposing to visit Washington with Bank of England official Kit McMahon in early January 1977 'if you felt it would be helpful in connection with the question of the sterling balances'[24] (Richardson 1976c).

Early in January 1977, US officials worked on various technical and procedural issues, including the size of the facility, the size of the American share of the facility, and the role of the IMF Managing Director in the arrangement in assuring that Britain continued to comply with IMF conditionality[25] (see US Federal Reserve System 1977a, 1977b). Although the British were again expressing public confidence about the likelihood of a sterling balance agreement (see *The Times*, 30 December 1976, 'Chancellor confident,' p. 2), it was not until 7 January that an anonymous US official indicated to the press that he was 'reasonably hopeful' about an agreement (*Financial Times*, 8 January 1977, 'US confident,' p. 1). On 10 January, G-10 central bankers (including Arthur Burns and Gordon Richardson) met at the BIS in Basle: late in the evening, a communiqué was issued announcing that 'agreement in principle has been reached . . . on a medium-term financing facility in the amount of $3 [billion] related to the official sterling balances' (*Financial Times*, 11 January 1977, 'Full text,' p. 11). The facility would be available for two years (renewable for a third year if all parties agreed), and the British would be permitted to draw on it as long as the UK continued to be eligible to draw on the IMF stand-by and if and when official sterling balances fell beneath their 8 December 1976 level of £2.165 billion (*Bank of England Quarterly Bulletin*, March 1977, p. 8; Bernstein 1983: 588; De Vries 1985, 1:475–6; US Federal Reserve System 1977c).

The central bankers envisioned a surveillance role for IMF Managing Director Witteveen in the arrangement:

> The UK will review regularly with the Managing Director of the IMF and with the governors of the participating central banks progress made in meeting the undertakings specified[26]. . . . If during the [two-year] period, the UK becomes ineligible to draw under the IMF stand-by, or in the judgment of the Managing Director is not making reasonable efforts to meet the undertakings[27]. . ., he will so notify the BIS as administrator of the facility. As a result eligibility to draw on the facility can be suspended.
>
> (US Federal Reserve System 1977c; De Vries 1985, 1:475–76)

Witteveen was 'enthusiastic' about his role in the arrangement (De Vries 1985, 1:476). Denis Healey, however, understandably minimized Witteveen's surveillance role in introducing the arrangement in Parliament, stating only that the Managing Director 'has been associated with these discussions and has been asked to assist in implementing the agreement' (UK Healey 1977a: 1261).

Following the announcement of 'agreement in principle' on sterling balances, the British authorities were able to borrow on commercial financial markets; in late January 1977, the Chancellor announced that the Bank of England had arranged a seven-year $1.5 billion loan from 13 British, German, and North American banks (*The Times*, 25 January 1977, 'Banks giving Britain,' p. 1). As Bank of England Governor Gordon Richardson (1977c: 51) explained, the UK's 1977 external deficit may be on a scale too large to be financed by the balance available . . . under the IMF stand-by. We therefore thought it prudent to ensure that our needs would be covered by medium-term finance. The terms under which the loan was made available . . . are an indication that the markets believe we have turned a corner.' Unmentioned, however was the fact that British commercial borrowing of this magnitude had only been possible after the IMF loan and sterling balances arrangement had been settled. Bundesbank Central Bank Council member Leonhard Gleske told Federal Reserve Board Governor Henry Wallich in February 1977 that, although discussions about the British commercial bank borrowing 'had been going on for some time' between German banks and the Bank of England, the German banks 'had waited until all pending negotiations – the IMF stand-by, the Bundesbank sterling balance arrangement – had been agreed upon. Presumably they meant to say that they did not mean to preempt any conditionality that might be imposed upon the UK through these official loan arrangements'[28] (Wallich 1977).

CONCLUSION

This chapter has outlined how the choices facing the British Government in December 1976 were structured so that the policy autonomy of the domestic authorities was constrained and how the various sources of external pressure on the Government – bilateral from the United States and Germany, multilateral from the IMF, and structural from the markets – worked in tandem to ensure that conditionality was enforced and that further policy change in Britain occurred. As the IMF official historian notes, the British clearly felt 'pushed' by the demands of the Fund (De Vries 1985, 1:478). The Government was shown to be incapable of obtaining a settlement on the 'on existing policies' terms that it had publicly announced as the basis for negotiations, and public expenditure had to be cut still further. The sterling balances arrangement was not announced simultaneously as the Prime Minister had wanted, but nearly a month after the IMF loan had been concluded. Moreover, the safety net was conditional upon British compliance with the terms of the letter of intent and thus served to reinforce and tighten IMF conditionality. Finally, financial markets proved unwilling to loan capital to the British until after the IMF and sterling balances arrangements were complete, further reinforcing external pressures for retrenchment upon the Government.

11 Conclusion

As the previous chapters have demonstrated, it was only with the explicit binding of the policy autonomy of the British economic authorities that the economic and political crises in Britain in 1976 were resolved. The constraints and parameters set for British economic policy through IMF conditionality were in effect for virtually the entirety of the Labour Government's remaining term of office. The IMF stand-by arrangement expired in January 1979; the sterling balances arrangement expired in February 1979 (De Vries 1985, 1:478); Labour was out of power in May 1979.

By way of conclusion, I wish to return to some of the broader questions that were raised in the first chapter and that have guided the case study chapters to argue that international cooperation theories can misidentify as 'cooperation' relations that are more accurately and more appropriately characterized as unwanted coercive pressures that can and do constrain sovereign policy autonomy. International regimes need to be more fully understood as structural manifestations of a hierarchically organized international political economy and as potential coercive power instruments. The literature is misleading when these coercive elements are misrepresented and when the non-voluntarist elements of 'cooperation' are underemphasized.

International economic and monetary relations during the mid-1970s were characterized by fundamental disagreements among advanced industrialized states about the rules and norms that should govern national economic management. On one hand, the British, the Italians, and (up through 1975) the IMF Managing Director argued that in light of the OPEC price shock, the swollen current account deficits of advanced industrialized states had to be financed, and that countries had to share and to 'accept the oil deficit' in the medium term in order to sustain economic activity and to avert potential global economic collapse (De Vries 1985, 1:314). On the other hand, the Americans, the Germans, and (after early 1976) the IMF Managing Director argued that easy financing was permitting deficit countries to postpone the necessary pain of adjustment and was thereby creating, tolerating, and even encouraging other kinds of risks to global monetary stability.

As US Treasury Secretary William Simon (1976j) argued in his address at the 1976 IMF annual meeting, '[a monetary] system means an agreed charter – a basic understanding among nations on the principles of behavior – that provides the framework in which we operate. But such a charter is only the beginning. Over time, the development of a system also involves the development of a code of behavior based on generally agreed-upon principles.' Deficit countries like the UK in the mid-1970s were perceived to be in violation of this 'code of behavior.' Senior officials in the US Government shared the opinion that, as US Federal Reserve Chairman Arthur Burns bluntly put it, the British Labour Government was a 'profligate Government' (Fay and Young 1978, 1:33). As Secretary Simon (1976a: 102) argued, 'to be sure, for a time an increased inflow of real resources from abroad may enable a country to postpone the hard choices among competing domestic claims. . . . But sooner or later, the bills come due – the adjustment I have spoken of . . . has to be made.' American officials in 1976 saw themselves as being in a position to ensure that the bills in London would indeed come due.

Economic policy retrenchment in Britain, involving repeated cutbacks in the Government's public expenditure plans and the move to publicly announced monetary targets, was largely the product of coercive external pressures exerted at multiple levels that served to constrict the policy autonomy of the governing authorities. At the structural level, pressures for policy change were exerted through the chronic lack of market confidence that was made manifest with the persistent downward pressure on sterling. Permanent Secretary to the Treasury Douglas Wass has acknowledged the power of these structural pressures when he commented in 1978 that 'if markets take the view that the policies pursued by a particular country are likely to damage assets held in that country or in that country's currency, they are likely to behave in ways which can actually enforce a policy change' (Keegan and Pennant-Rea 1979: 32). The lack of confidence in the British Government's ability to manage the economy was dramatic. In spite of intermittent but at times quite heavy support from the Bank of England, the pound fell from above $2 in March 1976 to trade in the mid-$1.50s by late October. In the 11 months up through November 1976, London required official financing of $7 billion to finance sterling balance outflows, almost all of which had to be obtained through foreign borrowing (BIS 1977: 89).

Market confidence can be elusive both conceptually and in terms of knowing the appropriate policy response, and as the British authorities discovered, once confidence is lost, it is difficult to determine the minimum policy changes necessary to assure its restoration. Accordingly,

over 1975 and 1976, the Government went through successive episodes of policy retrenchment. Public expenditure plans were scaled
back in the April 1975 Budget, in the public expenditure White Paper
released in February 1976, in the policy measures of July 1976, and in
the package that accompanied the IMF settlement in December 1976.
The Government implemented two years of restrictive incomes policy
agreements in which average male net incomes in real terms fell by
over 4 per cent in the first year, and by almost $\frac{1}{2}$ per cent in the
second (*Hansard*, 14 December 1978, cols. 381–2, Written Answers).
In the discussions surrounding both public expenditure cuts and incomes
policy, the maintenance and/or restoration of external confidence was
put forward repeatedly as the key reason for economic retrenchment.
Although Chancellor of the Exchequer Denis Healey assured Parliament
after the July 1976 expenditure reductions that 'the remaining obstacles
to our success are now removed' (Barnett 1982: 96), his optimism was
premature: only the explicit policy constraints imposed by subjecting
the Government to IMF conditionality turned the situation around. As
The Guardian perceptively commented a week after the public announcement of the IMF conditions, 'confidence is a splendidly unmeasurable,
unquantifiable, and unpredictable affair. No one will ever know if confidence would have returned without the [IMF] package. No one can
yet be sure what the effect of the package on confidence will be' (21
December 1976, 'Joel loses,' p. 12).

But it was not simply 'the market' that was convinced that further
retrenchment in Britain was necessary. US authorities held the British
Government's economic management in particularly low regard. In the
context of persistent market pressure on sterling, IMF conditionality
offered to American authorities an instrument through which they could
precipitate the macroeconomic policy changes they deemed necessary
in the UK. By attaching conditions to a short-term multilateral stand-
by extended to the UK for currency defense in June 1976, US officials
were able to push the British towards IMF discipline.

The American authorities' ideas about the kinds of changes they
would like to bring about were fundamental and wide-ranging, going
beyond the mere ensuring of 'responsible' national economic management. A background paper prepared for US Federal Reserve Chairman
Arthur Burns prior to the 1976 G-7 Economic Summit in Puerto Rico
outlined the broader American perspective and goals.

> Governments [in industrial states] strongly committed themselves to
> ameliorate social inequities at home and abroad and to achieve an

ever rising standard of living. However socially commendable, these commitments proved to be too ambitious in economic terms – both in what they attempted to achieve and in the expectations they raised among the public. Thus, the major task for the next several years is both economic and political – *not only to regain acceptable levels of output but also to set realistic goals that are accepted by the public at large.* Growth rates that will restore the industrial economies to high employment levels with sufficient price stability to be sustainable are clearly achievable, but they presuppose a reordering of priorities and a shift in resource allocation towards private investment.

(US Federal Reserve System 1976a: 3–4, emphasis in original)

The IMF-enforced retrenchment in the UK reflected the American preference for 'a reordering of priorities and a shift in resource allocation towards private investment' and necessitated a turn away from the ambitious policy goals set by the Labour Government when it came to power in 1974.

Finally, at the multilateral level, the IMF served as the instrument by which actual changes in British policy in late 1976 were brought about, with frank face-to-face negotiations about specific and binding constraints upon the Government's economic policy autonomy. Negotiations over policy retrenchment at the structural level are not possible because 'the market' is largely faceless. At the bilateral level, however, public government-to-government negotiations about the conduct of British macroeconomic policy would have been politically problematic and perceived to be an unacceptable infringement upon British sovereignty. In this context, American and German officials in 1976 'were relying on the Fund management and staff to assess the specific measures needed and to get UK officials to agree to them. . . . US Treasury officials . . . had come to regard the Fund as the only multi-country instrument that could make a serious attempt to lend on conditional terms and that might persuade a country to adopt the policies it recommended' (De Vries 1985, 1:470). And in fact, additional financing provided to the British in early 1977 from the US (the bilateral swap facility and the multilateral sterling balances safety net) was made available only after the IMF loan arrangements were finalized and was conditional upon Britain remaining in good standing *vis-à-vis* their obligations with the IMF.

Thus, it was through the application of IMF conditionality that the deflationary policy preferences of the markets, the US, and the IMF itself were realized in Britain over those of the legitimate elected Government. Resolution of the economic and political crisis on the on-existing-policies basis that was publicly stated by the Chancellor of the Exchequer proved not to be possible. The policy changes imposed upon Britain were contrary to the Cabinet's own initial assessment of what was appropriate. Restoration of confidence occurred only with the Government's capitulation to external demands for change.

By mid-1977, there were many indicators that confidence had in fact been restored and that the crisis was over. The Bank of England's convertible currency reserves swelled from $2.5 billion in December 1976 to $19 billion a year later; the Minimum Lending Rate fell from 15 per cent to 5 per cent over the same period; as early as January 1977, the British were able to obtain additional credit on financial markets with a $1.5 billion commercial bank loan (*Bank of England Quarterly Bulletin*, March 1978, Statistical Annex, Tables 23, 27). *Vis-à-vis* the IMF loan itself, following the SDR 1 billion ($1.15 billion) provided to the British immediately, there were additional drawings of SDR 320 million in May and August 1977 (De Vries 1985, 1: 476); in October 1977, however, the Chancellor announced that because of the Government's improved financial situation, Britain would not be drawing the SDR 310 million that was becoming available under the loan's phasing provisions, and no additional drawings on the stand-by were made (UK Healey 1977b: 1439–40; De Vries 1985, 1:476). *Vis-à-vis* the sterling balances safety net, the return in confidence was such that the Government, according to Denis Healey (1980: 21–2), 'never came close to activating the agreement' that had been arranged. In September 1977, IMF Managing Director Johannes Witteveen publicly characterized the economic progress that had been made in the UK as a 'success,' and the reportedly delighted Denis Healey noted that Witteveen's public comments were the first 'encouraging' remarks from the Managing Director that he could recall (*Financial Times*, 26 September 1977, 'Healey wins,' p. 1). By late 1977, sterling was again trading in the $1.80s and $1.90s; it rose above $2 in 1978.

The 1976 UK–IMF crisis proved to be of lasting significance both for the IMF and for the British Labour Party. For the IMF, the British loan had clearly not been a business-as-usual stand-by negotiation. After the crisis was resolved, Managing Director Witteveen complimented the head of the Fund team Alan Whittome for conducting 'the largest, longest, most difficult, and, perhaps, most momentous negotiation in the history of the Fund.' He also sent a special memorandum to the other members of the team, complimenting them for work 'conducted under the most intense glare of public and political interest of any mission in the Fund's experience' (De Vries 1985, 1:472). The intense publicity and crisis atmosphere surrounding the British loan had lasting effects with respect to the Fund's role as provider of conditional balance-of-payments financing. Advanced industrialized countries in the years that followed have avoided recourse to the Fund, as the UK–IMF episode fostered a belief that a conditional Fund stand-by was politically costly and something to be avoided if at all possible.[1] In the past two decades, the IMF's loan facilities have been used almost exclusively by developing and post-communist states; this is very different from the pattern and practice of Fund borrowing prior to 1976 when advanced industrial states like the UK, France, and Italy made regular use of the resources available through the Fund and were in fact its largest borrowers. The UK–IMF crisis in 1976 contributed to the widespread view that the IMF was the 'last of the last' places for states in difficulty to look for financing; once this impression was formed, national economic authorities would only turn to the Fund in the most desperate of circumstances, and then the Fund did tend to deal harshly with them. But the increasing frequency of harsh terms only reinforced the reticence to seek financing from the Fund, and thus a vicious circle of sorts was created out of the UK experience (interview material).

For the Labour Party, the 1976 crisis was a dramatic demonstration of the incompatibility of a Labour Government's domestic political imperatives with Britain's external economic constraints. Under intense bilateral, multilateral, and structural pressures, this incompatibility was resolved through a sacrifice of the domestic imperatives rather than a lessening of the international constraints. The humiliation of IMF conditionality gave the Conservatives an issue that was used relentlessly against Labour for the remainder of the 1970s and throughout the 1980s. For the Party itself, the IMF crisis and economic retrenchment were contributory factors underlying the trade union disenchantment and militancy of 1978–79 that led to Labour's disastrous electoral loss in May 1979, as well as the internal convulsions Labour experienced in the early 1980s. Labour would remain out of power for nearly two decades.

Notes

CHAPTER 1

1. The concept of an international regime will be discussed more extensively below; for now, regimes can be defined as 'sets of implicit or explicit principles, norms, rules and decision-making procedures around which actor expectations converge in a given area of international relations' (Krasner 1983:2).
2. This point is not lost on ministers in left-of-center governments, who have at times expressed it publicly while in power. The 1988–91 French Socialist Prime Minister Michel Rocard has commented that he regrets how 'finance takes the path over production' and that he would like to put in place a 'production ethic' in French economic policy. Such a proposal, however, could not come from the French left because of the requirements of external confidence; if such an idea did come from the left, from men 'filled with Marxism, with collectivism, with having been the purveyors of the gulag, the franc immediately loses four or five points' (*Le Monde*, 8 November 1989, 'Les Deux Rocards,' pp. 1, 12).
3. This phrasing is borrowed from Russett (1985: 228).
4. There is an enormous literature on the analytic insights that a public choice approach yields for the emergence and evolution of international regimes and for international cooperation more generally. Among others, see Snyder and Diesing (1977: 33–182); Stein (1983: 120–24); Keohane (1984: 65–84); Axelrod (1984); Milner (1992: 467–73); Martin (1992: 15–45); for a clarifying counter-view, see Green and Shapiro 1994.
5. In microeconomics, opportunities for bilateral coercion and manipulation within the marketplace are largely assumed away with the perfect competition assumption.
6. Lisa Martin (1992: 10), for example, defines 'cooperation' in her work 'in a loose sense, to refer to any joint activity among states.' For an informed discussion about various kinds of international cooperation – including the oxymoronic category of 'imposed cooperation' – see Milner (1992: 467–70).

CHAPTER 2

1. 1967–70 Chancellor of the Exchequer Roy Jenkins (1991: 274) regarding his efforts to ease the terms accompanying the UK's 1969 IMF borrowings.
2. For a useful distinction between 'negotiated' and 'imposed' international orders, see Young 1983: 99–101.
3. Ground had already been given on this question when it had been decided as early as 1947 (reconfirmed in 1948) that a member's 'entitled' purchases could be challenged by the Fund 'for good reasons' (Horsefield 1969, 1:189, 3:227; see also Dell 1981: 4, 7–9; Dam 1982: 120–1; Cohen 1983: 321).

4. For example, of the 101 stand-by arrangements approved between 1961 and 1965, 89 included phasing clauses; but of these there was only one instance in which phasing was applied to a developed borrower (a $100 million stand-by extended to Australia in 1961). The 12 stand-by arrangements that did not include phasing involved only six members – four developed OECD borrowers (Iceland, Japan, the UK, and the US), and two developing borrowers (Pakistan and the Philippines) (Horsefield 1969, 2:482, 490–1).
5. The staff did, however, make a detailed analysis of the UK situation; see De Vries (1987: 53–4).
6. The GAB, created in 1962 after involved negotiations between ten large OECD countries, was essentially an agreement among these countries to be ready to provide up to $6 billion to the IMF for the purpose of on-lending to each other (Horsefield 1969, 1:507–16; Deane and Pringle 1984: 33).
7. However, Clive Ponting (1989: 75) notes that to get the loan, the Chancellor had to 'give a private undertaking to the IMF that the government would "take such further action as may be necessary should existing policies not succeed".'
8. Additional factors that undermined sterling in mid-1967 included unfavorable interest rate differentials, the May 1967 rejection of the UK's Common Market application, and the closing of the Suez Canal following the June 1967 Six-Day War (De Vries 1976, 1:432).
9. IMF staff-member C. David Finch (1989: 10) strongly implies that the Fund forced UK devaluation when he writes that 'for the United Kingdom. . . , the tightening of conditionality was shown in 1967, when the IMF management withheld resources until the pound was devalued.' Finch attributes more influence to the IMF than do other first- and second-hand accounts of the devaluation (see De Vries 1976; Wilson 1971; Solomon 1977; Cairncross and Eichengreen 1983; Callaghan 1987; Burk et al., 1988; Ponting 1989).
10. Burk and Cairncross (1992: 10, fn 16) comment incorrectly that 'this stand-by [of November 1967] for the UK was the first for a large industrial member.' In fact, the Fund had arranged and approved repeated stand-bys for large industrial members – for the UK and France starting in 1956 and for the United States in 1963 (De Vries 1985, 1:426–30).
11. The seminar's terms of reference were 'to examine the theory of the relationship of financial factors on the national income and balance of payments, and the implications of these relationships for the techniques of economic forecasting' (Browning 1986: 269; see also Burk and Cairncross 1992: 144).
12. See De Vries (1976, 1:363–6 and 1985, 1:484–5) for a discussion of the IMF and monetarism.

CHAPTER 3

1. Tony Crosland (1971: 81), 1974–76 Minister for the Environment and 1976–77 Foreign Secretary.

2. The EEC published a report doubting whether the UK could hold sterling if it joined the Community; French Foreign Minister Couve de Murville made a careless public comparison of sterling's position and the French devaluation of 1958; interest rates had risen less than market expectations; and a £500 million current account deficit was forecast for 1967, with a similar deficit for 1968 (Burk et al., 1988: 50; Ponting 1989: 289; Wilson 1971: 443).

3. *In Place of Strife* was a highly controversial attempt in 1969 at industrial relations reform. For details, see Panitch (1976: 165–203), Ponting (1989: 350–71), Castle (1993: 413–25).

4. On the compromises involved in composing this passage, see Hatfield (1978: 226–8), Castle (1980: 18–20).

5. The UK had become a member of the European Community in January 1973 over official Labour Party opposition. For Labour moderates who supported UK membership against party policy, Europe was particularly difficult. The issue was very divisive and tended to marginalize the influence of Labour moderates in other areas of party policy (see Crosland 1982: 220–3; Jenkins 1991: 315–53; Hatfield 1978: 115–18, 129–30; Bilski 1977; George 1990: 76–7).

CHAPTER 4

1. IMF Managing Director Johannes Witteveen (1974d: 129) in a May 1974 speech.

2. According to Healey's memoirs (1989: 423), he was suggesting privately a figure of 'at least $25 billion' for the renewed and enlarged facility.

3. There were other elements in addition to the oil facilities that reflected the emergence of a 'lax international debt regime' (Bernstein 1983: 55). As the Fund historian notes (De Vries 1985, 1: 481), 'by the middle of 1974 policy governing the use of [Fund] resources was no longer as monolithic as it had been in earlier years. The Fund had developed a number of "windows" . . . from which a member might request drawings. There was a compensatory financing facility, a buffer stock financing facility, an oil facility, and an extended facility. A supplementary financing facility, which had a different character, was yet to come. Different conditions applied to each facility. The compensatory financing facility and the oil facility, for instance, were subject to what some Executive Directors and staff regarded as mild or modest conditionality, and others regarded as "virtually no conditionality"' (for more detail, see De Vries 1985, 1: 361–83, 399–421).

4. On Prisoners' Dilemma and international relations, see among others Snyder and Diesing (1977), Keohane (1984), Axelrod (1984).

5. Indeed, the head of the Japanese Economic Planning Agency Isamu Miyazaki was paraphrased in *The Financial Times* (11 June 1975, 'Japanese GNP,' p. 8), arguing impoliticly that 'Japan cannot help running a massive trade surplus with non-oil producing countries if it is to finance its deficit with oil exporting countries' (quoted also in Labour Party Research Department 1975a: 27).

CHAPTER 5

1. 'A Phoney Phase' is the title of a chapter of Chief Secretary of the Treasury Joel Barnett's memoirs (1982: 31–47).
2. The pay policy indexation mechanism (the so-called threshold agreements) automatically triggered a 40 pence per week pay increase for every 1 per cent by which prices rose above the target threshold rate of 6 per cent: by the time the policy lapsed, most workers had received eleven automatic pay increases (Browning 1986: 48–9; Gardner 1987: 45–6, 52; Castle 1980: 8).
3. Healey retrospectively acknowledges in his memoirs (1989: 393) that the Budget's export-orientation was inconsistent with the general world economic situation: 'My first budget made Britain's balance of payments worse; we exported less than we expected because world trade was shrinking. It is not possible for a country like Britain to grow alone when the rest of the world is contracting.' Although as early as April 1975 Healey was acknowledging that an absolute decline in the volume of total world imports 'seems to have set in' (UK Healey 1975a: 278), the contradiction this decline presented to the Government's export emphasis did not bring about a rethinking of the Government's economic strategy (see *The Times*, 11 January 1975, 'State and Industry,' p. 1; UK Healey 1975a: 278, 283; UK Healey 1975c: 70, 72– 3; UK Healey 1975d: 1401–2; Healey 1989: 400–1).
4. Middlemas (1991: 101) suggests that the loan from Iran was preferred to the clearing bank loan because of the 'unacceptable conditions' attached to the latter, but he does not elaborate. The Saudi loan was apparently secret, as Healey made no mention of it in Parliament at the time (Healey 1989: 423; see also UK Healey 1974d; Dell 1991: 116–17). At the height of the IMF crisis in November 1976, staff in the US Federal Reserve calculated the sources and the total amount of financing that the British had available. Included in this calculation was an 'indeterminate amount from [the] Saudi Arabian Monetary Authority (on a secret basis)' (Howard 1976a: Table 2).
5. For greater detail, see UK Healey (1974c: 258–67); *National Institute Economic Review*, November 1974, pp. 7–11; Barnett (1982: 51–2); Browning (1986: 63); Gardner (1987: 53); Dell (1991: 111–8).
6. These data are presented with the warning that published currency reserve figures should always be regarded warily. As the Bank for International Settlements (BIS 1977: 129) has cautioned, 'in the interpretation of countries' reserve figures it has to be borne in mind that such changes are not always a reliable guide to the size or even, in some cases, the direction of official intervention. For example, reserves can be affected by central-bank transactions with their own governments as customers or by income from the investment of foreign exchange holdings. In addition, changes in reserves are sometimes deliberately manipulated, for instance through the use of swaps or outright forward transactions' (see also Castle 1980: 441; Haines 1977: 55).
7. Presumably, the 'uninformed comment' included the remarks of the Chancellor, who had pointed out that average real pay increases of 8–9 per cent were occurring (UK Healey 1975a: 281).

CHAPTER 6

1. Minister of Trade Peter Shore (Hennessy 1986: 173).
2. See UK Foot (1975: 424); Wilson (1979: 114–15); Jones (1986: 296); Healey (1989: 394–5); Middlemas (1991: 94); Dell (1991: 152–4, 158–60).
3. The accuracy of Donoughue's account of these events is challenged by Treasury Minister Edmund Dell (1991: 160–6, 172–4), who argues that Donoughue makes too much of the Policy Unit's role in resolving the crisis and that Donoughue's distinction between a 'statutory' policy (with criminal sanctions against unions) and a 'voluntary' policy (with reserve powers against employers) is confused.
4. See also the endnote accompanying Figure 5.1.
5. On this question, see also Wilson (1979: 227); Pliatzky (1982: 148, 1989a: 42); Bernstein (1983: 328); Callaghan (1987: 414); Donoughue (1989: 42); Britton (1989: 42); Dell (1991: 198); Burk and Cairncross (1992: 22–9).

CHAPTER 7

1. US Treasury Secretary William Simon (1976b) in a confidential spring 1976 memo.
2. Japanese Finance Minister Masayoshi Ohira's speech (1975: 48–53) was also somewhat defensive, but he did not respond directly to Healey's criticisms.

CHAPTER 8

1. Journalists William Keegan and Rupert Pennant-Rea (1979: 162) characterizing the sterling depreciation that began in March 1976.
2. This point is a matter of disagreement: see Brittan (1977: 88); Keegan and Pennant-Rea (1979: 162); Whitehead (1985: 184); Browning (1986: 72–3); Gardner (1987: 60–1); Donoughue (1989: 42); Healey (1989: 426–7); Burk and Cairncross (1992: 27–9).
3. There were rumors in the press that Nigeria, an OPEC member and official sterling balance holder, was moving out of sterling (see *The Times*, 6 March 1976, 'Currencies face,' p. 1; *The Guardian*, 10 March 1976, 'Pound goes down,' p. 1; *The Financial Times*, 10 March 1976, 'Nigeria reduces,' p. 1; Middlemas 1991: 105; Burk and Cairncross 1992: 30–1).
4. See Benn (1989: 498); Castle (1980: 696–8); Labour Party (1976a: 12–14); *The Guardian*, 1 March 1976, 'Healey to crush,' p. 18; *The Times*, 5 May 1976, 'Chancellor rejects,' pp. 1, 2. Former Treasury adviser Professor Wynne Godley and the Cambridge Economic Policy Group (CEPG) in 1976 initiated a wider public debate about import controls; through this debate, some of the CEPG import control ideas were filtered into policy discussions within the Government (see Godley 1976a, 1976b; *Cambridge Economic Policy Review*, No. 2, March 1976; UK Healey 1976b: 243–4; Peter Jay, *The Times*, 29 March 1976, 'The radical Cambridge alternative,' p. 14; Samuel Brittan, *Financial Times*, 1 April 1976, 'Import controls,' p. 21; Wynne Godley, letter, *Financial Times*, 2 April 1976,

p. 19; Castle 1980: 316, 707; Benn 1989: 531, 580, 664–5; Dell 1991: 260; Burk and Cairncross 1992: 150–5).

5. See also the endnote accompanying Figure 5.1.

6. The magnitude of Bank of England currency intervention through 22 July 1976 is revealed in a table marked 'Restricted' that was prepared for US Federal Reserve Chairman Arthur Burns.

7. See *The Times*, 9 April 1976, 'Pound slides,' p. 1; *Sunday Times*, 11 April 1976, 'Sterling,' p. 61; *The Times*, 13 April 1976, 'Mr Healey accepts,' p. 1; *The Times*, 13 April 1976, 'Mr Scargill,' p. 2; *Bank of England Quarterly Bulletin*, June 1976, pp. 171–2.

8. As an assessment of the American view, this argument was correct; the US Treasury position was that 'only in the framework of [more forceful fiscal and monetary policy action] would the provision of external financing offer any lasting benefit or truly be in Britain's or the world's interests' (US Government 1976).

9. For overly brief discussion of the June central bank stand-by in their memoirs, see Healey (1989: 427–8); Callaghan (1987: 419).

10. Healey (1976a) wrote to Simon, 'I am pleased that agreement has been reached on the swap arrangements. . . . I would like to assure you, on behalf of the Government of the United Kingdom, that liquidation of any drawings under those arrangements will be made in full accordance with the agreed terms. If necessary to meet those obligations, the United Kingdom will make drawings in the required amounts from the International Monetary Fund in accordance with the Articles of Agreement of the Fund. DW Healey.'

11. For accounts of the range of the Cabinet debate, see Benn (1989: 588–600); Donoughue (1987: 91–2); Barnett (1982: 93–6).

12. Accounts of how the 2 per cent increase was proposed vary on some details; see Fay and Young (1978, 1: 35); Whitehead (1985: 186); Benn (1989: 599); Dell (1991: 229–30).

13. Burk and Cairncross (1992: 204) incorrectly describe the July forecast as a 'target.' It would not be officially so characterized until October (Hall 1983: 45).

CHAPTER 9

1. *Financial Times* editorial comment on the Government (28 September 1976, 'Reality in Currency Markets,' p. 18).

2. See *The Times*, 3 September 1976, 'Reserves fall,' p. 15; *The Times*, 9 September 1976, 'Urgent Downing Street talks,' p. 1; 'Industry fears,' p. 17; *Financial Times*, 14 August 1976, '£524 m trade gap,' pp. 1, 22; *Financial Times*, 8 September 1976, 'Record fall,' pp. 1, 48; Browning (1986: 80–1).

3. According to an anonymous IMF official, 'discreet discussions' were occurring as early as June (Bernstein 1983: 365).

4. In fact, it was quoted with relish in the subsequent books of US Federal Reserve Chairman Arthur Burns (1978: 470) who described it as a summary of 'the bankruptcy of mechanical Keynesianism,' and of US Treasury

Secretary William Simon (1978: 214) who pointed to it as a 'confession of governmental impotence' from a chastened European social democrat.

5. A call had been made for special deposits equivalent to 1 per cent of British banks' eligible liabilities in September; this amount was increased to 2 per cent in October and was expected to result in the immobilization of approximately £700 million (*Bank of England Quarterly Bulletin*, December 1976, p. 418; *Financial Times*, 17 September 1976, 'Bank tightens,' p. 1; *Financial Times*, 8 October 1976, 'Healey moves,' pp. 1, 44; Dell 1991: 238).

6. Other reportedly agreed upon terms were also outlined, including a 1977–78 PSBR limit of £8 billion, a domestic credit expansion limit of £6 billion, and a money supply growth limit of 10 per cent (*Sunday Times*, 24 October 1976, 'The Price Britain faces,' p. 1).

7. For more, see Fay and Young (1978, 2: 34); Healey (1980: 35); Bernstein (1983: 507–9); Donoughue (1985: 67, 1987: 92); Dell (1991: 239); Burk and Cairncross (1992: 74).

8. The other members of the IMF team reportedly were Hari Vittas, Assistant Chief of the British Commonwealth Division; Ed Brau, Assistant Division Chief in the Exchange and Trade Relations Department; Les Manison, an economist in the European Department; and Michael Deppler, an economist in the Research Department (*Sunday Times*, 7 November 1976, 'Six secrets,' p. 6).

9. Nor is it clear that the British were being honest with the Fund. The forecasts were leaked to the press on 1 November (*Financial Times*, 1 November 1976, 'Treasury forecasts,' p. 1), and Chief Secretary to the Treasury Joel Barnett (1982: 102) recounts that the forecasts had been complete 'for some two weeks' – i.e., in mid-October – before they were leaked.'

10. In other accounts (Fay and Young 1978, 2: 34; Barnett 1982: 102), this figure is £11.2 billion; Policy Unit member Gavyn Davies (1989: 43) has suggested that it was 'approaching £12 bn.'

11. On the question of Treasury loyalty, see also Fay and Young (1978, 2: 33–4); Bernstein (1983: 495–500); Whitehead (1985: 192–3); Donoughue (1987: 94, 1989: 43); Pliatzky (1989a: 43); Dell (1991: 250); Middlemas (1991: 99– 100); and Burk and Cairncross (1992: 72–3).

12. According to Dell (1991: 255), the IMF did not wish to see Lever; at the end of his visit, Lever told the press that he had not in fact seen any IMF officials (*Financial Times*, 17 November 1976, 'UK seeks talks,' pp. 1, 46; *The Times*, 17 November 1976, 'Lever hopes,' p. 27).

13. In a prescient background profile on Lever prepared for Treasury Secretary Simon in 1974, it was suggested that Lever's role in the Government 'may be that of the man who asks for the money from foreigners and is occasionally pushed forward to demonstrate orthodoxy and respectability' (US State Department 1974).

14. A seven-page memo of the Ford–Lever conversation was prepared subsequently, but it is classified and unavailable for research (see the withdrawal sheet in the White House Central Files, Subject File, CO160, Box 57, Ford Presidential Library).

15. In attendance were President Ford, Secretary of State Kissinger, Federal Reserve Chairman Burns, Under-Secretary Yeo, and several officials and

advisers (Daily Diary of the President, 19 November 1976). The agenda of the meeting and various attachments are classified and unavailable for research (see the withdrawal sheet, White House Central Files, Subject File, CO 160 10/1/76 – 11/30/76, Box 57, Ford Presidential Library).

16. This message (British Embassy 1976) is quoted above.

17. Burk and Cairncross (1992: 82, 111) argue that as a result of Lever's trip to Washington, 'the US government had in some sense agreed that they would help the UK government to secure a sterling balances agreement.' It is my view that they are incorrect. Ford's message (1976a) falls short of a US commitment to 'secure agreement.' Indeed, the White House Press Secretary was instructed that if he were asked directly whether the US would support sterling balances, he was to reply 'I have no comment on that.' As late as mid-December, an unnamed 'top American official' was quoted in the press stating that there 'has definitely not been a promise of the United States agreement' on sterling balances (Nessen 1976; *The Times*, 13 December 1976, 'No American pledge,' p. 19).

18. Reportedly, the IMF also wanted a lower exchange rate, but this is disputed by the leader of the IMF mission Alan Whittome. It is unclear who is correct (see Fay and Young 1978, 2: 34; Bernstein 1983: 507–9; Burk and Cairncross 1992: 74).

19. Burk and Cairncross (1992: 82, fn 99) write that 'it is not clear who initiated this meeting, the Prime Minister, the Chancellor, the CBI or the IMF mission.' According to an unnamed British Treasury official, 'it was Healey's idea' (Bernstein 1983: 513; see also UK Healey 1976h: 484).

20. Much of the subsequent discussion and analysis of the UK–IMF negotiations is made confusing by changing PSBR estimates that were made at different times and for different financial years (see Browning 1986: 131, fn 27 for a clarifying table). There were other macroeconomic variables of interest to the Fund (see Bernstein 1983: 507–10), but the difficulties over the terms of the loan centered on the size of the PSBR.

21. In Cabinet, Reg Prentice (Overseas Development) also advocated expenditure cuts (Holmes 1985: 97), but he was not close to Healey or Dell.

22. Crosland in Cabinet used the just released and more optimistic forecasts from the National Institute of Economic and Social Research that concluded that 'there is no case for any net contractionary policy action in 1977 or 1978: rather the contrary' (Bernstein 1983: 564; *National Institute Economic Review*, November 1976, p. 4).

23. Schmidt called Ford on 30 November, but the call was not completed (Daily Diary of the President, 30 November 1976). According to Pöhl, Schmidt sent a message to Ford at around the same time or soon thereafter that 'they should give up their tough position via London' (Burk and Cairncross 1992: 91).

24. In fact, a final decision was not taken until the following week: when Cabinet met on 25 November, Callaghan told ministers that 'Ford and Schmidt did not want a decision today' (Benn 1989: 658).

25. The copy of the document (Ford 1976b) upon which this account is based is a draft of Ford's response which was heavily edited by Treasury Secretary Simon. It is unclear whether Simon's alterations were incorporated into the final message sent to Callaghan.

CHAPTER 10

1. Foreign Secretary Tony Crosland to Cabinet (Whitehead 1985: 199; Benn 1989: 685).
2. In a memo written for President Ford, Simon listed his contacts in London as Alan Whittome, Denis Healey, Gordon Richardson, Derek Mitchell, Karl Otto Pöhl, 'plus a number of informal talks' (Simon 1976k).
3. Annual rate based on first ten months.
4. Although Witteveen (1987: 31) has cryptically remarked that 'it was decided' during his meetings in London, it is not clear whether a specific PSBR target for 1977–78 was actually agreed upon on 1 December; IMF historian De Vries (1985, 1: 472) is ambiguous while Alan Whittome claims to be unable to recall (Burk and Cairncross 1992: 94). Both Healey (1989: 431–2) and Callaghan (1987: 439–40), however, suggest that it remained uncertain whether the IMF would actually accept only £1 billion in expenditure cuts (see below; see also Callaghan 1976b; Benn 1989: 672; Burk and Cairncross 1992: 103).
5. For a fuller account of the Cabinet discussions, see Fay and Young (1978, 3: 33); Barnett (1982: 104–5); Bernstein (1983: 566–71); Whitehead (1985: 195–7); Benn (1989: 662–78).
6. On the last point, see Labour Party Research Department 1976; *Financial Times*, 4 November 1976, 'Labour document,' p. 18.
7. A two-page memo prepared for Ford regarding the conversation is classified and unavailable for research (see the withdrawal sheet in Presidential Handwriting File, Countries – United Kingdom, Box 7, Ford Presidential Library).
8. In the event, the wording of the Government's 15 December statement to Parliament regarding sterling balances (UK Healey 1976g: 1535–6) was nothing like Callaghan's suggested phrasing (see below).
9. Burk and Cairncross (1992: 103) have commented on the idle nature of the British threat to call an election, arguing that 'it would be strange if the threat . . . in itself had much influenced the IMF: why should they care if the British held an election on the subject?' There are two possible, albeit speculative, responses. First, with only £500 million in cuts separating the two sides, the IMF could afford to give in rather than risk calling the British bluff. Second, an election would have placed the Fund at the center of British electoral politics and would almost certainly have delayed and complicated the conclusion of the negotiations. In the unlikely event that Labour won the election, little would have changed; if Labour lost, however, the IMF would have been stigmatized in Britain. Although IMF negotiator Alan Whittome had told the British that it was 'not in the business of bringing governments down' (Pliatzky 1989: 44), the perception would have been that the Fund had driven Labour from power.
10. Proposals involved a weakening of the inflation-proofing of public sector pensions, nationalized industry pricing (electricity, gas, and telephone), regional employment subsidies, and the sale of British Petroleum shares (Benn 1989: 683–5; Barnett 1982: 107–9; Fay and Young 1978, 3: 34).
11. The ninth of December was also the due-date for the repayment of the

$1.5 billion drawing from the central bank stand-by. It is possible that American officials delayed responding to Healey's 5 December appeal until they were certain that the British had fulfilled their repayment obligations on time – which they did (see *The Times*, 10 December 1976, 'Loan being repaid,' p. 14). Yeo's call to Mitchell occurred late in the evening in London (Burk and Cairncross 1992: 117), after the close of financial markets in New York.

12. Richardson (1977b) acknowledged 'the conditions attached to our drawings . . . as set out in your letter' in his response to Burns.

13. On the differences in definition between an M3 target and a DCE ceiling, see Richardson (1977a: 49); OECD (1977: 25, fn 27); *National Institute Economic Review*, February 1977, pp. 40–3; Browning (1986: 270–3).

14. However, 'temporary selective measures' remained an option in 'cases where particular industries which are viable in the long-term are suffering serious injury as a result of increased imports' (Healey 1976e: para. 24).

15. 'The United Kingdom Government will consult the Fund in accordance with the policies of the Fund on such consultation on the adoption of any measure that may be appropriate. In any case, the United Kingdom authorities will reach understandings with the Fund before 16 January 1978 on their policy intentions for the remaining period of the stand-by arrangement' (Healey 1976e: para. 25).

16. Quarterly monitoring had accompanied the 1967 and 1969 arrangements: see Chapter 2.

17. The Government's Parliamentary survival was more directly threatened in March 1977 when left-wing Labour backbenchers threatened to abstain on the public expenditure White Paper containing the IMF cuts and the Opposition put down a motion of confidence. The Government survived only by concluding a formal agreement – the Lib–Lab Pact – that secured the support for Labour of the 14 Liberal MPs (see Mitchie and Hoggart 1978; Barnett 1982: 115–17; Whitehead 1985: 258–62; Callaghan 1987: 451–8; Benn 1990: 85–91).

18. Quarterly satisfaction of IMF conditions as the Treasury Plan envisioned would have been a significant tightening of conditionality; in the end, consultations concerning the fulfillment of the terms of the sterling balances agreement occurred at six-month intervals (De Vries 1985, 1: 478; see also Bernstein 1983: 587).

19. See *Financial Times*, 8 December 1976, 'Healey hint,' pp. 1, 34; *The Times*, 8 December 1976, 'Healey hint,' p. 1.

20. This message, dated 11 December and classified Top Secret, can be found in the 'President's Correspondence with Foreign Leaders' series in the Brent Scowcroft files at the Ford Presidential Library (personal correspondence, Karen B. Holzhausen, 2 June 1992). It is not available for research.

21. The text of the message is classified, but it is clear from the attached documents that it concerned sterling balances (see the withdrawal sheet in the White House Central Files, CO160 12/1/76 – 1/20/77, Box 58, Ford Presidential Library).

22. Treasury Secretary Simon, while not present, had sent to Ford a five-page paper entitled 'Alternative Proposals for Dealing with United Kingdom

Sterling Balances.' This paper, however, is classified and unavailable for research (see the withdrawal sheets in White House Central Files, FI9 12/1/76 – 1/20/77, Box 24, and in White House Central Files, CO160 12/1/76 – 1/20/77, Box 58, Ford Presidential Library).

23. The American representatives sent back long accounts of the Paris meetings to Washington; the reports are classified, however, and unavailable for research (see the withdrawal sheet in the Arthur Burns Papers, United Kingdom, Sterling Balance Problem, Nov 1976 – Jan 1977 (2), Box B113, Ford Presidential Library).

24. It is unclear whether this offer was accepted, although *The Financial Times* on 11 January 1977 reported that 'it is believed that British officials have come to Washington under a . . . cloak of secrecy' to discuss sterling balances ('International agreement,' pp. 1, 28).

25. A four-page paper was written in January 1977 entitled 'Possible Role of IMF Managing Director in Verifying UK Eligibility to Draw under Sterling Balances Facility.' This paper is classified, however, and unavailable for research (see the withdrawal sheet in the Arthur Burns Papers, United Kingdom Sterling Balance Problem, Nov 1976 – Jan 1977 (2), Box B113, Ford Presidential Library).

26. In return for the facility, the British were committed: '(i) To reduce the official sterling balances over [two years] to working levels. . . . (ii) To offer foreign currency "funding" securities in exchange for official holdings of sterling. . . . [and] (iii) To exercise restraint with respect to future increases in private sterling balances' (US Federal Reserve System 1977c; see also De Vries 1985, 1: 475).

27. An eleven-point paper had been written in the US Federal Reserve on what 'reasonable effort' might mean (US Federal Reserve System 1977b).

28. There are three memos dated late January and February 1977 among Arthur Burns' papers regarding the British commercial bank loan; all are classified and unavailable for research (see withdrawal sheet in Arthur Burns Papers, Federal Reserve Board Subject Files, 'United Kingdom, General – November 1976–1977, Box B113, Ford Presidential Library).

CHAPTER 11

1. There is the exception of a simultaneously negotiated Italian stand-by that was concluded in April 1977; see De Vries (1985, 1: 439–59). In early 1983, there was considerable speculation that the French Socialist Government of François Mitterrand and Pierre Mauroy might be compelled to seek a conditional IMF loan (see *The Guardian*, 19 March 1983, 'France,' p. 18; *Financial Times*, 25 March 1983, 'Defence of franc', p. 3; *Le Monde*, 2 April 1983, 'Fin de la mission,' p. 7; Milési 1985: 209; Bauchard 1986: 145; July 1986: 97). The French Socialists were able to avoid the Fund by committing themselves to a policy U-turn that was accompanied by a conditional loan extended through the European Community (see Cameron 1988; Muet and Fonteneau 1990).

Bibliography

Apel, Hans, 1974: 'Statement,' in IMF (1974: 115–19).

Apel, Hans, 1975: 'Statement,' in IMF (1975b: 43–8).

Artis, Michael, and David Cobham, eds, 1991: *Labour's Economic Policies, 1974–1979*. Manchester: Manchester University Press.

Axelrod, Robert, 1984: *The Evolution of Cooperation*. New York: Basic Books.

Bank of England, 1984: *The Development and Operation of Monetary Policy, 1960–1983*. Oxford: Clarendon Press.

Bank of England Annual Report.

Bank of England Quarterly Bulletin.

Barnett, Joel, 1982: *Inside the Treasury*. London: André Deutsch.

Bauchard, Phillippe, 1985: *La Guerre des deux roses: du rêve à la réalité, 1981–1985*. Paris: Bernard Grasset.

Benn, Tony, private political diaries and papers in the Benn Archives, London.

Benn, Tony, 1987: *Out of the Wilderness: Diaries 1963–67*. London: Hutchinson.

Benn, Tony, 1988: *Office without Power: Diaries 1968–72*. London: Hutchinson.

Benn, Tony, 1989: *Against The Tide: Diaries 1973–76*. London: Hutchinson.

Benn, Tony, 1990: *Conflicts of Interest: Diaries 1977–80*. London: Hutchinson.

Bernstein, Karen, 1983: The International Monetary Fund and Deficit Countries: The Case of Britain, 1974–77. PhD diss., Stanford University.

Bilski, Raphaella, 1977: 'The Common Market and the Growing Strength of Labour's Left Wing,' *Government and Opposition* (Summer) 12(2): 306–31.

BIS [Bank for International Settlements], 1977: *Bank for International Settlements: Forty-Seventh Annual Report, 1st April 1976 – 31st March 1977*. Basle: Bank for International Settlements.

Block, Fred, 1987: *Revising State Theory: Essays in Politics and Post-industrialism*. Philadelphia: Temple University Press.

British Embassy, 1976: memo to the White House, 17 November 1976. United Kingdom Subject File, 1976 (Sep–Dec), Series IIIB, Drawer 27, Folder 14, Simon Papers, Lafayette College.

Brittan, Samuel, 1977: *Economic Consequences of Democracy*. 2nd edn. Hants: Wildwood House.

Britton, Andrew, 1989: contribution to Burk et al. (1989).

Britton, Andrew, 1991: *Macroeconomic Policy in Britain, 1974–87*. Cambridge: Cambridge University Press.

Browning, Peter, 1986: *The Treasury and Economic Policy, 1964–1985*. London: Longman.

Bundesbank, 1976: *Report of the Deutsche Bundesbank for the Year 1975*. Frankfurt.

Bundesbank, 1977: *Report of the Deutsche Bundesbank for the Year 1976*. Frankfurt.

Burk, Kathleen, et al., 1988: 'Symposium: 1967 Devaluation,' *Contemporary Record* (Winter) 1(4): 44–53.

Burk, Kathleen, et al., 1989: 'Symposium: 1976 IMF Crisis,' *Contemporary Record* (November) 3(2): 39–45.

Burk, Kathleen and Alec Cairncross, 1992: *'Goodbye Great Britain': The 1976 IMF Crisis.* New Haven, CT: Yale University Press.

Burns, Arthur, 1976a: notes regarding June 1976 multilateral loan to the UK, *c.* 3–6 June 1976. Federal Reserve Board Subject File, United Kingdom: Loan from Group of Ten, June 1976, Box B113, Burns Papers, Ford Library.

Burns, Arthur, 1976b: proposed text for Denis Healey's statement to Parliament on 7 June 1976, marked *c.* 5/76 [but more probably early June 1976]. Federal Reserve Board Subject Files, Bank of England, 1976–77, Box B7, Burns Papers, Ford Library.

Burns, Arthur, 1976c: note from 'Catherine' to Burns, 7 June 1976, 12:30 p.m. Federal Reserve Board Subject File, United Kingdom: Loan from Group of Ten, June 1976, Box B113, Burns Papers, Ford Library.

Burns, Arthur, 1977: letter to Gordon Richardson, 8 January 1977. Federal Reserve Board Subject File, United Kingdom: Sterling Balance Problem, November 1976 – January 1977 (2), Box B113, Burns Papers, Ford Library.

Burns, Arthur, 1978: *Reflections of an Economic Policy Maker: Speeches and Congressional Statements: 1969–1978.* Washington, DC: American Enterprise Institute.

Butler, David, and Dennis Kavanagh, 1974: *The British General Election of February 1974.* London: Macmillan.

Butler, David and Dennis Kavanagh, 1975: *The British General Election of October 1974.* London: Macmillan.

Butler, David and Dennis Kavanagh, 1980: *The British General Election of 1979.* London: Macmillan.

Butler, David and Uwe Kitzinger, 1976: *The 1975 Referendum.* London: Macmillan.

Cairncross, Alec, 1975: 'The Financing of Public Expenditure,' pp. 18–20, and testimony, in *First Report from the Expenditure Committee: The Financing of Public Expenditure*, Vol. 2, Session 1975–76, in *Parliamentary Papers (House of Commons and Command)*, Vol. 28, Session 1975–76.

Cairncross, Alec, 1988: contribution to Burk et al. (1988).

Cairncross, Alec, and Barry Eichengreen, 1983: *Sterling in Decline: The Devaluations of 1931, 1949 and 1967.* Oxford: Basil Blackwell.

Callaghan, James, 1967: letter of intent to Pierre-Paul Schweitzer, 23 November 1967, in *Parliamentary Debates* (Commons), 30 November 1967, 5th ser., vol. 755 (1966–67), cols 648–52.

Callaghan, James, 1976a: letter to Gerald Ford, 23 November 1976. United Kingdom Subject File, 1976 (Sep–Dec), Series IIIB, Drawer 27, Folder 14, Simon Papers, Lafayette College.

Callaghan, James, 1976b: letter to Gerald Ford, 2 December 1976. United Kingdom Subject File, 1976 (Sep–Dec), Series IIIB, Drawer 27, Folder 14, Simon Papers, Lafayette College.

Callaghan, James, 1987: *Time and Chance.* London: Collins.

Cambridge Economic Policy Review [also called *Economic Policy Review*].

Cameron, David R., 1988: 'The Colors of a Rose: On the Ambiguous Record of French Socialism,' Harvard University, Center for European Studies Working Paper, 1988.

Carnoy, Martin, 1984: *The State in Political Theory*. Princeton, NJ: Princeton University Press.

Carr, Edward Hallett, 1939: *The Twenty Years' Crisis, 1919–1939: An Introduction to the Study of International Relations*. 2nd edn. London: Macmillan; reprint, New York: Harper & Row, 1964.

Castle, Barbara, 1980: *The Castle Diaries, 1974–76*. London: Weidenfeld & Nicolson.

Castle, Barbara, 1984: *The Castle Diaries 1964–70*. London: Weidenfeld & Nicolson.

Castle, Barbara, 1993: *Fighting All the Way*. London: Macmillan.

Central Statistical Office, *Monthly Digest of Statistics*. London: HMSO.

Coates, David, 1975: *The Labour Party and the Struggle for Socialism*. Cambridge: Cambridge University Press.

Coates, David, 1980: *Labour in Power? A Study of the Labour Government 1974–79*. New York: Longman, 1980.

Coates, David, 1989: *The Crisis of Labour: Industrial Relations and the State in Contemporary Britain*. Oxford: Philip Allan.

Cobham, David, 1991: 'Monetary Policy,' in Artis and Cobham (1991: 38–55).

Cohen, Benjamin J., 1983: 'Balance of Payments Financing: Evolution of a Regime,' in Krasner (1983: 315–36).

Colombo, Emilio, 1974: 'Statement,' in IMF (1974: 101–7).

Colombo, Emilio, 1975: 'Statement,' in IMF (1975b: 36–43).

Commission of the European Communities, 1990: *One Market, One Money: An Evaluation of the Potential Benefits and Costs of Forming an Economic and Monetary Union*. Printed in *European Economy* 44 (October 1990).

Committee of Twenty, 1974: 'Committee of 20 Agrees on Steps on Oil Crisis, SDRs, Fund Role,' *IMF Survey* 3 (21 January): 17, 22–3.

Cowhey, Peter F., 1990: 'The International Telecommunications Regime: The Political Roots of Regimes for High Technology,' *International Organization* (Spring) 44(2): 169–99.

Crawford, Malcolm, 1983: 'High Conditionality Lending: The United Kingdom,' in Williamson (1983: 421–39).

Crawford, Malcolm, 1989: 'Selective Memories,' *Business* (December): 173.

Crewe, Ivor, 1982: 'The Labour Party and the Electorate,' pp. 9–49 in Kavanagh, Dennis, 1982: *The Politics of the Labour Party*. London: George Allen & Unwin.

Crosland, Anthony, 1971: *A Social Democratic Britain*. Reprinted in Crosland (1974: 71–94).

Crosland, Anthony, 1974: *Socialism Now and Other Essays*. London: Jonathan Cape.

Crosland, Susan, 1982: *Tony Crosland*. London: Jonathan Cape.

Crossman, Richard, 1975, 1976, 1977: *The Diaries of a Cabinet Minister*. 3 vols. New York: Holt, Rinehart & Winston.

Dahl, Robert, 1961: *Who Governs? Democracy and Power in an American City*. New Haven, CT: Yale University Press.

Daily Diary of the President, 29 September 1976: File 9/27–30/76, Box 21, Ford Library.

Daily Diary of the President, 16 November 1976: File 11/15–30/76, Box 21, Ford Library.

Daily Diary of the President, 19 November 1976: File 11/15–30/76, Box 21, Ford Library.

Daily Diary of the President, 30 November 1976: File 11/15–30/76, Box 21, Ford Library.

Daily Diary of the President, 1 December 1976: File 12/1–8/76, Box 22, Ford Library.

The Daily Telegraph.

Dam, Kenneth W., 1982: *The Rules of the Game: Reform and Evolution in the International Monetary System.* Chicago: University of Chicago Press.

Davies, Gavyn, 1989: contribution to Burk et al. (1989).

Deane, Marjorie, and Robert Pringle, 1984: *Economic Cooperation from the Inside.* New York: Group of Thirty.

Dell, Edmund, 1980: 'Collective Responsibility: Fact, Fiction or Façade?,' pp. 27–48, in *Policy and Practice: The Experience of Government.* London: Royal Institute of Public Administration.

Dell, Edmund, 1987: *The Politics of Economic Interdependence.* London: Macmillan.

Dell, Edmund, 1991: *A Hard Pounding: Politics and Economic Crisis 1974–1976.* Oxford: Oxford University Press.

Dell, Sidney, 1981: *On Being Grandmotherly: The Evolution of IMF Conditionality. Essays in International Finance, No. 144.* Princeton, NJ: International Finance Section, Department of Economics, Princeton University.

The Department of State Bulletin.

DePorte, A. W., 1979: *Europe Between the Super-Powers: The Enduring Balance.* 2nd edn. New Haven, CT: Yale University Press.

Deutsch, Karl W., and J. David Singer, 1964: 'Multipolar Power Systems and International Stability,' *World Politics* (April) 16(3). Reprinted pp. 69–71 in Phil Williams, Donald M. Goldstein, and Jay M. Shafritz, eds, *Classic Readings of International Relations.* Belmont, CA: Wadsworth.

De Vries, Margaret Garritsen, 1976: *The International Monetary Fund 1966–1971: The System Under Stress.* 2 vols. Washington, DC: International Monetary Fund.

De Vries, Margaret Garritsen, 1985: *The International Monetary Fund, 1972–1978: Cooperation on Trial.* 3 vols. Washington, DC: International Monetary Fund.

De Vries, Margaret Garritsen, 1987: *Balance of Payments Adjustment, 1945 to 1986: The IMF Experience.* Washington, DC: International Monetary Fund.

Donoughue, Bernard, 1985: 'The Conduct of Economic Policy, 1974–79,' pp. 47–71 in King, Anthony, ed., 1985: *The British Prime Minister.* 2nd edn. Durham, NC: Duke University Press.

Donoughue, Bernard, 1987: *Prime Minister: The Conduct of Policy under Harold Wilson and James Callaghan.* London: Jonathan Cape.

Donoughue, Bernard, 1989: contribution to Burk et al. (1989).

Downs, Anthony, 1957: *An Economic Theory of Democracy.* New York: Harper & Row.

The Economist.

Emminger, Otmar, 1975: 'On the record,' *The Banker,* (March) 125(589): 327–9.

Esping-Anderson, Gosta, 1985: *Politics against Markets: the Social Democratic Rise to Power.* Princeton, NJ: Princeton University Press.

Evans, Peter B., Harold K. Jacobson, and Robert D. Putnam, eds, 1993: *Double-Edged Diplomacy: International Bargaining and Domestic Politics.* Berkeley: University of California Press.

Fay, Stephen, 1987: *Portrait of an Old Lady: Turmoil at the Bank of England.* London: Viking.

Fay, Stephen and Hugo Young, 1976: 'The Fall of Heath,' *The Sunday Times.* 3 Parts. 22 February 1976, pp. 33–4; 29 February 1976, pp. 33–4; and 7 March 1976, p. 34.

Fay, Stephen and Hugo Young, 1978: 'The Day the £ Nearly Died,' *The Sunday Times.* 3 Parts. 14 May 1978, pp. 33–5; 21 May 1978, pp. 33–5; 28 May 1978, pp. 33–4.

Featherstone, Kevin, 1988: *Socialist Parties and European Integration: A Comparative History.* Manchester: Manchester University Press.

Fforde, J.S., 1982: 'Setting Monetary Objectives,' in Bank of England (1984: 65–73). Reprinted in *Bank of England Quarterly Bulletin,* June 1983.

The Financial Times.

Finch, C. David, 1989: *The IMF: The Record and the Prospect: Essays in International Finance, No. 175.* Princeton, NJ: International Finance Section, Department of Economics, Princeton University.

Foot, Michael, 1986: *Loyalists and Loners.* London: Collins.

Foote, Geoffrey, 1985: *The Labour Party's Political Thought: A History.* 2nd edn. London: Croom Helm.

Foote, Geoffrey, 1988: *A Chronology of Post War British Politics.* London: Croom Helm.

Fourcade, Jean-Pierre, 1974: 'Statement,' in IMF (1974: 90–101).

Fourcade, Jean-Pierre, 1975: 'Statement,' in IMF (1975b: 92–102).

Ford, Gerald R., 1976a: letter to James Callaghan, 20 November 1976. United Kingdom Subject File, 1976 (Sep–Dec), Series IIIB, Drawer 27, Folder 14, Simon Papers, Lafayette College.

Ford, Gerald R., 1976b: letter to James Callaghan, 24 November 1976. United Kingdom Subject File, 1976 (Sep–Dec), Series IIIB, Drawer 27, Folder 14, Simon Papers, Lafayette College.

Forester, Tom, 1979: 'Neutralising the Industrial Strategy,' pp. 74–94 in Coates, Ken, ed., 1979: *What Went Wrong: Explaining the Fall of the Labour Government.* Nottingham: Spokesman.

Gardner, Nick, 1987: *Decade of Discontent: The Changing British Economy since 1973.* Oxford: Basil Blackwell.

Gardner, Richard N., 1980: *Sterling–Dollar Diplomacy in Current Perspective: The Origins and the Prospects of Our International Economic Order.* New expanded edn. New York: McGraw-Hill, 1969; reprint, New York: Columbia University Press.

George, Stephen, 1990: *An Awkward Partner: Britain in the European Community.* Oxford: Oxford University Press.

Gilpin, Robert, 1987: *The Political Economy of International Relations.* Princeton, NJ: Princeton University Press.

Godley, Wynne, 1976a: 'The Case,' *The Sunday Times,* 28 March 1976, p. 63.

Godley, Wynne, 1976b: 'What Britain Needs,' *The Times,* 1 November 1976, p. 14.

Gold, Joseph, 1970: *The Stand-By Arrangements of the International Monetary Fund: A Commentary on Their Formal, Legal, and Financial Aspects.* Washington, DC: International Monetary Fund.

Gold, Joseph, 1979: *Legal and Institutional Aspects of the International Monetary System: Selected Essays.* Washington, DC: International Monetary Fund.

Green, Donald P. and Ian Shapiro, 1994: *Pathologies of Rational Choice Theory: A Critique of Applications in Political Science.* New Haven, CT: Yale University Press.

Group of Ten, 1975: 'Communiqué of the Ministerial Meetings of the Group of 10,' *IMF Survey* (20 January) 3: 19.

The Guardian.

Haas, Ernst B., 1983: 'Words Can Hurt You; or, Who Said What to Whom about Regimes,' in Krasner (1983: 23–59).

Haggard, Stephen, and Beth A. Simmons, 1987: 'Theories of International Regimes,' *International Organization* (Summer) 41(3): 491–517.

Haines, Joe, 1977: *The Politics of Power.* London: Jonathan Cape.

Hall, Maximillian, 1983: *Monetary Policy since 1971: Conduct and Performance.* London: Macmillan.

Ham, Adrian, 1981: *Treasury Rules: Recurrent Themes in British Economic Policy.* London: Quartet Books.

Hatfield, Michael, 1978: *The House the Left Built: Inside Labour Policy-Making 1970–75.* London: Victor Gollancz.

Healey, Denis, 1974a: 'Statement,' in IMF (1974: 74–81).

Healey, Denis, 1974b: letter to William Simon, 12 November 1974. United Kingdom Subject File, 1974–76 (Aug), Series IIIB, Drawer 27, Folder 13, Simon Papers, Lafayette College.

Healey, Denis, 1975a: letter to H. Johannes Witteveen, 18 December 1975. House of Commons Library.

Healey, Denis, 1975b: letter to H. Johannes Witteveen, 18 December 1975. House of Commons Library.

Healey, Denis, 1975c: 'Statement,' in IMF (1975b: 74–9).

Healey, Denis, 1975d: statement in debate on the economy, in Labour Party (1975: 200–5).

Healey, Denis, 1976a: letter to William Simon, 6 June 1976. United Kingdom Subject File, 1974–76 (Aug), Series IIIB, Drawer 27, Folder 13, Simon Papers, Lafayette College.

Healey, Denis, 1976b: letter to Arthur Burns, 7 June 1976. Federal Reserve Board Subject File, United Kingdom: Loan from Group of Ten, June 1976, Box B113, Burns Papers, Ford Library.

Healey, Denis 1976c: speech, 21 October 1976, printed in *The Times*, 22 October 1976, p. 24.

Healey, Denis, 1976d: letter to William Simon, 5 December 1976, attached to a covering letter from Peter Ramsbotham, 6 December 1976. United Kingdom Subject File, 1976 (Sep–Dec), Series IIIB, Drawer 27, Folder 14, Simon Papers, Lafayette College.

Healey, Denis 1976e: letter, 15 December 1976. House of Commons Library.

Healey, Denis, 1980: *Managing the Economy: The Russell C. Leffingwell Lectures, October 11, 15, and 18, 1979.* New York: Council on Foreign Relations.

Healey, Denis, 1987: untitled, in *Institutional Investor*, International edition (June): 66–8.

Healey, Denis, 1989: *The Time of My Life*. London: Michael Joseph.

Heffer, Eric, 1986: *Labour's Future: Socialist or SDP Mark 2?* London: Verso.

Henkin, Louis, 1968: *How Nations Behave: Law and Foreign Policy*. 2nd edn. New York: Columbia University Press.

Hennessy, Peter, 1986: *Cabinet*. Oxford, Basil Blackwell.

Hennessy, Peter, 1989: *Whitehall*. New York, Free Press.

Holmes, Martin, 1985: *The Labour Government, 1974–79: Political Aims and Economic Reality*. London: Macmillan.

Hormats, Robert, 1976: memo to Brent Scowcroft, 11 November 1976, regarding Proposed Presidential Visit with Harold Lever. White House Central Files, CO160 10/1/76 – 11/30/76, Ford Library.

Horsefield, J. Keith, et al., 1969: *The International Monetary Fund 1945–1965: Twenty Years of International Monetary Cooperation*. 3 vols. Washington, DC: International Monetary Fund.

Howard, David H., 1976a: 'The External Financial Position of the UK Public Sector,' 16 November 1976. International Finance General December 1976, Box B64, Burns Papers, Ford Library.

Howard, David H., 1976b: 'Sterling Holdings of non-residents held in the United Kingdom,' 22 November 1976. International Finance General December 1976, Box B64, Burns Papers, Ford Library.

Howard, David H., 1976c: 'Monetary Policy in the United Kingdom,' 22 November 1976. Federal Reserve Board Subject File, International Finance – General, Dec 1976, Box B64, Burns Papers, Ford Library.

Ikenberry, G. John, 1992: 'A world economy restored: expert consensus and the Anglo-American postwar settlement,' *International Organization* (Winter) 46(1): 289–321.

IMF [International Monetary Fund], 1974: *International Monetary Fund: Summary Proceedings of the Twenty-Ninth Annual Meeting of the Board of Governors, September 30–October 4, 1974*. Washington, DC: International Monetary Fund.

IMF, 1975a: *Annual Report of the Executive Directors for the Fiscal Year Ended April 30, 1975*. Washington, DC: International Monetary Fund.

IMF, 1975b: *International Monetary Fund: Summary Proceedings of the Thirtieth Annual Meeting of the Board of Governors, September 1–5, 1975*. Washington, DC: International Monetary Fund.

IMF, 1976a: *Annual Report of the Executive Directors for the Fiscal Year Ended April 30, 1976*. Washington, DC: International Monetary Fund.

IMF, 1976b: *International Monetary Fund: Summary Proceedings of the Thirty-First Annual Meeting of the Board of Governors, October 4–8, 1976*. Washington, DC: International Monetary Fund.

IMF, 1989a: *Government Finance Statistics Yearbook*. Washington, DC: International Monetary Fund.

IMF, 1989b: *International Financial Statistics Yearbook*. Washington, DC: International Monetary Fund.

IMF Survey.

The International Herald Tribune.

Jackson, Peter M., 1991: 'Public Expenditure,' in Artis and Cobham (1991: 73–87).

Jay, Peter, 1988: contribution to Burk et al. (1988).

Jenkins, Roy, 1969: letter of intent to Pierre-Paul Schweitzer, 22 May 1969, in *Parliamentary Debates* (Commons), 23 June 1969, 5th ser., vol. 785 (1968–69), cols 1008–10.

Jenkins, Roy, 1989: *European Diary, 1977–1981*. London: Collins.

Jenkins, Roy, 1991: *A Life at the Centre*. London: Macmillan.

Jessop, Bob, 1978: 'Capitalism and Democracy: The Best Possible Political Shell?' in Littlejohn, Gary, et al., eds, 1978: *Power and the State* London: Croom Helm.

Jessop, Bob, 1982: *The Capitalist State: Marxist Theories and Methods*. New York: New York University Press.

Jessop, Bob, 1990: *State Theory: Putting Capitalist States in their Place*. University Park, PA: Pennsylvania State University Press.

Jones, Jack, 1986: *Union Man: The Autobiography of Jack Jones*. London: Collins.

July, Serge, 1986: *Les Années Mitterrand: Histoire baroque d'une normalisation inachevée*. Paris: Bernard Grasset.

Katzenstein, Peter S., ed., 1978: *Between Power and Plenty: Foreign Economic Policies of Advanced Industrial States*. Madison, WI: University of Wisconsin Press.

Keegan, William and Rupert Pennant-Rea, 1979: *Who Runs the Economy? Control and Influence in British Economic Policy*. London: Maurice Temple Smith.

Keeley, James F., 1990: 'Toward a Foucauldian Analysis of International Regimes,' *International Organization* (Winter) 44(1): 83–105.

Keohane, Robert O., 1983: 'The Demand for International Regimes,' in Krasner (1983: 141–171).

Keohane, Robert O., 1984: *After Hegemony: Cooperation and Discord in the World Political Economy*. Princeton, NJ: Princeton University Press.

Keohane, Robert O., and Joseph S. Nye, 1977: *Power and Interdependence: World Politics in Transition*. Boston: Little, Brown.

Kogan, David and Maurice Kogan, 1982: *The Battle for the Labour Party*. 2nd edn. London: Kogan Page.

Krasner, Stephen D., 1978: 'United States Commercial and Monetary Policy: Unravelling the Paradox of External Strength and Internal Weakness,' in Katzenstein, ed., 1978: 51–87.

Krasner, Stephen D., ed., 1983. *International Regimes*. Ithaca, NY: Cornell University Press.

Krasner, Stephen D., 1988: 'Sovereignty: An Institutional Perspective,' *Comparative Political Studies* (April) 21(1): 66–94.

Krugman, Paul R., 1988: 'Sustainability and the Decline of the Dollar,' pp. 82–99 in Bryant, Ralph C., Gerald Holtham, and Peter Hooper, eds, 1988: *External Deficits and the Dollar: The Pit and the Pendulum*. Washington, DC: Brookings Institution.

Labour Party, 1972: *Labour's Programme for Britain: Annual Conference 1972*. London: The Labour Party.

Labour Party, 1973a: *Labour's Programme for Britain: Annual Conference 1973*. London: The Labour Party.

Labour Party, 1973b: *Report of the Seventy-Second Annual Conference of the Labour Party*. London: The Labour Party.

Labour Party, 1973c: *Paying for Labour's Programme: A Background Document*. London: The Labour Party.

Labour Party, 1974a: *Let Us Work Together – Labour's Way Out of the Crisis: The Labour Party Manifesto, 1974.* London: The Labour Party.

Labour Party, 1974b: *Britain will Win with Labour: The Labour Party Manifesto, October 1974.* London: The Labour Party.

Labour Party, 1974c: *Report of the Seventy-Third Annual Conference of the Labour Party, London, November 27–30, 1974.* London: The Labour Party.

Labour Party, 1975: *Report of the Seventy-Fourth Annual Conference of the Labour Party, Blackpool, September 29 – October 3, 1975.* London: The Labour Party.

Labour Party 1976a: *Labour's Programme for Britain: Annual Conference 1976.* London: The Labour Party.

Labour Party, 1976b: *Report of the Seventy-Fifth Annual Conference of the Labour Party, Blackpool, September 27 – October 1, 1976.* London: The Labour Party.

Labour Party Research Department, 1975a: 'Economic Report, November 1975.' RE: 336/November 1975. London: Labour Party Research Department.

Labour Party Research Department, 1975b: 'Import Controls: The Issue of Retaliation.' RE: 363/November 1975. London: Labour Party Research Department.

Labour Party Research Department, 1976: 'The Problem of Sterling.' RE: 800/October 1976. London: Labour Party Research Department.

Labour Party Study Group, 1973: *Opposition Green Paper: The National Enterprise Board: Labour's State Holding Company: Report of a Labour Party Study Group.* London: The Labour Party.

Labour Weekly.

Larre, René, 1976: message to Arthur Burns, 9 December 1976. Federal Reserve Board Subject File, Bank for International Settlements – General, May 1976 – Jan 1978, Box B3, Burns Papers, Ford Library.

Lever, Harold, 1989: contribution to Burk (1989: 45).

Lindblom, Charles E., 1977: *Politics and Markets: The World's Political-Economic Systems.* New York: Basic Books.

Lindblom, Charles E., 1982: 'The Market as Prison,' *The Journal of Politics* (May) 44(2): 324–36.

London Press Service.

Lowi, Theodore J., 1967: 'The Public Philosophy: Interest-Group Liberalism,' *American Journal of Political Science* (March) 61(1): 5–24.

Lowi, Theodore J., 1969: *The End of Liberalism: The Second Republic of the United States.* 2nd edn. New York: Norton.

McConnell, Grant, 1966: *Private Power and American Democracy.* New York: Alfred A. Knopf; reprint, New York: Vintage Books.

McCormick, Frank E., 1976: 'Reported Foreign Exchange Market Intervention,' 22 July 1976. Folder 'International Economic Developments: Briefing Book 7/23/76,' Box B60, Burns Papers, Ford Library.

McCracken, Paul, et al., 1977: *Towards Full Employment and Stability: A Report to the OECD by a Group of Independent Experts.* Paris: Organisation for Economic Co-operation and Development.

MacDougall, Donald, 1987: *Don and Mandarin: Memoirs of an Economist.* London: John Murray.

MacDougall, Donald, 1988: contribution to Burk et al. (1988).

McMahon, Kit, 1986: *Market Forces: Stamp Memorial Lecture Delivered Before the University of London on Thursday, 20 November 1986.* London: University of London.

Macpherson, C.B., 1977: *The Life and Times of Liberal Democracy.* London: Oxford University Press.

Maier, Charles S., 1978: 'The Politics of Productivity: Foundations of American International Economic Policy After World War II,' in Katzenstein (1978: 23–49).

Malkiel, Burton G., 1976a: memorandum for the President, 21 May 1976, Subject: International Financial Conditions. US Council of Economic Advisers Records, Alan Greenspan Files, White House Correspondence, Box 2, May 1976, Ford Library.

Malkiel, Burton G., 1976b: memorandum for the President, 25 June 1976, Subject: International Financial Conditions. US Council of Economic Advisers Records, Alan Greenspan Files, White House Correspondence, Box 2, June 1976, Ford Library.

Martin, Lisa, 1992: *Coercive Cooperation: Explaining Multilateral Economic Sanctions.* Princeton, NJ: Princeton University Press.

Marx, Karl, and Friedrich Engels, 1848: *Manifesto of the Communist Party.* Reprinted, pp. 469–500 in Tucker, Robert C., ed., 1972: *The Marx-Engels Reader.* 2nd edn. New York: Norton.

Middlemas, Keith, 1990: *Power, Competition and the State, Volume 2: Britain, 1961–74.* London: Macmillan.

Middlemas, Keith, 1991: *Power, Competition and the State: Volume 3. The End of the Postwar Era: Britain since 1974.* London: Macmillan.

Milési, Gabriel, 1985: *Jacques Delors.* Paris: Pierre Belfond.

Miliband, Ralph, 1961: *Parliamentary Socialism: A Study in the Politics of Labour.* 2nd edn. London: Allen & Unwin.

Miliband, Ralph, 1969: *The State in Capitalist Society.* New York: Basic.

Milner, Helen, 1992: 'International Theories of Cooperation among Nations: Strengths and Weaknesses,' *World Politics* (April) 44 (3): 466–96.

Mitchie, Alistair and Simon Hoggart, 1978: *The Pact: The Inside Story of the Lib-Lab Government, 1977–8.* London: Quartet Books.

Le Monde.

Monthly Digest of Statistics.

Morganthau, Hans J., 1948: *Politics Among Nations: The Struggle for Power and Peace.* 6th edn. New York: Knopf.

Muet, Pierre-Alain, and Alain Fonteneau, 1990: *Reflation and Austerity: Economic Policy under Mitterrand.* New York: Berg.

National Institute Economic Review.

Nessen, Ron, 1976: 'Assistance to the United Kingdom,' 23 November 1976. Ron Nessen Files, Foreign Guidance for Press Briefings, United Kingdom, Box 125, Ford Library.

The New York Times.

Newman, Michael, 1983: *Socialism and European Unity: The Dilemma of the Left in Britain and France.* London: Junction Books.

The Observer.

O'Connor, James, 1973: *The Fiscal Crisis of the State.* New York: St. Martin's Press.

Ohira, Masayoshi, 1975: 'Statement,' in IMF (1975b: 48–53).

OECD [Organisation for Economic Co-operation and Development], 1975: *OECD Economic Surveys: United Kingdom*. Paris: Organisation for Economic Co-Operation and Development.

OECD, 1976: *OECD Economic Surveys: United Kingdom*. Paris: Organisation for Economic Co-Operation and Development.

OECD, 1977: *OECD Economic Surveys: United Kingdom*. Paris: Organisation for Economic Co-Operation and Development.

OECD, 1978: *OECD Economic Surveys: United Kingdom*. Paris: Organisation for Economic Co-Operation and Development.

OECD, 1985: *Exchange Rate Management and the Conduct of Monetary Policy*. Paris: Organisation for Economic Co-operation and Development.

OECD, 1988: *Why Economic Policies Change Course: Eleven Case Studies*. Paris: Organisation for Economic Cooperation and Development.

OECD, 1989a: *Historical Statistics: 1960–1987*. Paris: Organisation for Economic Co-operation and Development.

OECD, 1989b: *National Accounts: Main Aggregates, Volume 1*. Paris: Organisation for Economic Cooperation and Development.

OECD Economic Outlook.

Oye, Kenneth A., 1986: 'Explaining Cooperation under Anarchy: Hypotheses and Strategies,' pp. 1–24 in Oye, Kenneth A., ed., *Cooperation under Anarchy*. Princeton, NJ: Princeton University Press.

Panitch, Leo, 1976: *Social Democracy and Industrial Militancy: The Labour Party, the Trade Unions, and Incomes Policy, 1945–1974*. Cambridge: Cambridge University Press.

Parliamentary Debates (Commons).

Parliamentary Papers (House of Commons and Command).

Pempel, T.J., and Keiichi Tsunekawa, 1979: 'Corporatism without Labour? The Japanese Anomaly,' pp. 231–70 in Schmitter, Philippe C. and Gerhard Lehmbruch, eds, 1979: *Trends toward Corporatist Intermediation*. Beverly Hills, CA: Sage.

Pliatzky, Leo, 1982: *Getting and Spending: Public Expenditure, Employment and Inflation*. Oxford: Basil Blackwell.

Pliatzky, Leo, 1989a: contribution to Burk et al. (1989).

Pliatzky, Leo, 1989b: *The Treasury under Mrs. Thatcher*. London: Basil Blackwell.

Pöhl [Poehl], Karl Otto, 1976: 'Statement,' in IMF (1976b: 106–9).

Polsby, Nelson, 1963: *Community Power and Political Theory*. New Haven, CT: Yale University Press.

Ponting, Clive, 1989: *Breach of Promise: Labour in Power 1964–1970*. London: Hamish Hamilton.

Prestowitz, Clyde V., Jr, 1988: *Trading Places: How We are Giving our Future to Japan and How to Reclaim It*. Paperback edn. New York: Basic Books.

Przeworski, Adam, 1980: 'Material Interests, Class Compromise, and the Transition to Socialism,' pp. 162–88 in Roemer, John, ed., 1986: *Analytical Marxism*. Cambridge: Cambridge University Press.

Przeworski, Adam, 1985: *Capitalism and Social Democracy*. Cambridge: Cambridge University Press.

Przeworski, Adam and John Sprague, 1986: *Paper Stones: A History of*

Electoral Socialism. Chicago: University of Chicago Press.

Przeworski, Adam and Michael Wallerstein, 1988: 'Structural Dependence of the State on Capital,' *American Political Science Review* (March) 82(1): 11–29.

Putnam, Robert D., 1988: 'Diplomacy and Domestic Politics: The Logic of Two-Level Games,' *International Organization* (Summer) 42(3): 427–60. Reprinted in Evans, Jacobson, and Putnam (1993: 431–68).

Putnam, Robert D., and Nicholas Bayne, 1984: *Hanging Together: Cooperation and Conflict in the Seven-Power Summits*. Rev. and enlarged edn. Cambridge, MA: Harvard University Press.

Richardson, Gordon, 1976a: 'Speech,' 18 June 1976, in *Bank of England Quarterly Bulletin*, September 1976, pp. 323–7.

Richardson, Gordon, 1976b: 'Speech,' 21 October 1976, in *Bank of England Quarterly Bulletin*, December 1976, pp. 453–4. Reprinted in *The Times*, 22 October 1976, p. 24.

Richardson, Gordon, 1976c: telex to Arthur Burns, 24 December 1976. Federal Reserve Board Subject File, Bank for International Settlements: Meeting, Basle, Jan 1977, Box B5, Burns Papers, Ford Library.

Richardson, Gordon, 1977a: 'Speech,' 17 January 1977, in *Bank of England Quarterly Bulletin*, March 1977, pp. 48–50. Reprinted in Bank of England (1984: 49–50).

Richardson, Gordon, 1977b: letter to Arthur Burns, 21 January 1977. Federal Reserve Board Subject File, United Kingdom: Sterling Balance Problem, Nov 1976 – Jan 1977 (2), Box B113, Burns Papers, Ford Library.

Richardson, Gordon, 1977c: 'Speech,' 31 January 1977, in *Bank of England Quarterly Bulletin*, March 1977, pp. 50–2.

Richardson, Gordon, 1978: 'Reflections on the Conduct of Monetary Policy.' Reprinted in Bank of England (1984: 51–8).

Ruggie, John, 1983: 'International Regimes, Transactions, and Change: Embedded Liberalism in the Postwar Economic Order,' in Krasner (1983: 195–231).

Russett, Bruce, 1985: 'The Mysterious Case of Vanishing Hegemony; or, Is Mark Twain Really Dead?' *International Organization* (Spring) 39(2): 207–231.

Scowcroft, Brent, 1976a: memorandum to Alan Greenspan, 24 February 1976, Subject: British Economic Policy. White House Central Files, Subject File, CO 160 1/1/76 – 2/29/76, Box 57, Ford Library.

Scowcroft, Brent, 1976b: schedule proposal, 12 November 1976. White House Central Files, Subject File, CO160 10/1/76 – 11/30/65, Box 57, Ford Library.

Seidman, L. William, 1976: agenda, 1 December 1976, prepared for a meeting on 2 December 1976 between Gerald Ford, William Simon, and L. William Seidman. White House Central Files, CO160, 12/1/76 – 1/20/77, Box 58, Ford Library.

Seyd, Patrick, 1987: *The Rise and Fall of the Labour Left*. London: Macmillan.

Sheldon, Robert, 1988: contribution to Burk et al. (1988).

Shore, Peter, 1988: contribution to Burk et al. (1988).

Silkin, Arthur, 1977: 'The "Agreement to Differ",' *The Political Quarterly* 46: 65–73.

Simon, William E., 1974: 'Statement,' in IMF (1974: 81–90).

Simon, William E., 1975a: 'Statement,' in IMF (1975b: 108–18).

Simon, William E., 1975b: 'International Economic Co-operation. 2. As the United States Sees It,' *The Banker* (December) 125: 1463–67.

Simon, William E., 1976a: 'Statement,' in IMF (1976b: 87–103).

Simon, William E., 1976b: memo for the Economic Policy Board, undated (probably March or April 1976). L. William Seidman Files, E.P.B. Subject File, Monetary – International, Box 77, Ford Library.

Simon, William E., 1976c: testimony, 1 June 1976, pp. 6–21, in *Hearings before the Subcommittee on International Trade, Investment, and Monetary Policy of the Committee on Banking, Currency and Housing, House of Representatives,* Ninety-Fourth Congress, Second Session, on H.R. 13955, A Bill to Provide for Amendment of the Bretton Woods Agreements Act, and for Other Purposes. Washington, DC: US Government Printing Office, 1976.

Simon, William E., 1976d: memo to Gerald Ford, 7 June 1976, Subject: Financial Support for the United Kingdom. United Kingdom Subject File, 1974–76 (Aug), Series IIIB, Drawer 27, Folder 13, Simon Papers, Lafayette College.

Simon, William E., 1976e: memo to Gerald Ford, 13 July 1976. Germany Subject File, 1974–76, Series IIIB, Drawer 22, Folder 62, Simon Papers, Lafayette College.

Simon, William E., 1976f: outline of Healey and Witteveen proposals, undated (probably late November 1976). United Kingdom Subject File, 1976 (Sep–Dec), Series IIIB, Drawer 27, Folder 14, Simon Papers, Lafayette College.

Simon, William E., 1976g: letter to Denis Healey, 14 December 1976. United Kingdom Subject File, 1976 (Sep–Dec), Series IIIB, Drawer 27, Folder 14, Simon Papers, Lafayette College.

Simon, William E., 1976h: 'Calls and Appointments Sheets: 1976, (Nov 1–11).' Series X, Drawer 54, Folder 12, Simon Papers, Lafayette College.

Simon, William E., 1976i: 'Calls and Appointments Sheets: 1976, (Dec),' Series X, Drawer 54, Folder 14, Simon Papers, Lafayette College.

Simon, William E., 1976j: speech, 5 October 1976, reprinted in 'Department of the Treasury News,' 4 October 1976. Board of Governors, International Monetary Fund and the International Bank for Reconstruction and Development, Manila: 1976 (October 4), Series V, Drawer 40, Folder 82, Simon Papers, Lafayette College.

Simon, William E., 1976k: memo to Gerald Ford, undated [probably late November or early December]. Subject: Visit to London. L. William Seidman Files, Memorandum to the President, June 1976 – December 1976 (6), Box 77, Ford Library.

Simon, William E., 1978: *A Time for Truth.* New York: Reader's Digest Press.

Skocpol, Theda, 1985: 'Bringing the State Back In: Strategies of Analysis in Current Research', pp. 3–37 in Evans, Peter, Dietrich Rueschemeyer and Theda Skocpol, eds, 1985: *Bringing the State Back In.* Cambridge: Cambridge University Press.

Skocpol, Theda and Kenneth Finegold, 1984: 'State, Party, and Industry: From Business Recovery to the Wagner Act in America's New Deal', pp. 159–92 in Bright, Charles and Susan Harding, eds, 1984: *Statemaking and Social Movements: Essays in History and Theory.* Ann Arbor, MI: University of Michigan Press.

Smith, Peter, 1989: 'On Macroeconomic Policy,' pp. xiii–xvi in Marshallsay, Diana and Peter G. Richards, eds, 1989: *Ford List of British Parliamentary Papers*. Cambridge: Chadwyck-Healey.

Snyder, Glenn H., and Paul Diesing, 1977: *Conflict Among Nations: Bargaining, Decision Making, and System Structure in International Crises*. Princeton, NJ: Princeton University Press.

Solomon, Robert, 1977: *The International Monetary System, 1945–1976: An Insider's View*. New York: Harper & Row.

Southard, Frank A., Jr, 1979: *The Evolution of the International Monetary Fund: Essays in International Finance, No. 135*. Princeton, NJ: International Finance Section, Department of Economics, Princeton University.

Spaventa, Luigi, 1983: 'Two Letters of Intent: External Crises and Stabilization Policy, Italy, 1973–77,' in Williamson (1983: 441–73).

Stein, Arthur, 1983: 'Coordination and Collaboration: Regimes in an Anarchic World,' in Krasner (1983: 115–40).

Stiles, Kendall W., 1991: *Negotiating Debt: The IMF Lending Process*. Boulder, CO: Westview Press.

Strange, Susan, 1971: *Sterling and British Policy: A Political Study of an International Currency in Decline*. London: Oxford University Press.

Strange, Susan, 1976: *International Economic Relations of the Western World, 1959–1971*. London: Oxford University Press.

Strange, Susan, 1983: '*Cave! hic dragones*: A Critique of Regime Analysis,' in Krasner (1983: 337–54).

Strange, Susan, 1988: *States and Markets*. London: Pinter Publishers.

The Sunday Telegraph.

The Sunday Times.

Taylor, Andrew, 1987: *The Trade Unions and the Labour Party*. London: Croom Helm.

The Times.

Tribune.

Truman, E. M., 1976: 'An Analysis of Two Approaches to the "Sterling Balance Problem",' 23 November 1976, attached to a memo from Ted Truman to Arthur Burns, 23 November 1976. Arthur Burns Papers, Federal Reserve Board Subject File, Box B113, United Kingdom, Sterling Balance Problem, Nov 1976 – Jan 1977 (1), Ford Presidential Library.

TUC [Trades Union Congress], 1973: *Report of 105th Annual Trades Union Congress*. London: Congress House.

TUC, 1974a: *Collective Bargaining and the Social Contract*. Reprinted in TUC (1974b: 284–91).

TUC, 1974b: *Report of 106th Annual Trades Union Congress*. London: Congress House.

TUC, 1975: *Report of 107th Annual Trades Union Congress*. London: Congress House.

TUC, 1976a: *Report of 108th Annual Trades Union Congress*. London: Trades Union Congress.

TUC, 1976b: *Economic Review, 1976*. London: Trades Union Congress.

TUC, 1977a: *Report of 109th Annual Trades Union Congress*. London: Trades Union Congress.

TUC, 1977b: *Economic Review, 1977*. London: Trades Union Congress.

TUC–Labour Party Liaison Committee, 1973: *Economic Policy and the Cost of Living*. Reprinted in TUC (1973: 312–15).

TUC–Labour Party Liaison Committee Minutes. London: Labour Party Research Department.

UK Michael Foot, 1975: Attack on Inflation, 22 July 1975. *Parliamentary Debates* (Commons), 5th ser., vol. 896 (1974–75), cols 423–31.

UK Denis Healey 1974a: Budget Statement, 26 March 1974. *Parliamentary Debates* (Commons), 5th ser., vol. 871 (1974), cols 277–328.

UK Denis Healey 1974b: Economic Situation, 22 July 1974. *Parliamentary Debates* (Commons), 5th ser., vol. 877 (1974), cols 1048–56.

UK Denis Healey 1974c: Budget Statement, 12 November 1974. *Parliamentary Debates* (Commons), 5th ser., vol. 881 (1974–75), cols 241–80.

UK Denis Healey 1974d: Saudi Arabia (Chancellor's Visit), 13 December 1974. *Parliamentary Debates* (Commons), 5th ser., vol. 883 (1974–75), cols 982– 88.

UK Denis Healey, 1975a: Budget Statement, 15 April 1975. *Parliamentary Debates* (Commons), 5th ser., vol. 890 (1974–75), cols 273–322.

UK Denis Healey, 1975b: Domestic Inflation, 1 July 1975. *Parliamentary Debates* (Commons), 5th ser., vol. 894 (1974–75), cols 1189–1200.

UK Denis Healey 1975c: Attack on Inflation, 21 July 1975. *Parliamentary Debates* (Commons), 5th ser., vol. 896 (1974–75), cols 46–75.

UK Denis Healey, 1975d: International Monetary Fund Borrowings, 10 November 1975. *Parliamentary Debates* (Commons), 5th ser., vol. 899 (1974–75), cols 920–6.

UK Denis Healey, 1975e: Employment, 17 December 1975. *Parliamentary Debates* (Commons), 5th ser., vol. 902 (1975–76), cols 1400–19.

UK Denis Healey, 1976a: Public Expenditure, 9 March 1976. *Parliamentary Debates* (Commons), 5th ser., vol. 907 (1975–76), cols 254–72.

UK Denis Healey, 1976b: Budget Statement, 6 April 1976. *Parliamentary Debates* (Commons), 5th ser., vol. 909 (1975–76), cols 232–82.

UK Denis Healey, 1976c: £ Sterling, 7 June 1976. *Parliamentary Debates* (Commons), 5th ser., vol. 912 (1975–76), cols 912–27.

UK Denis Healey, 1976d: Public Expenditure, 22 July 1976. *Parliamentary Debates* (Commons), 5th ser., vol. 915 (1975–76), cols 2010–36.

UK Denis Healey, 1976e: Public Expenditure, 2 August 1976. *Parliamentary Debates* (Commons), 5th ser., vol. 916 (1975–76), cols 1234–54.

UK Denis Healey, 1976f: Economic Situation, 11 October 1976. *Parliamentary Debates* (Commons), 5th ser., vol. 917 (1975–76), cols 36–54.

UK Denis Healey, 1976g: Economic Situation (Government Measures), 15 December 1976. *Parliamentary Debates* (Commons), 5th ser., vol. 922 (1976–77), cols 1525–58.

UK Denis Healey, 1976h: Economic Situation, 21 December 1976. *Parliamentary Debates* (Commons), 5th ser., vol. 923 (1976–77), cols 482–503.

UK Denis Healey, 1977a: Sterling Balances, 11 January 1977. *Parliamentary Debates* (Commons), 5th ser., vol. 923 (1976–77), cols 1260–69.

UK Denis Healey, 1977b: Economic Situation, 26 October 1977. *Parliamentary Debates* (Commons), 5th ser., vol. 936 (1976–77), cols 1437–40.

UK Roy Jenkins, 1967a: International Monetary Fund (Standby Credit), 30 November 1967. *Parliamentary Debates* (Commons), 5th ser., vol. 755 (1966–67), cols 643–52.

UK Roy Jenkins, 1967b: International Monetary Fund (Letter of Intent), 5 December 1967. *Parliamentary Debates* (Commons), 5th ser., vol. 755 (1966–67), cols 1196–1202.

UK Roy Jenkins, 1969a: Budget Statement, 15 April 1969. *Parliamentary Debates* (Commons), 5th ser., vol. 781 (1968–99), cols 991–1043.

UK Roy Jenkins, 1969b: International Monetary Fund (Standby Facilities), 23 June 1969. *Parliamentary Debates* (Commons), 5th ser., vol. 785 (1968–69), cols 1001–10.

UK Parliament, 1975: *The Attack on Inflation.* Cmnd. 6151. July 1975.

UK Parliament, 1976: *Public Expenditure to 1979–80.* Cmnd. 6393. February 1976.

UK Harold Wilson, 1975: Attack on Inflation, 11 July 1975. *Parliamentary Debates* (Commons), 5th ser., vol. 895 (1974–75), cols 901–28.

UK Harold Wilson, 1976: Government Economic Strategy, 11 March 1976. *Parliamentary Debates* (Commons), 5th ser., vol. 907, cols 634–42.

US Congress, Senate, Committee on Foreign Relations 1976: *Hearings before the Committee on Foreign Relations on S. 3454 to Provide for Amendment of the Bretton Woods Agreements Act, and for Other Purposes.* 94th Cong., 2nd Sess.

US Council of Economic Advisers, 1976a: Case Report – International Economic Summit 6/27–28/76, Part 1: 'International Economic Policy Issues,' Tab B: 'International Financial and Monetary Issues,' undated. Council of Economic Advisers Records, Burton G. Malkiel Files, Subject File, Puerto Rico Summit (1), Box 136, Ford Library.

US Council of Economic Advisers, 1976b: memo for the President, 29 October 1976, International Financial Conditions. White House Central Files, Subject File, FI9, 1/1/76 – 11/30/76 Executive, Box 24, Ford Library.

US Federal Reserve System, 1976a: 'Policy Problems,' Part 2, Tab 1, 'Economic Activity and Policies in Major Industrial Countries,' 4 June 1976. Federal Reserve Board Subject File, International Economic Summit, Puerto Rico, June 1976, Briefing Book (1), Box B62, Burns Papers, Ford Library.

US Federal Reserve System, 1976b: table, Comparison of Plans for Dealing with Sterling Balances, 11 December 1976. Federal Reserve Board Subject File, United Kingdom – Sterling Balances Problem, Nov 1976 – Jan 1977 (2), Box B113, Burns Papers, Ford Library.

US Federal Reserve System, 1977a: Points to be Raised with Under-Secretary Yeo, Revised, 5 January 1977. Federal Reserve Board Subject File, Treasury Dept, Jan–Feb 10, 1977, Box B103, Burns Papers, Ford Library.

US Federal Reserve System, 1977b: Notes on 'Reasonable Effort,' 8 January 1977. Federal Reserve Board Subject File, United Kingdom – Sterling Balances Problem, Nov 1976 – Jan 1977 (2), Box B113, Burns Papers, Ford Library.

US Federal Reserve System, 1977c: Agreement of Participating Central Banks on Main Components of Sterling Balance Facility, 10 January 1977. Federal Reserve Board Subject File, United Kingdom – Sterling Balances Problem, Nov 1976 – Jan 1977 (2), Box B113, Burns Papers, Ford Library.

US Government, 1976: earlier draft of 'Remarks on International Financial and Monetary Issues for Use by the President at the Economic Summit,' Tab B ('International Financial and Monetary Issues') of US Briefing Book for the International Economic Summit in Puerto Rico, *c.* early June 1976.

L. William Seidman Files, Foreign Trips File, International Economic Summit, 6/27–28/76 – Briefing Papers – Comments on, Box 317, Ford Library.

US Information Service, 1976: Official Text, 23 June 1976, US Embassy in London, 'Excerpts from a statement by US Secretary of the Treasury William Simon to the Organization for Economic Cooperation and Development,' 22 June 1976.

US State Department, 1974: background profile on Harold Lever, May 1974. United Kingdom Subject File, 1974–76 (Aug), Series IIIB, Drawer 27, Folder 13, Simon Papers, Lafayette College.

US State Department, 1976a: cable to Burton Malkiel and Henry Wallich, 9 June 1976. Council of Economic Advisers, Burton G. Malkiel Files, Subject Files, OECD – Economic Policy Committee – June–July 1976, Box 132, Ford Library.

US State Department, 1976b: 'Bilateral Relations and the Situation in the United Kingdom,' 7 July 1976. White House Central Files, Subject File, CO160 7/7/76, Box 57, Ford Library.

Volcker, Paul A., 1976: memo to Governor Henry Wallich, 'Possible Approach to Sterling Balance Problem,' 9 December 1976. Federal Reserve Board Subject File, United Kingdom: Sterling Balance Problem, Nov 1976 – Jan 1977 (1), Box B113, Burns Papers, Ford Library.

The Wall Street Journal.

Wallich, Henry C., 1976a: memo to Catherine, 25 June 1976, with attachments. Federal Reserve Board Subject File, Bank of England, 1976–77, Box B7, Burns Papers, Ford Library.

Wallich, Henry C., 1976b: note to Arthur Burns, 13 December 1976, regarding the wording of Denis Healey's 15 December House of Commons statement concerning progress on sterling balances. Federal Reserve Board Subject File, United Kingdom – Sterling Balances Problem, Nov 1976 – Jan 1977 (2), Box B113, Burns Papers, Ford Library.

Wallich, Henry C., 1977: memo to Chairman Burns, 16 February 1977. Subject: Information received by foreign central banks concerning large foreign loans made by their commercial banks. Federal Reserve Board Staff Files, Wallich, Henry C. (3) 1977, Box C16, Ford Library.

Waltz, Kenneth N., 1959: *Man, The State, and War: A Theoretical Analysis.* New York: Columbia University Press.

Waltz, Kenneth N., 1964: 'The Stability of a Bipolar World,' *Daedalus* (Summer) 93(3). Reprinted pp. 62–8 in Phil Williams, Donald M. Goldstein, and Jay M. Shafritz, eds, *Classic Readings of International Relations.* Belmont, CA: Wadsworth.

Waltz, Kenneth N., 1969: 'International Structure, National Force, and the Balance of World Power,' pp. 304–14 in Rosenau, James, ed., 1969: *International Politics and Foreign Policy: A Reader in Research and Theory.* Rev. edn. New York: Free Press.

Waltz, Kenneth N., 1979: *Theory of International Politics.* Reading, MA: Addison-Wesley.

Wass, Douglas, 1976: 'Statement,' in IMF (1976b: 79–82).

Wass, Douglas, 1984: *Government and the Governed: BBC Reith Lectures 1983.* London: Routledge & Kegan Paul.

White House Press Secretary 1976: press release, Press Conference of William Simon, Puerto Rico, 28 June 1976. US Council of Economic Advisers Records,

Burton G. Malkiel Files, Subject File, Puerto Rico Summit (2), Box 136, Ford Library.

Whitehead, Phillip, 1985: *The Writing on the Wall: Britain in the Seventies*. London: Michael Joseph.

Whitehead, Phillip, 1987: 'The Labour Governments, 1974–79,' pp. 241–73 in Hennessy, Peter, and Anthony Seldon, eds, 1987: *Ruling Performance: British Governments from Attlee to Thatcher*. New York: Basil Blackwell.

Williamson, John, ed., 1983: *IMF Conditionality*. Washington, DC: Institute for International Economics.

Wilson, Harold, 1971: *The Labour Government 1964–1970: A Personal Record*. London: Weidenfeld & Nicolson and Michael Joseph.

Wilson, Harold, 1976: *The Governance of Britain*. London: Weidenfeld & Nicolson and Michael Joseph.

Wilson, Harold, 1979: *Final Term: The Labour Government, 1974–76*. London: Weidenfeld & Nicolson and Michael Joseph.

Witteveen, Johannes, 1974a: 'Oil Prices, Inflation, Stagnation,' *IMF Survey* (21 January) 3: 17, 20–22.

Witteveen, Johannes, 1974b: 'Managing Director's Proposal,' *IMF Survey* (4 February) 3: 41.

Witteveen, Johannes, 1974c: 'Witteveen Assesses,' *IMF Survey* (4 February) 3: 43–5.

Witteveen, Johannes, 1974d: 'Respective Roles,' *IMF Survey* (6 May) 3: 129, 133–6.

Witteveen, Johannes, 1974e: 'Presentation,' in IMF 1974: 18–28. Reprinted in *IMF Survey* (14 October) 3: 323–8.

Witteveen, Johannes, 1974f: 'Statement,' in IMF (1974: 272–4).

Witteveen, Johannes, 1974g: 'Fund's Role,' *IMF Survey* (9 December) 3: 380–2.

Witteveen, Johannes, 1975a: 'Presentation,' in IMF (1975b: 20–9). Reprinted in *IMF Survey* (15 September) 4: 259–62.

Witteveen, Johannes, 1975b: 'Statement,' in IMF (1975b: 248–51).

Witteveen, Johannes, 1976a: 'Complementary Roles,' *IMF Survey* (3 May) 5: 138–40.

Witteveen, Johannes, 1976b: 'Presentation,' in IMF (1976b: 12–21). Reprinted in *IMF Survey* (18 October) 5: 307–12.

Witteveen, Johannes, 1976c: 'Witteveen: Recovery Firmly Established,' *IMF Survey* (19 July) 5: 209, 219–22.

Witteveen, Johannes, 1987: untitled, in *Institutional Investor*, International edition (June): 27–35.

Yeo, Edwin, H. 1976a: memo to William Simon, 6 June 1976. United Kingdom Subject File, 1974–76 (Aug), Series IIIB, Drawer 27, Folder 13, Simon Papers, Lafayette College.

Yeo, Edwin H., 1976b: 'Recovery Seen Sparking Exchange Rate Variability,' *Journal of Commerce*, 14 June 1976, Section 2, p. 1.

Young, Oran R., 1983: 'Regime Dynamics: The Rise and Fall of International Regimes,' in Krasner (1983; 93–113).

Young, Oran R., 1986: 'International Regimes: Towards a New Theory of Institutions', *World Politics* (October) 39(1): 104–22.

Young, Oran R., 1989: *International Cooperation: Building Regimes for Natural Resources and the Environment*. Ithaca, NY: Cornell University Press.

Index

Alternative Economic Strategy, 3–4,
93–4, 135, 153, 200, 202–4, 219,
238n.4
Apel, Hans, 71–2, 123–4

Balance of Payments Financing, 17–18,
21–7, 36–40, 45–6, 62–78, 85,
121–30, 228, 233, 236n.2, 236n.3,
236n.5
OPEC and, 64, 68
private financial markets and, 70,
124–5, 129, 226–7
United Kingdom and, 28–47, 49,
53–4, 80, 83–5, 87–8, 91–2, 96,
99–100, 107–10, 112–13, 143,
150, 167, 226–7, 237n.3, 239n.8
Bank for International Settlements (BIS),
221, 223–5, 237n.6
creditor in G-10 central bank
financing, 144
Bank of England, 33, 84, 149, 159, 194,
214
currency reserves 29, 49–50, 89, 91,
114–15, 137–8, 143, 149, 158–60,
174, 204, 212, 232, 237n.6
intervention on exchanges, 89–90,
133, 137–8, 140, 149, 159–60,
164, 229, 239n.6
'practical monetarism' and, 156
sterling depreciation, 116–17, 133,
238n.5
view on sterling, 140, 158, 164
Barber, Anthony, 66
Barnett, Joel, 83, 85, 92, 95, 112,
120, 153, 154, 176, 211, 237n.1,
240n.9
Basnett, David, 219
Belgium
creditor in G-10 central bank
financing, 144
Benn, Tony, x, 61, 81, 95, 98, 145, 162,
169, 175, 185, 189–90, 191, 197,
199–200, 206
alternative economic strategy, 93–4,
153, 200, 202
expenditure cuts, 152, 200
Labour Party leadership elections,
134–5

Bennett, Jack, 73
Block, Fred, 8
Booth, Albert, 175, 185
Brau, Ed, 240n.8
Bretton Woods System, 17, 20–3, 62–3
British Petroleum, 185, 195, 201, 204,
207, 210, 211, 218
Brittan, Samuel, 156
Britton, Andrew, 116–118
Burk, Kathleen, x, 235n.10, 239n.13,
241n.17, 241n.19, 242n.9
Burns, Arthur, 143–4, 148, 155, 167,
192, 208, 213–14, 229, 230–1,
239n.4, 244n.28
conditionality and, 130, 208, 214,
230–1, 243n.12
oil facility and, 74
sterling balances and, 169, 177–8,
180–1, 222–5, 240n.15

Callaghan, James, 1, 3, 81, 94, 98, 105,
162–3, 169, 193, 217
backbenches and, 219
becomes Prime Minister, 134–5
cabinet strategy, 184–5, 196, 199, 202,
204–5, 208, 211
Crosland and, 184, 187, 196–7, 203–4,
206
defense and, 170–1, 188
devaluation (1967) and, 32–3, 48–52
expenditure cuts and, 145, 151,
153–4, 162, 199, 205, 208, 211,
242n.4
Foot and, 197
Ford and, 1, 177, 180, 187–9, 203,
205, 207–9, 221–2, 224, 242n.7,
243n.20
G-7 summit in Puerto Rico, 149–51
G-10 central bank credit and, 146,
239n.9
Healey and, 168, 182, 189, 191, 197,
199, 202, 205, 209, 211
IMF and, 138, 145, 152–3, 161–2,
164–5, 169, 175, 177, 179,
182–5, 187–9, 190, 196–9, 202,
205, 207–10, 242n.4
import protection and, 169, 203,
214–15